Scottish Theatre
Since
the Seventies

Also available: *The Scottish Novel since the Seventies*, edited by Gavin Wallace and Randall Stevenson (Edinburgh University Press, 1993)

SCOTTISH THEATRE
SINCE THE SEVENTIES

Edited by
Randall Stevenson
and
Gavin Wallace

Edinburgh University Press

Edinburgh University Press
22 George Square, Edinburgh

Typeset in Garamond
by Hewer Text Composition Services, Edinburgh, and
printed and bound in Great Britain by The Alden Press, Oxford

A CIP record for this book is
available from the British Library

ISBN 0 7486 0781 1

Contents

              The Sense of the Past in Scottish Theatre
              Ian Brown (Queen Margaret College)   84

Eight   In the Jungle of the Cities
              Randall Stevenson   100

Nine   Fantasists and Philosophers
              Sarah C. Rutherford   112

Ten   The New Wave
              Peter Zenzinger   125

Eleven   Loose Canons: Identifying a
              Women's Tradition in Playwriting
              Audrey Bain   138

              PART III   POLITICS AND PRACTICES

Twelve   From Cheviots to Silver Darlings
              John McGrath interviewed by Olga Taxidou   149

Thirteen   Epic Theatre in Scotland
              Olga Taxidou   164

Fourteen   Scottish Drama and the Popular Tradition
              Femi Folorunso   176

Fifteen   Talking in Tongues: Scottish Translations 1970–1995
              Bill Findlay   186

Sixteen   Directing for the Scottish Stage
              Ian Brown (Traverse Theatre)   198

Seventeen   Economics, Culture and Playwriting
              David Hutchison   206

              The Scottish Theatre since 1970: A Bibliography
              Alison Lumsden   215

                                        About the Contributors   225

                                                       Index   230

Acknowledgements

The editors are grateful to contributors who have worked punctually and efficiently throughout. We have also gained enormously from working with Jackie Jones of Edinburgh University Press: anyone who has done so knows she is the best publisher in the world, and her insight, inspiration, and imaginative encouragement have shaped and sustained the production of this book at every stage. Olga Taxidou's eternal energy, thoughtfulness and generous commitment to the project have likewise been instrumental in helping the editors achieve their goals, and in pointing out several we could not have seen for ourselves.

Our work in compiling this volume is dedicated to the memory of Garth Sterne, great theatregoer, who died in January 1996.

Introduction

Snakes and Ladders, Snakes and Owls: Charting Scottish Theatre

Randall Stevenson

Country: Scotland. Whit like is it? And whit like's its theatres? Ah dinna ken whit like *your* theatre is. Here's mines.

It's Rikki Fulton and John Shedden stamping onto the stage of the MacRobert Centre as if they'd always owned it – the opening moment of *Let Wives Tak Tent*, on Scottish Theatre Company's first-ever first-night in 1981.

It's two hundred spectators furtively searching their pockets for a hanky at the end of Edwin Morgan's overwhelming adaptation of *Cyrano de Bergerac* at the Traverse in 1992.

It's stumbling over an old bear in a prehistoric peat-bog in the promenade performance *Border Warfare* at the Tramway in 1989.

It's an audience packed into an impromptu Fringe venue in 1976, engrossed in the religious struggles and acrimonies of Donald Campbell's *The Jesuit*.[1]

It's strolling over the Victoria Bridge in 1981, past Gorbals Cross – a September sunset colouring the grubby Clyde and the Glasgow sky – to the Citizens' Theatre and its delicate shadings of past and present in Robert David MacDonald's Proust-adaptation *A Waste of Time*.

It's the audience rising as one to give the Maly Theatre of Leningrad a standing ovation for *Brothers and Sisters* in Glasgow's year as European City of Culture, 1990.

It's Elizabeth MacLennan wringing the hearts of a packed Citizens' in the closing scene of Ena Lamont Stewart's *Men Should Weep*, revived as part of 7:84's 'Clydebuilt' season in 1982.

It's Scottish Mime Theatre driving round the Highlands with their feet sticking out the windows of their van into the warm summer air of 1979.

It's . . . and it's . . .

But it's enough, for now. You'll have noticed already that the list is highly personal, and you've maybe also spotted that it's parodic – of La Corbie's opening survey of Scotland in Liz Lochhead's *Mary Queen of Scots Got Her Head Chopped Off* (1987). Above all, though, it's *partial*. Any full catalogue of good Scottish productions over the past two or three decades – even just a list of highlights, personal favourites and greatest hits – would be much longer than the one above. Even if your personal list goes back for less than twenty years – perhaps even if it goes back for only one or two – there is now enough imagination, originality, variety, and confidence in Scottish theatre to provide an exciting range of achievements more or less annually.

This is all the more worth celebrating as it is such a new state of affairs. It often seems that it's *only* in the past quarter century or so that there's been much Scottish theatre to celebrate at all. Earlier, the rarity of good drama often left commentators on the Scottish scene victims of gloom and melancholy: some of their views are revealing enough – or picturesque enough – to be worth quoting at length. In an influential study of Scottish literature published in 1919, G. Gregory Smith laments that

> There is the third literary kind, Drama; but of this there is as little (or as much) to be said as Niels Horrobow was able to say of the owls and snakes of Iceland. Scientific duty compelled that worthy to set apart a chapter to tell us 'There are no owls in the whole island', and another to intimate with like brevity that 'No snakes of any kind are to be met with throughout the whole island . . . it is owing to the excessive cold that no snakes are found'. An excellent pattern for an account of Scottish drama![2]

As the Glasgow Repertory Theatre – an early inspiration for James Bridie, probably the best-known twentieth-century Scottish dramatist – was still working only five years before he wrote, Gregory Smith might have recorded a less extreme chill prevailing across the dramatic landscape. And the climate showed some signs of improving again, with the work of the Scottish National Players between the wars, the Curtain

Theatre and Bridie's plays in the 1930s, and the successes of Glasgow Unity Theatre in the 1940s. Yet one of Unity's own playwrights, George Munro, still remarks of the contemporary Scottish scene

> 'Here be deserts and wild beastes', wrote medieval cartographers: and so, cryptically, would I write Scotland's name upon any Theatre chart . . . dramaturgically speaking, Scotland is in the bronze age, still.[3]

Deserts – usually frozen – and wild beastes – menacing or just missing – continue to appear in assessments of Scottish theatre later in the century. Something of Gregory Smith's gloomy pattern still shapes the Foreword to David Hutchison's pioneering study, *The Modern Scottish Theatre* (1977), Christopher Small remarking that

> A history of the modern Scottish theatre – or one, indeed, of the Scottish theatre ancient and modern – would seem likely at first blush to be a short one; even, like the celebrated chapter on Snakes in the History of Iceland, to be encompassed in a single terse negative sentence.

Fortunately, Small is also able to point to 'early shoots and flowers' appearing in the frozen deserts:[4] twenty years later, it is clear that Scottish drama in the seventies experienced not just a 'first blush' but a whole new dawn, one still shedding light on the landscape today. Commentators earlier in the century less gloomy than Gregory Smith helpfully foresaw how this might occur: that most distinguished of Scottish writers, Hugh MacDiarmid, was one. Apart from roundly rubbishing the reputation of J. M. Barrie – highly successful on the London stage at the turn of the century – MacDiarmid had relatively little to say about the theatre, perhaps not surprisingly. Surveying much the same barren theatrical scene which troubled Gregory Smith, MacDiarmid might justly have wondered why the drama seemed untouched by the Scottish literary renaissance his own work had helped initiate in fiction and poetry in the 1920s. Nevertheless, MacDiarmid's 'R. F. Pollock and the Art of the Theatre' (1926) is a prescient essay, more or less predicting the need for the Traverse Theatre, and foreseeing directions Scottish playwrights needed to follow if they were to catch up with the nation's novelists and poets. These were not to be found by following J. M. Barrie's road to London, with only a patronising backward glance at Scotland, nor by sharing the Scottish National Players' rather idealised, countrified vision of their nation. Instead, MacDiarmid demands a drama concentrating on the real nature and particularities of Scottish experience – 'a distinctively Scottish form, the dramatic equivalent of the *differentia* of Scots psychology'.[5]

His essay does not go far in defining these *differentia* in Scots experience, psychological or otherwise, but most are obvious enough. As in many a small country – and more than in some – there are in Scotland areas of shared experience, common political outlook, language and history, which set the country apart from its neighbours and offer dramatists forms and interests particularly appealing to Scottish audiences. Obvious or not, these were areas playwrights did explore in the 1970s, finding in them an energy and immediacy which helped the theatre match Scottish fiction and poetry at last: though a dramatic renaissance was missing from MacDiarmid's heyday, it has emerged clearly in the last twenty-five years.

While Part I of this study considers recently influential theatres and theatre companies, essays in Part II examine dramatists' approaches to these areas and *differentia*, with Sarah Rutherford adding a study of playwrights who have continued Scottish literature's long-established habits of philosophical speculation and transition into fantasy. Of all these areas examined in Part II – language, history, shared experience and outlook – it is probably Scots speech that is the most fundamental influence on the drama, and it is discussed in Bill Findlay's study of translation in Part III as well as Lindsay Paterson's essay in Part II. That production of *The Jesuit*, for example, owed its power probably less to the play's emotive issues than to hearing them discussed in tones and terms immediately familiar from the streets outside the theatre – still a fairly new experience in 1976. In one way, much of this novelty might be thought to have since worn off: Scots language has been used by most of the writers discussed in Part II, and as Peter Zenzinger notes in his essay, a new generation has reproduced a wider than ever range of speech-forms, urban and rural, bringing to the stage accents and dialects rarely heard on it before, such as the stylised Doric employed by Rona Munro in *Saturday at the Commodore* (1989). In another way, however, elements of novelty and immediacy still remain. In television, radio, or most other channels of communication, even within Scotland, it is still fairly rare, even surprising, to hear Scots spoken. Think of your own reactions when you found the first lines of this Introduction written in a kind of Scots. Think, too, of the significance of finding *only* the first couple of lines in that form, before English took over.

Divisions between the standard English used for most official purposes and the roguish, marginal existence enjoyed by Scots have of course been much discussed by students of Scottish affairs, Hugh MacDiarmid included, as have their contributions to splits and antisyzygies in the Scottish imagination and soul. In the theatre, however, the use of Scots has little to do with splitting and everything to do with solidarity – with a collective cocooning of stage and audience in a community of speech which often includes, by implication, a sense of shared outlooks, values, and emotions. One of MacDiarmid's poems, 'Gairmscoile', concludes that

> It's soon, no' sense, that faddoms the herts o' men
> . . . the rouch auld Scots I ken
> E'en herts that ha'e nae Scot'll dirl rich thro'
> As nocht else could.

Scots in the theatre does indeed have a peculiar hold over the emotions, a power to 'faddom the hert' of audiences and draw them into complicity with stage action, almost independently of what the 'sense' or direction of that action is itself. Donald Campbell's focusing of sympathies in *The Jesuit,* for example, had as much to do with which characters spoke in Scots and which did not as it did with what each of them actually said.

As MacDiarmid helps to indicate, such powers exist almost regardless of audiences' ability or inclination to speak the language themselves. Probably not one spectator in ten shared the full range of vocabulary or expression so dextrously deployed by Edwin Morgan in that translation of *Cyrano de Bergerac,* or by Liz Lochhead in hers of *Tartuffe* (1986). Yet this did not for a moment stop audiences laughing or weeping at attitudes and actions made to seem so immediate, so familiar, by the ways they were expressed and discussed. Rather like MacDiarmid's development of the language in his poetry, stage Scots does not need to be a completely authentic reflection of the speech of its audience – something which could probably not be achieved in any case, given the range of dialects and regional variations in modern Scotland. On the contrary, as Liz Lochhead remarks in her Introduction to *Tartuffe,* authors have often created 'a totally invented . . . theatrical Scots'.[6] It is not authenticity, but difference – difference from standard English in particular – which gives this language its power to communicate a distinctively Scottish experience, highlighting the *differentia* MacDiarmid mentions. Variously developed in the work of Donald Campbell, Bill Bryden, Roddy McMillan, Stewart Conn and others in the 1970s, it is a resource which has greatly empowered the progress of Scottish theatre over the past quarter century.

Scottish history has offered almost equal – and equally various – dramatic potential, as Ian Brown of Queen Margaret College suggests in his survey in Part II. At one level, Scotland's past boasts stories, incidents and a historical *dramatis personae* quite colourful and exciting enough to spin out an evening in the theatre if presented with even moderate competence – or so at least many an author seems to suppose. Straightforward dramatic accounts of the life of Mary Queen of Scots, for example, had been written in great numbers before her life was treated more analytically, and more imaginatively, by Liz Lochhead in *Mary Queen of Scots Got Her Head Chopped Off*, or by Ian Brown himself in *Mary* (1977). There are ways, however, in which almost any treatment of history creates implications reaching well beyond the straightforward excitement of a good story. Shakespeare's history plays were no doubt intended as entertainment, and yet – deliberately or not – they also clarified and confirmed the contemporary ruling class's hold on its power over England. W. B. Yeats plundered myths of Ireland's past not only to carry off a gallus story or two, but to find heroic exemplars and role-models which would arouse the political feelings of his contemporaries in early twentieth-century Dublin. Given Scotland's politics in recent decades, its drama has been likelier to critique extant structures of power than to confirm them, ending up closer as a result to the model of Yeats than of Shakespeare. Hector MacMillan's *The Rising* (1973), for example, is set in the 1820s, yet its story of attempts to set up a Scottish assembly in Edinburgh could hardly fail to resonate with nationalist sentiments in 1970s' Scotland. Though performed at a later stage in the evolution of such feelings, much the same is true of James Kelman's *Hardie and Baird* (1990) or Peter Arnott's *Thomas Muir's Voyage to Australia* (1986), each concerned, like MacMillan's play, with workers' insurrections in 1820s' Scotland.

As Ian Brown's essay suggests – even in its title (taken from a play by John McGrath) – many recent Scottish dramatists have been 'plugged into history' as much or more than those just mentioned, directing towards the present powers drawn from shared, often highly emotive, awareness of Scotland's past. The outstanding example has been John McGrath's work with 7:84 (Scotland), most famously in *The Cheviot, the Stag and the Black, Black Oil* (1973), which recalled the Highland Clearances in order to direct audiences' attention upon the oil industry's current encroachment on Scottish life. This and later productions discussed by Linda Mackenney in Part I made 7:84 one of the most significant participants in the 1970s renaissance, alongside the Traverse Theatre's discovery of new writers and Bill Bryden's work with a Scottish company and Scottish dramatists at the Royal Lyceum in the early years of the decade. Determination to reach audiences as fully and directly as possible led 7:84 to redefine both the nature of Scottish theatre – reintroducing popular performance forms, such as the ceilidh format used in *The Cheviot* – and where it could take place. Lessons in geography, as well as in history, have been a part of 7:84's

influential legacy: using community centres, clubs, and village halls –
initially throughout the Highlands, and later in the Lowlands as well –
the company re-established touring as an opportunity and an obligation
for Scottish companies. Scottish Mime Theatre would not have been
rolling round the Highlands in 1979 if 7:84 had not shown the way, and
many companies have followed since. Borderline, Benchtours, Winged
Horse, Guiser, Clyde Unity and many others have all benefited from
7:84's example of what can be achieved by a small but determined
company, working on limited resources in impromptu venues.[7]

7:84's immediacy of contact with audiences has been matched in
other ways, in the 1970s and since, by playwrights drawing upon
another of the *differentia* of Scottish experience, to be found in the
life of its cities. City life, of course, is hardly uniquely Scottish, but
shared nowadays by the majority of the world's population. Yet there
are clear particularities in Scottish working life, and in the towns and
cities in which it takes place – most obviously in Glasgow and the West,
the setting of most of the plays 'In the Jungle of the Cities' assesses in
Part II. Glasgow's huge expansion after the industrial revolution left the
city with problems more numerous and more extreme than experienced
elsewhere, though with a sense of identity and community strengthened
by the very pressures these problems created. Poverty, slums, squalor,
crime, and the hard conditions imposed by heavy industry also shaped
a working-class radicalism more determined than elsewhere, and often
more successful – most clearly in the rent strikes and agitations of the
Red Clydeside period early in the twentieth century, though there were
many legacies and contemporary movements for playwrights to explore
in the 1970s. All these factors – none unique, yet each specifically
accented within Scotland – offer dramatic opportunities comparable
to those of Scots language. The kind of powerful hold exercised over
spectators by a language familiar to them can also be established by
accurate depiction of the lives they lead, the streets they walk in, the
places they work, the homes where they live, eat and sleep. Accurate
representation of this kind also, of course, encompasses language as much
as set or action. The distinctive accents of the city – its expressions rubbed
hard by working life – provide particular points of contact for urban
audiences, adding to the powers and immediacies of Scottish theatrical
language and performance already discussed.

As well as examining the rise of the city play, 'In the Jungle of the
Cities' points to ways this was based upon – or rediscovered – earlier
Scottish drama with similar concerns. Much the same could be said of
the other areas of interest so far discussed. Just as the work of Glasgow
Unity playwrights such as Robert McLeish and George Munro offered

examples to later plays set in the cities, so recent uses of Scots language and history may be seen to follow from the work of three dramatists, Robert McLellan, Robert Kemp and Alexander Reid, all of whom had written extensively for the stage by the 1950s. *The King of Scots* (1951) and other history plays Kemp wrote in bland, pseudo-Shakespearean English were probably less useful as models than the vigorous language and comic invention of McLellan's *Jamie the Saxt* (1937) – examining a period Stewart Conn returns to, in something of the same style, in *The Burning* (1970), and also a particular influence on the work of Donald Campbell. Each of these playwrights illustrates the potential of theatrical Scots: Kemp in his use of it as a medium for translation (it was his version of Moliere's *L'Ecole des Femmes*, *Let Wives Tak Tent*, which provided Scottish Theatre Company with that opening night in 1981); McLellan in almost everything he wrote; and Reid in various Scots plays published in the 1950s.

In an Introduction written for two of these, Reid restates the kind of priorities MacDiarmid had indicated thirty years earlier when he remarks that

> The return to Scots is a return to meaning and sincerity. We can only grow from our own roots and our roots are not English . . . If we are to fulfil our hope that Scotland may some day make a contribution to World Drama . . . we can only do so by cherishing, not repressing our national peculiarities (including our language).[8]

His remarks probably seem more significant now – in the light of the dramatic revival which has grown up since the 1970s – than when they were made in 1958. One swallow doesn't make a summer, and an owl or two even less so, as poor old Niels Horrobow might have reflected, and in the 1950s and much of the 1960s, drab times for Scottish theatre, there were few birds ready to fly in the directions Reid suggests; few writers ready to follow the examples provided by his own work, or by McLellan or Kemp.[9] Gloomier commentators have often attributed the barrenness of the theatrical landscape to the non-existence or discontinuity of a tradition which might have helped to foster contemporary drama, and even some of those taking a more positive view have regretted the absence of viable models from earlier years. Edwin Morgan complains in 1967 about the 'slow, broken, and disturbed' development of Scottish theatre in general. Writing ten years later, in his Introduction to *The Modern Scottish Theatre*, David Hutchison still suggests that 'Scottish dramatists have had to cope with the great problem of the absence of a significant dramatic tradition within which to work'.[10] Models, traditions, and influences obviously help literature to come into being, but as some literary theorists have remarked,[11] successful works of literature also *create* models, traditions and influences for themselves, at least in the sense of revealing ones which may always have existed, perhaps without anyone much noticing their potential. The appearance of 'early shoots and flowers' Christopher Small records in the 1970s – and the drama which has grown up and flourished since – has in this way revealed roots for itself, often in work which had previously been thought simply dead and buried.

Perhaps the clearest example of this was in the 1982 'Clydebuilt' season (further described by Linda Mackenney in Part I) in which 7:84 exhumed some plays – such as Ena Lamont Stewart's *Men Should Weep* (1947) – of genuine and continuing power, while also helping explain the success of their *own* brand of theatre. Original though they had seemed in the 1970s, it turned out that 7:84 had also been *re*discovering interests and idioms long available to the Scottish stage, redeploying them in ways particularly heightening their contemporary political relevance. The question of tradition remains a complex one for the Scottish Theatre, and as Femi Folorunso argues in Part III, the apparent absence of one may just be the result of searching for it in all the wrong places, overlooking forms of popular entertainment – ones often used by 7:84 – which have always played an important part in Scottish life. At any rate, not only the 'Clydebuilt' season but Scottish drama's general revival in recent decades has cast a warmer, backward glow over some of the earlier parts of the twentieth century. When a full history of Scottish theatre is written,[12] it should show that earlier landscapes were less icy and deserted than commentators sometimes supposed, and that – however impressive its recent progress – Scottish theatre did not appear entirely out of thin or desert air in 1970.

While the 'Clydebuilt' season helped recreate a kind of confidence in the past, by the end of the 1970s there was also widespread confidence in the present and future of Scottish theatre. By the end of the decade, playwrights had used extensively most of the specific strengths and *differentia* – of language, history, city life – discussed above, their interests in them further encouraged by changes in the political and economic outlook of Scotland itself. The origin of some of these changes is indicated by the setting – an oil rig – and title of Tom Gallacher's *The Sea Change*, staged at the Traverse in 1976, and by his later explanation that, 'the burgeoning riches of oil off the Scottish coast accomplished a sea change in the Arts as well . . . Scottishness was an asset, not a liability.' The mercenary soldier in Stewart Conn's *Play Donkey* (1977) likewise remarks of 'Fighting for wur freedom, after all these centuries' that there 'Might even have been a chance of . . . getting paid for it, now there's all that oil'.[13] The Piper Alpha oil-rig disaster of 1988 offered final confirmation – if any were still required – that John McGrath's warnings about the black, black oil were more sensible than the kind of welcome it received in the 1970s. Nevertheless, the oil fuelled a mood of political nationalism, or at least of national self-interest in the 'asset' of Scottishness, which contributed at many levels to the dramatic revival of the time. Whatever the strengths or weakness of its tradition, however clear or otherwise its collective characteristics, for any nation a dramatic revival is possible only when it has sufficient interest in itself, and a sufficient sense of self, to wish to see its life staged and scrutinised in its theatres.[14] In Scotland by the end of the 1970s these conditions seemed to have been fulfilled.

Further evidence of this appears in the foundation in 1980 of Scottish Theatre Company, an organisation which still seems to have offered the best chance – in this millennium – of creating the kind of National Theatre whose perennial hold on dramatic dreams and aspirations Roger Savage discusses in Part I. The company began promisingly enough with a first season going on from the success of that Rikki Fulton-inspired *Let Wives Tak Tent* to include new work by Tom McGrath – *Animal* – and Bill Bryden – *Civilians* – before ending gloomily with an adaptation of Henrik Ibsen's *Ghosts*. Later seasons saw a memorable revival of McLellan's *Jamie the Saxt*; ambitious productions of Brecht and Barrie; new plays from Catherine Lucy Czerkawska and Marcella Evaristi; and much besides. Yet Scottish Theatre Company never quite attracted the audiences it had predicted for itself, and whatever the admirable wisdom of the Scottish Arts Council in helping to set it up, it was a wisdom which ran out in 1987, the company expiring when its support was withdrawn – ironically just after one of its greatest successes, a production of Sir David Lindsay's *Ane Satyre of the Thrie Estaitis* (1540) which won the critics prize at the Warsaw International Theatre Festival.

In the fate of Scottish Theatre Company and 7:84 – much of its role taken over by its offshoot, Wildcat, by the end of the decade – might be read the wider fate of Scottish theatre in the 1980s. Neither nationalism, nor a socialism equally buoyant in the 1970s, easily survived the failure of the Devolution Bill and the re-election of a Tory government in 1979, and the 'seventies surge' in the theatre has sometimes been thought to have declined or expired along with the spirit of the nation. Thus *Scottish Theatre since the Seventies* is a title with a different resonance from its companion volume, *The Scottish Novel since the Seventies* (1993). However later progress is assessed, it is the 1970s *themselves* which are often considered one of the best-ever periods of Scottish drama, whereas

it is largely *since* 1979 – in a new renaissance led by Alasdair Gray and
James Kelman that the Scottish novel once again developed as strongly
as it did in MacDiarmid's day, in the 1920s and 1930s. What history
refuses, it is sometimes supposed, culture and imagination provide: thus
the political independence which failed to appear in 1979 has been
substituted by a flourishing cultural independence, widely manifest in
fiction and in many other art-forms as well – though perhaps less in the
drama. As a private act of creation, shared with disparate individual
readers, fiction is perhaps better equipped to garner and reintegrate
political or imaginative energies fragmented at the end of the 1970s.
As a public, highly social form, one in which the collective feeling of
the audience is always an important centre of gravity, drama was perhaps
more likely just to reflect a decline in national feelings, rather than creating consoling sublimations of their flagging energies. More immediately,
there were obvious financial constraints, under Tory rule, which affected
theatres a good deal more seriously than most publishers of fiction.

Yet a misleading and far too gloomy picture would be offered by
suggesting Scottish drama climbed various ladders in the 1970s only to
slip (adapting Gregory Smith a little) down sundry snakes ever since.
Most of the items in that opening list of highlights, after all, come
from the 1980s and 1990s, and there may be even more in yours
– not just because memory is short, but because Scottish drama has
genuinely moved on to new achievements since 1980, and indeed has
had to move on. Some of the features of Scottish life drama in the
1970s reflected – communities in class, urban life, outlook or politics
– have greatly changed, and the theatre, particularly the theatre of the
left, as John McGrath remarks in Part III, has found itself with new
sets of circumstances to address, and a need for new tactics in doing
so. Some of these circumstances are in themselves dispiriting, but the
search for new tactics, new visions, ought to be less so, especially given
the strength of foundations the 1970s laid.

Femi Folorunso points to their usefulness when he outlines in Part
III an inherently popular aspect in all Scottish drama, which he sees as
bound by its nature and circumstances to ask – more or less explicitly
– some version of that most widely-relevant question: 'Scotland: whit
like is it?' This was a question running through a lot of drama in the
1970s, sometimes fairly much in the foreground, and of course it has
regularly reappeared there since. Liz Lochhead's *Mary Queen of Scots Got
Her Head Chopped Off*, for example, could perhaps hardly avoid opening
with a summary anatomy of Scotland, given the play's interest in a figure
supposed to define so much of the nation's nature. But in much recent
drama, the nation's nature – the issue of whit like Scotland is – has been

allowed to fade into a background or secondary interest, if even a very significant one at all. Those various *differentia* – linguistic, historical, urban – have been allowed to develop as dramatic devices rather than necessarily subjects or issues in themselves.

Playwrights in the 1970s, in other words, built a stage on which their successors can perform, without always drawing attention to the methods of its construction or even the land on which it is based. Peter Zenzinger's essay shows how freely and successfully such possibilities have begun to be used by a 'New Wave' of dramatists working in subsequent decades. Their new interests include, for example, issues of gender politics which have a clear, urgent Scottish focus, but also reach firmly across national boundaries. In another essay in Part II, Audrey Bain sees such issues informing an 'emergent tradition' of women's writing for the Scottish theatre, one which draws on its established strengths while also reshaping and extending them towards new interests and discourses. In these and many other areas, there is probably more chance now than in the 1970s for playwrights to realise Alexander Reid's ambition for Scotland 'to make a contribution to World Drama' while retaining a particular relevance to the nation itself. This was a possibility anticipated by Sandy Neilson, director of that production of *The Jesuit*, when working for Scottish Theatre Company in 1981. He remarked in an interview that during the 1970s, playwrights

> had plenty to say about Scotland . . . In any form of development in drama, you're going to go through the classic syndromes of . . . playwrights writing about, first of all, their own identity . . . you're normally going to get, to begin with, [a] fairly introspective sort of drama – who are we?, who are the Scots?, how do we actually relate, culturally speaking, to all these other people around us? Surely we have an identity and a voice of our own. Then, eventually, that gets written out and . . . we can then go on and expand the subjects to become truly international, yet with a distinctive Scottish voice.[15]

A small nation with sharp particularities of language, history and culture, Scotland offers an ideal context through which – as John McGrath also suggests in Part III – the international can be imaginatively grounded in the local. Perhaps most clearly in the work of C. P. Taylor, there is already evidence of how this may be achieved by Scottish dramatists. Playwrights and theatre companies in years to come may realise still more fully the potential for interaction between local and cosmopolitan culture, further fulfilling MacDiarmid's ambition to 'see the Infinite/And Scotland in true scale to it'.[16]

*   *   *

If there are reasons for optimism about contemporary writing – about building stages metaphorically – there is surely reason for enormous, almost unqualified enthusiasm about building them literally; about the general provision of theatres and performance spaces across Scotland. As Mark Fisher notes in Part I, there has recently been a 'vast increase' in the availability of stage spaces, with a new Festival Theatre in Edinburgh; new buildings for the Traverse, and in Pitlochry and Dundee; and a new auditorium in Aberdeen. Refurbishments have also established fresh theatre spaces – such as the Tron in Glasgow – or improved old ones, such as the Citizens' Theatre in Glasgow, the Royal Lyceum in Edinburgh, and His Majesty's in Aberdeen. Most spectacularly, perhaps, the conversion of Glasgow's old Transport Museum into the Tramway Theatre has created one of the most flexible, exciting playing areas in Europe. It attracted Peter Brook's *Mahabharata* in 1988; it was employed particularly imaginatively by John McGrath in *Border Warfare* (1989) and *John Brown's Body* (1990), outstanding productions Olga Taxidou analyses in Part III; and it provided a challenging venue for various companies throughout Glasgow's year as European City of Culture in 1990.

These recent developments stand alongside some longer-established successes. The Edinburgh Festival is now the largest of its kind in the world, with hundreds of performances taking place daily every August. Glasgow's Mayfest provides a distinctive alternative to its larger neighbour, and outshines it theatrically from time to time – when the Maly Theatre came back in 1994, for example. As David Hutchison discusses in Part I, since 1968 the Citizens' brilliant stylishness in staging European drama and English classics *has* consistently outshone anything offered by other repertory companies in the United Kingdom. For even longer – since its foundation in 1963, when it was the only professional studio theatre in Britain – the Traverse has provided an equivalent excitement in the capital, hugely influencing styles and assumptions about theatre throughout Britain and beyond. Its long-sustained policy of encouraging new writing has been highly effective locally: like C. P. Taylor and Stanley Eveling in the 1960s, many recent Scottish dramatists owe their discovery and the progress of their early careers largely to the Traverse Theatre.

The oldest of these developments, the Edinburgh Festival, is barely fifty. Most are a lot younger. The advance in Scottish theatre has been so recent, and so rapid – seemingly still accelerating – that speculation almost inevitably arises about what fuels it, or why it ever occurred at all. Obviously, there are practical explanations: the vision of a few individuals in Edinburgh in 1947, and in various ways and places since; the relative wisdom of the Scottish Arts Council; the generosity of city councils, especially in Glasgow and Edinburgh, if not exactly in showering gold into the laps of their theatres and festivals, at least in helping them to sufficient funds and facilities to maintain a more or less viable existence. But the growth of theatre has been strong and widespread enough to suggest that – rather than in any significant way *creating* a demand – measures of civic or governmental planning have satisfied an existing one; one for which there may well be deeper sources or explanations. Christopher Small indicates one when in 'looking backward over Scotland's barren theatrical landscape' he suggests laying 'some of the blame for its infertility upon the Kirk'.[17] It is now widely accepted that for centuries the church drained away Scotland's dramatic potential in a direct way – by suppressing theatres, or designating them temples of Satan – but also by submitting churchgoers to weekly sermons of fire and brimstone, or figural conflict between the Beast and the Lord, Heaven and Hell, quite dramatic enough to overwhelm anything the stage itself could offer. If Scottish theatre has recently enjoyed dramatic successes, these may belong to an increasingly secular age, able at last to blow away fumes of brimstone, whether as threat or spectacle. More subtly, the theatre's recent advance might be seen not only as an escape from religious suppression, but as a filling of spaces, and a fulfilling of functions, left vacant by the Church's retreat. As its great grey hand has gradually loosened its grip on Scotland, areas of life constricted by its doctrines have once again opened up for the kind of negotiation with morals and emotions which theatre has always facilitated. Given ancient origins in collective celebration of libidinal, transgressive energies, theatre is perhaps likeliest to thrive in any society stirring away from moral constraint. Comparisons might be made with recent fiction by Alasdair Gray, Andrew Greig, Irvine Welsh, or Duncan McLean, incorporating within the Scottish novel hitherto-taboo subject-areas such as sexual relations, or – in the case of James Kelman – the expletives connected with them.

Whether or not the dramatic energy which flows around the arts festivals of the world has recently been drawn to Scotland, and Scotland to it, by a need to fill the holes religion has left, there is little doubt that Scotland's own arts festivals have in the past thirty years made it a genuine player on the great stage of the world, and one of the world's great stages – a role which Glasgow's nomination as European City of Culture perhaps helped to confirm. Just as Scotland's footballers have so regularly qualified for the World Cup over the past quarter century, so Scottish theatre has acquired a regular, natural place at the highest level. And of course it is tempting to conclude on such a note of achievement: with a picture of theatrical Jacob's ladders sprouting all over the Scottish landscape, leading step by golden step to a dramatic heaven – even one perhaps just vacated by the Church of Scotland. But there are still plenty of snakes on the scene. Some of their ugly heads may have been visible even in that opening list of highlights. It referred, you'll recall, to one production by a Soviet theatre, a mime-and-movement company, two translations, one revival and an adaptation: as you probably noticed, only two items out of eight were plays by contemporary Scottish dramatists. Your list no doubt contains different highlights, but it would be surprising if these included much more work by Scottish playwrights. Two items out of eight, 25 per cent of the total, would be a high estimate of the proportion of indigenous material annually presented on Scottish stages. There is a substantial gap, in other words, between the success of 'theatre in Scotland', and the success of 'Scottish drama' – in the sense of work written by, for, and about Scottish people.

There may even be times when the strength of the former works against the latter. Mark Fisher sees a generation of Scottish playwrights who have been partly passed over by the success of their theatres. In another essay in Part I, Owen Dudley Edwards points out that the Edinburgh Festival and its Fringe have never consistently favoured or encouraged Scottish writing, however positively they may have done so on occasion. Indeed, the kind of glossy international productions the Festival offers, or the sophisticated European theatre on view at the Tramway or the Citizens' – often criticised, as David Hutchison observes, for ignoring Scottish material – might be thought to make audiences occasionally less patient with local products, perhaps seeming on occasion rather a dour porridge after the *menus gastronomiques* on offer elsewhere. Any analogy between theatre and football, in other words, should perhaps not refer to the successes of the World Cup, achieved entirely with Scottish talent, but more to the clubs of the Premier League, where native players sometimes find themselves sidelined by expensive foreign stars.

The clubs, of course, hope that foreign and native players will profitably combine and interact, and there are likewise surely ways in which the imported and the home-grown can coalesce rather than compete on the Scottish stage. It is simply inaccurate, first of all, to criticise the Citizens' for passing over Scottish material, when for a long time past the writer it has most frequently performed has been its own – Scottish – dramaturg and translator, Robert David MacDonald. Worse, it just seems improvident. A glance around theatres or bookshops in any of the smaller countries of Europe would reveal a great deal of translated material; part of such nations' attempts to understand or locate themselves within international culture, engage with its diversities, or just borrow some of its exciting energies. For these and other reasons Bill Findlay explores in Part III, translation has been a rapidly expanding part of Scottish theatre, and MacDonald has contributed as much as anyone to its progress. For two decades, his work has brought to Gorbals Cross the best of European drama – sometimes also European fiction, as on that Proustean summer evening in 1981 – and the effect on audiences, and in shaping a new generation of playwrights, has been immense.

Other combinations of foreign and native energies are not hard to find: look no further than the example of Communicado Theatre Company.[18] Whether in staging Scottish or international material, their productions over the past decade or so have been shaped by a wide range of performance styles: these have perhaps owed most to the kind of physical theatre, heavily dependent on mime and movement, which has grown up in Poland under the influence of figures such as Jerzy Grotowski and Tadeusz Kantor – the latter's Cricot 2 Theatre familiar to Edinburgh audiences from visits to the city organised by Richard Demarco. The breadth of Communicado's interests was illustrated by the opening show of Glasgow's year as European City of Culture, *Jock Tamson's Bairns*. Devised by a largely Scottish company, with the help of a Scottish poet and playwright, Liz Lochhead, *Jock Tamson's Bairns* incorporated Scottish legend and a Scottish ritual – the Burns Supper – within a performance idiom whose dependence on choreography, movement and tableaux would have seemed familiar enough to theatre-goers from Warsaw, Lublin or Krakow; though perhaps at times a little naïve. A more convincing integration of the company's international and domestic interests appeared in their powerful production of *Blood Wedding* for the Edinburgh Fringe in 1988. This relied on movement skills performers had acquired from Jaques Lecoq's mime school in Paris, but also on Scottish accents and dialects which drew out from Garcia Lorca's language subtleties and powers often lost to performances in standard English, as well as suggesting a convincing, familiar rural setting for the play. Though few Scottish companies have been as successfully eclectic in style as Communicado, many directors in Scottish theatre share something of their influences – Jon Pope at the Citizens', for example, with a penchant for German Expressionism and a period of training in Poland in the 1980s. Kenny Ireland's work at the Royal Lyceum shows a comparable capacity to combine the solid needs of repertory theatre with much more innovative, experimental possibilities.

Maybe a defence of Scottish theatre's internationalism could be taken a stage or two further. For whatever reasons, post-Presbyterian or otherwise – such an argument might run – Scotland badly needs its theatre. And it *has* its theatre, already, and a very internationally-oriented one, too, bringing to Scotland's needs all the imagination, charm and vision of the world. So why worry if Scottish drama – plays by, for, and about the people of Scotland themselves – sometimes seems to lag behind? Well – since you ask! – because there *are* some very clear limits to any such argument. As suggested earlier, it's rare to hear Scots spoken in the media: it's likewise rare, in film or television particularly, to find much focus on Scottish issues or affairs, however much Hollywood may recently have rediscovered the romance of Scotland as a moneyspinner. Theatre offers one of the last public arenas – and maybe one of the best – for raising and debating issues of immediately local, regional or national concern. And if it functions as a context in which a society can examine its sense of self, and the stresses upon it, then there are surely enough stresses, whether historic, political, or economic, in contemporary Scotland – quite apart from the more moral or perhaps universal ones the church left behind – to require a particular Scottish focus for the drama. Since specifically Scottish issues – *differentia* of language, history, life – greatly contributed to the growth of Scottish drama in the 1970s, remaining thereafter an essential part of its base, it would be wrong for them to be too far lost sight of now.

They won't be, of course. But more might be done to encourage the work of the playwrights who will keep them in view, and to help close some of the gaps between Scottish dramatists and the Scottish stage. Scotland is fortunate to have in the Traverse a theatre genuinely committed to the work of local dramatists, and in the Scottish Society of Playwrights an organisation which has helped to look after their interests since its foundation in 1973, but there are still many difficulties strewn in the path of anyone writing for the stage, as a novice or even as an established author.[19] These are further discussed in David Hutchison's concluding piece, along with a radical strategy which might help to solve some of them. In another essay in Part III, Ian Brown outlines measures currently in place at the Traverse for supporting Scottish writing: in particular, the unusual but vital opportunity his theatre offers for an author to work closely with a particular director and company of actors, and towards performance in a familiar theatre space. He also gives a fascinating – sometimes disturbing – insight into the finances and daily running of a modern theatre. If Scotland has sometimes seemed to lag dramatically behind the rest of Europe, it is partly at least because its theatre companies are so painfully underfunded that they have almost never had the chance to compete with, or even dream of, the kind of general resourcing – of extended rehearsal periods in particular – which is a matter of course for the likes of the Maly Theatre and many other heavily state-subsidised companies around the continent. Ian Brown's question 'what use will beautiful empty theatres be without companies working in them?' is a grim reminder of difficulties which still afflict the Scottish stage, despite its many successes; of the snakes still brazenly entwining the best of ladders, as if sure they must all be staffs of Asklepius.

Ian Brown points out another difficulty when he discusses the shortage of worthwhile theatre criticism; often of any beyond the ephemeral, sometimes unreliable comments which appear in a handful of newspapers. As he suggests, theatre practitioners and theatre audiences might benefit from better, more substantial advice; clearer, more constructive contextualising of their work. *Theatre Scotland* magazine has helped in recent years to fill this gap, as *Scottish Theatre News* did during its short life (1981–7), but it is surprising how seldom drama in Scotland has been considered properly and at length, and how relatively few items there are for Alison Lumsden's bibliography of theatre criticism. For that matter, her bibliography of published plays is also fairly short, one of the problems of studying, teaching or writing about Scottish drama being the difficulty of finding copies of the scripts required. At any rate, it is this gap between theatrical promise and worthwhile commentary that the present volume is intended to close. From the point of view of their various specialisms – as playwright, journalist, researcher, director, academic, critic or historian – each of its contributors answers in one way or another that opening question, 'Scottish theatre: whit like is it?' Their answers, of course, are a great deal more comprehensive and less impressionistic than anything provided by that opening list of highlights. Yet even so, in a single short volume they can do no more than provide a preliminary survey of the wide and partially charted territory they survey, and there are whole areas on its frontiers – such as dance and mime, performance art, or radio and television drama – which have to be left for other volumes.

But such exclusions might in another way serve for rejoicing rather than regret. It should be a matter of satisfaction that a full account of the nation's drama is already too much for a single book, given how often it has risked being stigmatised by the kind of single sentence earned by owls and snakes in Iceland. Each of the pages that follows banishes still further these creatures of ill omen: think of them slouching off, melancholy beasts, further and further as the millennium approaches, and of all that may take their place, and enjoy every sentence as you read.

NOTES

1. *The Jesuit* was first staged at the Traverse Theatre, Edinburgh, but moved for the duration of the Edinburgh Festival to 'The Other Traverse', the old University Chaplaincy Centre in Forrest Road, which has since become the Bedlam, headquarters of Edinburgh University Theatre Company.

2. G. Gregory Smith, *Scottish Literature: Character and Influence* (London: Macmillan, 1919), pp.105–6. Smith moves towards a rather less pessimistic assessment later in his survey.

3. George Munro, 'The Adventures of a Playwright', unpublished typescript, Mitchell Library, Glasgow, pp.5, 7.

4. Christopher Small, Foreword to David Hutchison, *The Modern Scottish Theatre* (Glasgow: Molendinar Press, 1977), pp.[iii], vii.

5. Hugh MacDiarmid, 'R. F. Pollock and the Art of the Theatre' in *Contemporary Scottish Studies* (1926; rpt. Manchester: Carcanet, 1995), p.181. MacDiarmid's views of J. M. Barrie appear in an essay in the same volume.

6. Liz Lochhead, Introduction to *Tartuffe: A Translation into Scots from the Original by Molière* (Edinburgh and Glasgow: Polygon and Third Eye Centre, 1985).

7. Gerry Mulgrew, director of Communicado Theatre Company, records that '*The Cheviot, the Stag and the Black, Black Oil* opened the door and provided the focus for a distinct and intelligent Scottish theatre. It engendered a whole popular movement whose reverberations are still being felt today'. 'The Poor Mouth', *Chapman 43–4: On Scottish Theatre*, (Spring 1986), pp.64–5. Sandy Neilson talks of '7:84's monumental work in pioneering new venues throughout the country with their historic tour of *The Cheviot* and subsequent productions. They opened to a large and hungry audience outside the two cities who had effectively been starved of professional theatre and it now became possible to form small scale companies who found themselves with a platform large enough to sustain and justify their existence'. 'Theatre Revival: A Director's View', ibid, p.17.

8. Alexander Reid, Introduction to *Two Scots Plays* (London: Collins, 1958).

9. What openings did exist for Scottish work at the time were to be found at the Citizens', which staged some Scottish material, and at the Gateway Theatre in Edinburgh. Founded and administered by Robert Kemp, it produced work by McLellan and Reid, as well as Kemp's own, and occasionally plays by other contemporary dramatists such as Ronald Mavor, James Scotland and Ada F. Kay. Some of the theatre's role, and its audience, passed on through the Edinburgh Civic Theatre Trust to the Royal Lyceum Theatre in 1965.

10. Edwin Morgan, 'Scottish Writing Today II: The Novel and the Drama', *English* (Autumn 1967), p.229; Hutchison, *The Modern Scottish Theatre* (note 4), p.3.

11. See Harold Bloom, *The Anxiety of Influence: A Theory of Poetry* (Oxford: Oxford University Press, 1973).

12. It nearly has been, with Bill Findlay, ed., *A History of Scottish Theatre* (Edinburgh: Polygon) due to appear late in 1996. The Scottish Theatre Archive established in Glasgow University Library by Linda Mackenney has also helped re-open Scotland's theatrical past to contemporary analysis.

13. Tom Gallacher, 'To Succeed at Home', *Chapman* (see note 7), p.89; Stewart Conn, *Play Donkey*, Act II, sc.xiii.

14. Neil Gunn put this more strongly when he remarked that 'In Dublin, Irish National

life was so strong that it created a drama out of itself . . . but we cannot expect anything like that in Scotland, because there has been neither a sense of national conflict nor of national travail. There has not been that sense of high movement of the country's spirit out of which great drama is made . . . What do we want a national theatre for if we have nothing in ourselves, nothing national, to express there?' 'Nationalism in Writing II: The Theatre Society of Scotland', *Scots Magazine* 30, iii (1938), pp.197, 198. Scotland may not be about to enter a phase of 'high movement of the country's spirit', but it seems possible that by the end of the century its political situation may have changed enough to recreate some of the dramatic self-interest Gunn felt missing in 1938, and which did appear in the 1970s. Scottish theatre should benefit as a result.

15. Sandy Neilson, interviewed by Owen Dudley Edwards for BBC Television, 'Spectrum: A Theatre for Scotland', 8 March 1981. Like much of the interview material, this section was cut from the broadcast programme, and is to be found in an unpublished typescript in the possession of the interviewer, pp.25–6. I am grateful to Owen Dudley Edwards for having made this material available.

16. Hugh MacDiarmid, 'A Drunk Man Looks at the Thistle' (1926), rpt. in *The Hugh MacDiarmid Anthology*, ed. Michael Grieve and Alexander Scott (London: Routledge and Kegan Paul, 1972), p.98.

   Scottish plays, and Scottish theatre companies, have still not made much impact abroad. For further discussion of some of the difficulties involved, and some of the potentials, see Neil Wallace, 'Theatre out of Print', *Theatre Scotland*, I, 2 (Summer 1992), pp.23–6.

17. Small, Foreword (note 4), p.v.

18. Communicado, of course, were responsible for other successes already discussed – Edwin Morgan's *Cyrano de Bergerac* and Liz Lochhead's *Mary Queen of Scots Got her Head Chopped Off*.

19. For a full account of the Scottish Society of Playwrights, see Audrey Bain, 'Striking it Rich', *Theatre Scotland*, III, 11 (Autumn 1994), pp.16–24. Many playwrights have described the difficulties of survival, David Hutchison quoting from John Clifford's 'New Playwriting in Scotland', *Chapman* (note 7). David Greig also writes on the subject in 'Internal Exile', *Theatre Scotland* III, 11 (Autumn 1994), pp.8–10.

Part I

STAGES AND COMPANIES

One

A Scottish National Theatre?

Roger Savage

Should a national theatre be set up in Scotland? 'No', some will say. 'The place has got one already – a national theatre with a small 'n' and a small 't', that is. All the various activities of a theatrically healthy nation add up to that nation's national theatre. It's true that in Scotland a deal more cash to lubricate the system in matters like forward-planning, script-commissioning, cast-sizes and rehearsal-spans wouldn't come amiss, but there's a lot of life and diversity in Scottish playwriting and play-staging for all that. That's all Scotland has and all it *needs* to have where national theatrics is concerned.' Other folk, rather fewer perhaps, would agree that Scotland already has its national theatre, though they would put the words in capitals. 'Scotland is part of a wider British entity and that entity has its prime theatre on the south bank of the Thames in London. Granted, you might be tempted once in a while to think of it as the English National Theatre; but its full name – call them if you don't believe me – is the Royal National Theatre of Great Britain and Northern Ireland.[1] So the space is taken.'

Other folk still, intrigued by those capital letters perhaps, but less prepared to accept that the union of crowns and parliaments involves the merging of national identities, might well feel they could only decide whether Scotland needed a National Theatre or not if they had a tolerably clear idea of what such a beast, should it come into existence, might be like and what place it might have in the millennial landscape. Precedents from around the world certainly suggest a whole menagerie of possibilities. A national theatre can be a Comédie-Française: an august institution created by a Sun King as a manifestation of personal/national *gloire* and surviving fairly painlessly to become the chief citizens' theatre of the nation after a civic revolution. But equally it can be an expression of such a revolution, or at least of a deep social change; as with, say, the

national theatres of Bulgaria and Senegal, established after the decamping
of the Turks from the one country and the French from the other. It
can be a theatre dedicated to staging a particularly renowned corpus or
canon of local drama, as the Japanese National Theatre in Tokyo does
– it's the state's *kabuki-bunraku* house – and as the Stratford wing of
Britain's 'other' National, the Royal Shakespeare Company, was set up
to do. Contrariwise, it can be founded as part of a movement towards
the *creation* of such a corpus in a land so far fairly innocent of significant
home-grown playwriting, as with the Abbey Theatre in Dublin, opened
in 1904 by the Irish National Theatre Society Ltd and soon fathering
major pieces by Synge and O'Casey.

Then Nationals have come into existence to highlight, perpetuate,
give status to the quite distinct language which unites a people,
as with the Polish National Theatre, founded by King Stanislas
Augustus in 1765, or the Finnish one, which moved into a fine
purpose-built playhouse in Helsinki in 1902; though also they may
grow wings which confirm national linguistic splits. (Belgium has
had, in effect, two quasi-Nationals: the Théâtre National for the
French speakers, the Koninklijke Schouwberg for the Flemings.) To
add to the plurality and to the need to decide what your notional
National might be like before you pass judgement on it, Nationals
can either be shamelessly high-cultural affairs or *théâtres nationaux
populaires*: go-out-and-grab-the-people outfits like Jean Vilar's TNP
of the 1950s and 1960s. They can operate on a very grand scale – the
three-auditorium RNT in London for instance – or on a very modest
one. (It's said that in the early days of the Yakut State Theatre up near
the Arctic Circle, firewood for heating the house was happily taken in
payment for a ticket.) And the thrust of the word 'national' at their
mast-heads can vary widely too. An NT can quite reasonably proclaim
itself as national in the manner of most national galleries or national
orchestras or national opera companies. Though it may choose, that
is, to show a degree of local piety and own-backyard specialisation,
it will mainly be concerned to use its resources to put a prestigious
collection of international cultural treasures strikingly on display, with
sheer artistic quality and cosmopolitan comprehensiveness at a greater
premium than the expression of an ethnic identity. (It's an idea which
goes back to the pioneering *Nationaltheater* set up by Lessing's circle
in Hamburg in the 1760s.)

But just as plausibly, a National can be 'national' in quite other
senses. National in immigration-law terms – 'native born and bred'
– and so characterising a theatre which only uses indigenous talent
in its casts and production-teams. Or national as in 'national*ist*',

which would imply a theatre dedicated to celebrating the unique social characteristics and concerns of a particular country, perhaps in a radical, confrontational way, perhaps in a cosier, more touristic one. Or national as in 'national*ised*': a theatre where it's the money beyond the box-office take – money from a monarch's privy purse perhaps, or the resources of some philanthropic subscription-fund, or the tax-accumulation of central government – which foots a lot of the bill and as a *quid pro quo* probably calls at least some of the tune, directly or indirectly.

At various times this century, both before and since the setting up of the NT (later the RNT) on Thames, folk have dreamed of a Scottish theatre that might be National in a shifting variety of these senses. When the Glasgow Rep was founded in 1909, it claimed that one of its objectives was encouraging 'the initiation and development of a purely Scottish drama' through the provision of 'a stage and acting company . . . peculiarly adapted' to it: *one* sort of SNT in the egg, surely. Four years later the Scottish National Theatre Society was formed, though it didn't become active until the inter-war years, when its declared aims were, first, 'to develop Scottish National Drama through the production by the Scottish National Players' – the Society's unpaid barnstorm-troupers – 'of plays of Scottish Life and Character'; second, 'to encourage in Scotland a public taste for good drama of any type'; and third, 'to found a Scottish National Theatre' – to which end, said the Society's magazine encouragingly (this being an age well before Arts Councils, Millennium Funds or National Lotteries), 'donations and legacies are invited' for a fund to be 'devoted to the foundation and endowment . . . of a Scottish National Theatre in Glasgow'.[2] The inspiration here was clearly the Abbey in Dublin, and behind it the Scandinavian Nationals and all those Nationals within an overarching Habsburg domain that had sprung up in Eastern Europe in the nineteenth century: the Hungarian in 1840, the Serbian in 1868 and so on. Indeed, the motto set very boldly over the proscenium arch of the Národní Divadlo, the Czech national playhouse in Prague (built by enthusiastic public subscription in the 1860s and 1870s), would have seemed especially resonant to members of the old SNTS: NÁROD SOBĚ – 'a nation to itself', with perhaps the triple suggestion of a country making itself the gift of a theatre, a country speaking meaningfully to itself there, and a country existing primarily *unto* itself.[3]

Still unhatched, the Scottish national egg rolled erratically on. For example, in 1938 the Theatre Society of Scotland was founded with the aim of bringing 'an endowed professional theatre' into existence in the empty but potentially fruitful space between amateur dramatics on the one side and London-based commercial touring product on the other. Bricks and mortar were envisaged (for a playhouse and an adjoining drama school as well), plus a company made up exclusively of Scots actors. Among the *literati* of the time, Neil Gunn was sympathetic but in a rather guarded, sceptical way (was there enough national ferment in the Scottish *soul?*), while Fred Urquhart was more positive; though, having given a proselytising article on the subject the title 'The Case for a Scottish National Theatre', he admitted in the article itself to being 'chary . . . about the word "National" – it savours too much of the madness which all over Europe today is the cause of bitterness and strife.'[4] During and after the Nazi War that Urquhart was glimpsing, others kept the egg rolling. Companies began to think of themselves as the SNT *de facto* if not *de jure*, or as potential SNTs in waiting or in the making: in the 1940s James Bridie's Citizens' Theatre and its working-class rival Glasgow Unity (the proto-Nationals of two different Scotlands); in the 1960s and 1970s the Edinburgh Royal Lyceum under several diverse managements.[5] Alongside this, proposals and plans were earnestly mooted and floated. In 1948 for instance, the Edinburgh branch of the Saltire Society drew up a scheme for the establishment of an SNT in the national capital: both a company (envisaged as performing a shamelessly cosmopolitan, high-cultural repertoire) and a building, which would be funded jointly by government and public subscription. And about forty years later there was another flurry of proposing, debating and resolving, with articles apropos in the magazines *Chapman* and *Theatre Scotland*[6] and a conference on the desirability of a Scottish National Theatre organised in May 1987 by members of an offshoot of the Saltire Society, the *soi-disant* Advisory Council for the Arts in Scotland, which had been founded in 1981. A unanimous resolution was passed, viz. that conference 'considers that there is a pressing need for a Scottish National Theatre company to consolidate the Scottish tradition in all aspects of the theatre, calls upon all theatre companies in Scotland to cooperate towards this objective of national importance, [and] urges the Scottish Arts Council and all levels of government and other potential funding bodies to give active support.'[7] One result of this was a 'National Theatre for Scotland Campaign'. Launched in the early 1990s and making its stand in print in 1994 with a spirited pamphlet *The Scottish Stage* compiled by Donald Smith, it is still campaigning, since, for all the talk, ink and incubation, the Scottish egg has still not hatched. The dream of an SNT remains, for better or worse, just that.

Why has it been this way? Sheer contingencies of luck (bad), money (lack of), factionalism and bureaucratic stalling have doubtless had an effect; but in a broader and deeper sense the reason may well be that quite a few of the really effective stimuli behind the creation of lively national theatres elsewhere have simply not obtained in Scotland. Of course direct court patronage in the French manner, though it had been strong enough in the sixteenth century to engender Lindsay's formidable *Satyre of the Thrie Estaitis*, pretty much came to an end in the early seventeenth when the court itself went south with King James VI; so the taking-over for the nation of a long-established, pre-eminent and tradition-rich Comédie-Ecossaise – one which would doubtless have been battle-scarred through perpetual skirmishings with the Kirk! – was never a starter.

But equally, Scotland has not had the kind of clear-cut revolution or defining moment of secession which might be marked by the founding of an SNT *à la* Bulgaria or Senegal. Then there is something of a falling-between-stools in the matter of dramatic corpus and canon. In the late twentieth century certainly, neither the RSC model nor that offered by the Abbey Theatre seems quite to fit the scene north of the border. There is no Scottish dramatist who is iconic in quite the way Shakespeare in England or Molière in France have become, and hence no single corpus of playscripts crying out for institutionalised performance by a Scottish NT. (Edinburgh's most eye-catching memorial to a writer, the Scott Monument in Princes Street, commemorates a novelist, not a playwright, albeit a novelist the stage-versions of whose works – presented with great success in the nineteenth century at the Theatre Royal in the significantly named Shakespeare Square nearby – gave strong currency to ideas of 'national drama', and have led the Theatre Royal itself to be described by some as 'Scotland's first national theatre'.[8]) At the same time, however, only the very short-sighted could fail to notice that dramatists in Scotland since at least the time of J. M. Barrie (and more especially since the 1960s) have been remarkably productive, and pretty often staged as well – if not necessarily re-staged or put into print. The Scottish Society of Playwrights when founded in 1973 didn't have to search or scrape for members; and one interesting development from that 1987 conference was the drawing-up and picking-over of quite extensive lists of plays by Scots (many though not all of them consciously reflecting 'Scottish Life and Character'): plays which had had at least one run and were arguably worth reviving as the millennium drew on. With so much playwriting staining the silence without an SNT, an Abbey-type clarion-call of enablement – 'Now at last there's an outlet for Scottish talent; go home and script!' – might seem surplus to requirements in the 1990s.

Again, the language factor, so crucial elsewhere – in Finland, Poland, Hungary among other places – has not packed the punch needful to deliver an NT for Scotland. Perhaps if the country's Gaelic-speaking community (a community with a lot of enthusiasm for amateur drama) had been ten times larger in the last hundred years and if it had been more focused on a big, busy town or two, a quasi-Flemish Gaelic theatre might have come into being, forming one half of a double-yoked Belgian-type SNT. But with the statistics being what they are – only one in fifty people in Scotland are Gaelic speakers – the problems of getting a Gaelic National Theatre up and running are vividly enough shown by the short life of Fir Chlis, the first professional Gaelic-speaking theatre company in Scotland, which lasted only three years after its founding in 1978.[9] As for the country's majority language, Scots, even in its older and broader forms it is not in the same league of grammatical, lexical difference from the language of its hegemonic neighbour south of the border as the Finnish and Polish which led Finns and Poles to set up national theatres to celebrate, preserve, extend and give international status to their native tongues and declare their distinctness from the surrounding Prussian and Russian and Swedish and such. Scots and English are far closer to each other. The chameleon skill which is developed out of professional necessity by so many Scots-born actors, the ability to move with ease between forms of Broad Scots, Urban Scots and RADA/Home-Counties English, can stand as symbolic of that closeness. (Symbolic, too, of a hierarchical relationship; few English-born actors would feel the necessity of developing the same skill in reverse.)

If these are some relevant arguments as to why Scotland has not hatched a National Theatre in the past, do they add up to a clinching super-argument that there could never be such a theatre in the future? Not necessarily. Indeed, some of the arguments start trains of thought which could be apropos for anyone wanting to make a serious case for an SNT to the Scottish Arts Council (who have traditionally kept the concept at arm's length), or St Andrew's House, or the Palace of Westminster. Thus while it is true that Scotland has had as yet no National-Theatre-generating grand event of secession, revolution or even devolution, the country could be said right now to be in the middle of a phase of high national self-consciousness and of deep concern over matters of social-political-cultural identity. Is this not just the situation which merits the setting up of a kind of Civic Forum of the Imagination: a stage on which to play out dreams, visions, nightmares of nationality and nationhood past, present and future? Who knows: such a theatre, touring extensively and finding resonances of one kind and another all over Scotland, might do the state some cohesive service. It was Tom McGrath, playwright and *dramaturg*, who asked in a wryly sceptical piece about national theatrics: 'Is there a theatre company that can pull this land together?' In fact it's a notion that had been put forward more gravely many years earlier:

> A standing theatre would be a material advantage to a nation. It would have a great influence on the national temper and mind by helping the nation to agree in opinions and inclinations. The stage alone can do this because it commands all human knowledge, exhausts all positions, illumines all hearts, unites all classes . . . If the poets were allied in aim – that is, if they selected well and from national topics – there would be a national stage, and we should *become a nation.*

(No, it's not an inter-war Scottish ideologue; it's Friedrich Schiller on the German theatre in 1784.)[10]

Again, though it would be myopic to say that Scotland in the late twentieth century has no real corpus of native drama and so needs an SNT to create one, it could reasonably be argued that there is currently no proper way of reviving and revisiting the best Scottish plays, of keeping them in the national bloodstream as they deserve, and that a properly funded SNT could be charged with that responsibility (as the improperly funded, accident-prone and oddly short-lived Scottish Theatre Company charged itself in the 1980s under the brave directorates of Ewan Hooper and Tom Fleming). Further, while it is true that there is no Comédie-Ecossaise ready to take over as an SNT, there has been a remarkable tradition of Scots acting, rooted in music-hall and variety and with strong links to pantomime and TV sit-com, which arguably deserves to be preserved and built on, contributing vital things to the acting style of a putative national company. It is intriguing how well this tradition has served some actual classics of the Comédie-Française when they have been done in lively Scots-language adaptations: *L'Ecole des Femmes, Le Malade Imaginaire, Tartuffe* and so on. (Lady Gregory's 'Kiltartan Molière' for the Abbey Theatre has been finely upstaged by the *echt*-tartan Molière of Robert Kemp, Victor Carin, Liz Lochhead and the others.) Indeed, perhaps the most important train of thought started by the non-emergence so far of an SNT has to do with the Scots language. Granted that the non-Gaelic tongue (or rather range of tongues) spoken north of the border is nearer to Sassenach-English than Finnish is to any of the Baltic languages surrounding it; but for all that, from the perspective of many Scots the distance between the two is great enough. A prestigious theatre which spoke to its people in their own tongue, which consistently used the intonations and rhythms, idioms and structures, resonances and overtones of Scots for a greater realism, a richer fantasy, a more immediate rapport in acting and playwriting than would otherwise be possible: could an SNT not admirably be that? Couldn't it properly take the name of National if it announced 'Here we speak Scots, speak it in all its varieties, speak it to creative ends, speak it well?'

Well, maybe. Certainly if someone was asked whether they thought Scotland needed a National Theatre with a capital NT and said they would like some details of the nature of the beast before deciding, then it's in such terms that it could most plausibly be described to them: as a theatre expertly talking to the Scots – and anyone else who cared to listen – *in* Scots, talking primarily about Scottish issues (however broadly defined), building on the tried and trusted strengths of Scottish acting, making forays of revival into the corpus of drama of Scots written between 1540 and 1995, and extending that corpus with adventurous stagings of promising new Scots pieces, along perhaps with Scots adaptations of relevant drama from elsewhere.

Yet the question remains, is it feasible, indeed is it really desirable, to build something called The Scottish National Theatre on this ideological raft in the 1990s? It may be most desirable that *some* company like this should exist, be decently subsidised, tour extensively and have its work widely known: to emancipate Scots fully as a dramatic medium, to provide a focus for vernacular acting, to keep national achievement in playwriting before the public eye, to hold a mirror up to Scottishness on the edge of the millennium. It could be a resurrected Scottish Theatre Company perhaps, with better funding, a sounder venue policy and a greater preparedness to be politically controversial. But whether that company should be labelled 'The SNT', with all the kudos and centrality which that would imply, is another matter. Doing so might seem to institutionalise the view that theatrical work by Scots which foregrounds issues of national identity is *inherently* more valuable than work which doesn't. And that is surely too narrow a view. By its lights Sean O'Casey has *ipso facto* to be a better Irish dramatist than Samuel Beckett, Arthur Miller a better American one than Tennessee Williams. In Scottish terms and simply taking the highest-profile example of the last quarter-century, such a view would marginalise the achievement of an author like Robert David MacDonald, the playright-adaptor-translator (born in Elgin) whose remarkable work with Giles Havergal and Philip Prowse at the Glasgow Citizens' has been idiosyncratic, highly cosmopolitan, flamboyantly unlocal – and pretty consistently staged in shameless South-British RP. Politically quite incorrect from certain perspectives, it has none the less paid the citizens of Glasgow the

serious compliment of treating their city as a *European* one first
and foremost.[11] The Cits at its best and the company which
we have hypothesised as mainlining consistently on the Scottish
Condition should surely bloom and contend like the flowers of
Chairman Mao, not be institutionally rank-ordered, with the Cits
and companies like it being consigned to the B position, as arguably they *would* be by the Act of Parliament and Royal Assent
needful to create a Scottish National Theatre along the lines considered here. Unless of course that Act did the proper dialectical thing and at the same time created a Scottish *Inter*national
Theatre!

That would hardly be feasible; but even an SNT on its own would
raise feasibility problems. Could a reliable source of beyond-box-office
funding be found for it which would give it *Lebensraum* and yet
pose no threat to the funding of other Scottish theatres? Could
a base be found for it (and in what city?) which would give
it a good home and yet not tie it too tightly *to* that home?
Would the nucleus of talent for the company be new-created or
be found in one of the present Scottish companies, which, by
achieving greatness, would have more greatness thrust upon it?
Crucially, is there a handful of consequential men and women
out there sufficiently wise, knowledgeable, steely, visionary, impartial
and confidence-inspiring to form the SNT's board of trustees, make
proper decisions about these matters and convince the theatrical
profession, the municipalities and so on that the decisions are the
right ones? Just as important, would it be possible to find an Artistic
Director creative and charismatic enough and yet at the same time
Ideologically Sound enough to make the whole thing work from
season to season? The kind of *apparatchik* who would be prepared
to carry out some of the more detailed policies that have been
framed with the best of intentions for an SNT recently[12] doesn't
easily inhabit the same skin as the kind of obsessive enthusiast and
quester after personal theatrical grails – great at getting the best
out of complex human relationships among actors and production
teams, at juggling with contingencies, at moulding and nurturing
organic ensemble – who tends to deliver the really good productions.
(MacDonald's *Chinchilla* is required reading – and, if possible, viewing
– here.)[13]

Again, if finally the SNT egg is to be hatched in the late twentieth
century, how does one prevent the creature that emerges from being
an overlusty cuckoo in the quite crowded and not very sturdy nest
of the current theatrical scene in Scotland? When the SNT idea

was first mooted and for some decades afterwards, the country had little to speak of in the way of an indigenous theatrical profession where 'straight' theatre was concerned, and nothing in the way of public subsidy. Bridie's state-assisted creation of the Citizens' Theatre in the 1940s and the staggered births since then of the various local-authority-and-Arts-Council-supported civic reps, regional troupes and smaller, more specialised outfits have changed all that. There is now quite a scatter of such companies in Scotland, all of them in a sense 'national' in that they can think beyond a purely box-office break-even in return for declaring a serious artistic policy to a public purse-holder. Could an SNT – by definition prestigious, upmarket, probably with quite enviable working conditions and certainly with a high public profile at home and eventually abroad – be added to them without drawing to itself much of the finest talent now available to the other companies in a way that would be nationally counterproductive? There is an old Russian (or is it cod-Russian) folk tale about the hollow tree in a forest glade which was able to provide house-room cumulatively for a whole succession of very diverse but accommodating creatures, until the arrival one day of a beast with an all-too-apt-name: Mr Bear-Squash-You-All-Flat. It couldn't happen here. Or could it?

NOTES

1. See, for example, an essay by the RNT's current director, Richard Eyre, 'What's the National Theatre For?', in his *Utopia and Other Places* (London: Bloomsbury Publishing, 1993), pp.173–81, esp. p.175.
2. *The Scottish Player*, I, 4 (1923), p.3. For the Glasgow Rep and the SNTS, see David Hutchison, *The Modern Scottish Theatre* (Glasgow: Molendinar Press, 1977), chapters 3 and 5.
3. *The Scottish Player*, 1, 6 (1923), p.2 declared that 'we can do what Ireland, Norway and Bohemia have done.' Laurence Senelick, ed., *National Theatre in Northern and Eastern Europe, 1746–1900* (Cambridge: Cambridge University Press, 1991), in the series 'Theatre in Europe: a Documentary History', is a happy hunting ground for Continental sources and analogues to Irish and Scottish notions of national theatre.
4. Gunn, 'Nationalism in Writing: II The Theatre Society of Scotland', *The Scots Magazine*, xxx (1938), pp.194–8; Urquhart, 'The Case for a Scottish National Theatre', *SMT Magazine and Scottish Country Life*, May 1939, pp.61–2.
5. For the Lyceum aspect of this from 1956 to 1977, see Chapters 8–10 of Donald Campbell, *A Brighter Sunshine: A Hundred Years of the Edinburgh Royal Lyceum Theatre* (Edinburgh: Polygon Books, 1983).
6. See, for example, the double number of *Chapman* (Nos. 43–44, 1986) devoted to theatre in Scotland, and the articles by Tom McGrath ('Blowing the Changes') and Joy Hendry ('Towards a National Theatre: Edited Highlights from the Recent AdCAS Conference') in *Chapman*, No.49 (1987), pp.60–66 and 68–75; also Alasdair Cameron, 'National Interests', *Theatre Scotland*, Vol.I, No.4 (1993),

pp.17–22, and the anon. compilation of views on a Scottish dramatic canon, 'The Hot One Hundred', *Theatre Scotland*, II, 8 (1994), pp.17–22. Cf. pp.205–7 of Randall Stevenson, 'Recent Scottish Theatre: Dramatic Developments?', in *Scotland: Literature, Culture, Politics*, ed. P. Zenzinger, *Anglistik & Englischunterricht*, Vols 38/39 (1989), pp.187–213.

7. Hendry, 'Towards a National Theatre' (see previous note), p.75.
8. For example, Donald Mackenzie, *Scotland's First National Theatre* (Edinburgh: Stanley Press, 1963), pp.13, 22, 28, 56.
9. See N. M. MacDonald, 'Gaelic Theatre – The Future?', *Chapman*, Nos.43–44 (1986), pp.147–9. A new Gaelic theatre company, Drama nah–Alba, is being set up by the National Gaelic Arts Project. See *Theatre Scotland* 4, 13, (Spring 1995), p.3.
10. McGrath, 'Blowing the Changes' (see note 6 above), p.61; Schiller, 'The Stage as a Moral Institution' (1784), tr. in B. Dukore, ed., *Dramatic Theory and Criticism: Greeks to Grotowski* (New York: Holt Rinehart & Winston, 1974), pp.444–5 (italics mine). Loren Kruger makes interesting use of Schiller's essay in his provocative study of NTs in three countries, *The National Stage: Theatre and Cultural Legitimation in England, France, and America* (Chicago: University of Chicago Press, 1992), esp. pp.83–94.
11. See, for example, Cordelia Oliver, *Glasgow Citizens' Theatre, Robert David MacDonald and German Drama* ('The Celebratory Lecture Given at the Ceremony to Award the Goethe Medal 1984 to Robert David MacDonald') (Glasgow: Third Eye Centre, 1984).
12. For example, Donald Smith, 'Scripting the Future', in *The Scottish Stage: A National Theatre Company for Scotland*, compiled D. Smith (Edinburgh: Candlemaker Press, 1994), pp.22–9.
13. Text in *A Decade's Drama: Six Scottish Plays* (Todmorden, Lancs: Woodhouse Books, 1980), pp.65–113.

Two

Cradle on the Tree-Top: the Edinburgh Festival and Scottish Theatre

Owen Dudley Edwards

> Hush-a-bye, baby, on the tree-top!
> When the wind blows, the cradle will rock.
> When the bough breaks, the cradle will fall:
> Down will come baby, cradle and all.
> — Popular Nursery Rhyme

> Hush-a-by lady, in Alice's lap!
> Till the feast's ready, we've time for a nap.
> When the feast's over, we'll go to the ball –
> Red Queen, and White Queen, and Alice, and all!
> — Lewis Carroll, *Through the Looking-Glass and What Alice Found There (1871)*

> O hush thee, my babie, thy sire was a knight,
> Thy mother a lady, both lovely and bright;
> The woods and the glens, from the towers which we see,
> They are all belonging, dear babie, to thee.
> . . .
> O hush thee, my babie, the time soon will come
> When thy sleep shall be broken by trumpet and drum;
> Then hush thee, my darling, take rest while you may,
> For strife comes with manhood, and waking with day.
> — Sir Walter Scott, 'Lullaby of an Infant Chief' (1815)

The place of the Edinburgh Festival in Scottish Theatre may be usefully likened to the place of England in Scottish nationalism: flamboyant in impact, sometimes pivotal in effect, but not fundamental in essence.

For purposes of this enquiry, by 'Festival' we mean the Edinburgh International Festival (as organised in the official service of the city) and the Edinburgh Festival Fringe (as occurring with the permission of the city): where it is necessary to distinguish them, the distinction will be made, but the necessity is far less frequent than either of them imagine. Hereinafter, they are 'EIF' and 'Fringe' when distinct: in unison, they are 'Festival'. And that last coding describes the reality: each is now unthinkable without the other, and each is in great part the product of the other. The Fringe first gathered *around* the EIF in 1947 (implicitly) and in 1948 (explicitly); the EIF, wishing in 1960 to define its parameters, declared them (with the aid of Messrs Alan Bennett, Peter Cook, Dudley Moore, and Jonathan Miller) to be *Beyond the Fringe*; the Fringe, conscious that in 1967 the EIF had been declared a Mausoleum in the *New Statesman* by Tom Nairn, grew into a protest movement all the sharper as the EIF establishment snorted and sneered its contempt; the EIF in 1979, breaking sharply from its elitist past, proclaimed an identity of purpose with the Fringe; the Fringe in the 1990s, swollen to Gargantuan size, began to ask itself questions of identity when a beleaguered Festival Director returned to the politics of diversion with an attack on Fringe quality. As we go to press, new EIF and Fringe Directors, eyeing one another in spirits of mutual emulation, prepare to celebrate the 50th birthday of the city as Festival City while all too much aware that their own personal birthdays as Edimbourgeoisie are in each case less than five.[1]

How Scottish is the Festival? 'We're here for a work-oot!' thundered a Scottish Fascist acquaintance (there are very few Scottish Fascists: this is one) on being discovered at Marco's Leisure Centre, Grove Street (Fringe Venue 98): 'We dinna go to see that English rubbish!' His views impressively mirror certain English critics who will elbow-jerk their indifference to Scottish productions or, if constrained to attend, will have all blinkers in place from bum on seat to interval walk-out. 'You're a pack of fucking bourgeois wankers!' yelled Mr James Kelman at a Festival meeting of Fringe performers, directors and impresarii, only to be informed (in accents as richly proletarian as those he strove to maintain), that his analysis had more relevance to his own present mode of discourse, given his professed utter ignorance of all productions at that Festival so far. 'East-windy . . . West-endy . . . all top hat and nae knickers . . . and feart of its own fart': the Glasgow hymn to Edinburgh, to be pronounced with such variations as occasion demands. But the view from Aberdeen will not be much more dazzled by Glaswegian Scottishness as against Edinburgh's, and the voice of Inverness may melt with irony at the Caledonian authenticities of Aberdeen. In any case, if Scottish theatre is to be worth having, it has no natural reason to fear an international audience in a Scottish town, nor to imagine it loses Scottish perspective by ability to project to international horizons.

But can it get them? Scotland may conquer its own parochialism: at least it knows it's there. But it then has to conquer England's, and England doesn't know *that's* there. And is the rest of the world aware of Scotland, theatrical or otherwise? 'English première. Irish company debut' announced one production in its self-description note in the 1995 Fringe Brochure. 'Scotland, England' conclude innumerable American-originating envelopes for Festival business: however ignorantly, they thereby assume a more federal structure than England has hitherto conceded. Above all, how many Festival visitors assume they have supped their fullest potential of Scottish theatre when they have been numbered among the audience at the Tattoo?

The conventional wisdom is not sanguine. David Hutchison's *The Modern Scottish Theatre* (1977), still the automatic first port of call for any voyager around the subject, breathes atmospherics more East-windy than West-endy:

> The Edinburgh Festival's contribution to Scottish theatre has been disappointing . . . There have always been a fairly respectable number of plays performed each year. Criticism has tended to be directed at the quality of drama rather than the quantity . . .
>
> Among the Festival's outstanding productions were those in the 1948, 1949, 1951 and 1959 of Lindsay's *The Three Estates*, presented again in 1973, but these productions could not be said to have generated any great response from contemporary Scottish writers. The official Festival usually presents a Scottish play, but all too often the plays chosen are such that they would never have appeared were there not the necessity to put on Scottish work of some description. The Festival Fringe has however proved a nursery for some of the most interesting contemporary Scottish writers, and although the productions may have been on occasion inadequate, at least the experimental facility, missing for so much of the time in Scotland, is available for a few weeks of the year in Edinburgh.[2]

Time has, happily, borne improvements as well as losses. The EIF greatly improved its choice of Scottish plays, including (under Frank Dunlop) memorable Japanese and Chinese productions of 'the Scottish play' itself, William Shakespeare's *Macbeth*: if its historical errors would make Hollywood blush, they seem less out of place in eastern Asiatic settings. (A sardonic award-winner on the Fringe, *The Real Lady Macbeth*, opined that the ill-luck dogging *Macbeth* arose from just retribution by the spirit world: in any case neither EIF nor Fringe has suffered conspicuously from such ill-luck, although Lyceum productions during the year certainly require any excuses they can get.)

David Hutchison was inaccurate even for 1977 in one matter. *Ane Satyre of the Thrie Estaitis* by Sir David Lyndsay of the Mount (*c.* 1486–1555) certainly has had 'great response' from Scottish writers since its revival: for a start, Sydney Goodsir Smith's *The Wallace* (1960) showed what a poet could do in the tradition of Scottish pageant and propaganda within the Hall of the General Assembly of the Church of Scotland, where Tyrone Guthrie had staged the twentieth-century revivals of Lyndsay's play. Dunlop revived it in tandem with *The Thrie Estaitis* in the mid-1980s. In the 1960s and 1970s the Hall itself had been turned over chiefly to Shakespeare spectaculars striving more for classical honours than original reconstructions: Dunlop used it increasingly for Scottish subjects, thrice with his own direction – Schiller's *Maria Stuart,* J. M. Barrie's *Peter Pan,* and Stevenson's *Treasure Island.* Dunlop was an outstanding director of children's theatre, and it is regrettable that the Barrie (never performed at the EIF) should have been aborted because of budget confusion, and the Stevenson failed chiefly through miscasting of Long John Silver and loss of rehearsal time. As a result, the boy Jim Hawkins (with whom the audience of all ages naturally identified) disappeared from the production after racing around the Hall perimeter to capture the *Hispaniola,* while the adult narrator was given all speeches in his subsequent alliance-or-vendetta with Silver. (Previously, in fight sequences, Adult Narrator jumped in to rescue Boy Hawkins – a clever reminder that Adult recollection improves on the limits of Boy's prowess.)

But the idea of a youthful identification-figure holding that great audience in thrall, while bringing to life epic events, reached fruition with adaptations of Scots novels in the regime (though this time not under the direction) of Dunlop's successor, Brian McMaster: first, Lewis Grassic Gibbon's *Sunset Song* trilogy, and then Alasdair Gray's *Lanark,* the two great modern Scottish sagas, were adapted for the TAG Theatre Company by Alastair Cording. These were productions which strangely revived a staple of pre-movie theatre, much less dependent on the kind of ensemble work established by the RSC *Nicholas Nickleby* (and sustained by innumerable imitations on and off the Fringe), and much more on audience recognition of its own performance as audience when the play required it. Purists complained, especially with *Lanark*: some Scots critics read the book and resented the play for having to leave out much of it, some English critics had not read the book and resented the play for not having left out more or all of it. Cording's achievement was in fact a very Irish one, the establishment of an unsympathetic but unanswerably determined auctorial protagonist sworn to silence, exile, cunning, artifice, relatives of varying want of understanding, teachers of ditto, the swim of a number of birds, the size of a number of policemen, and Odysseys around priests, men, women, and cities, to be juxtaposed in the gigantic alien world of the artist's imagination. *Lanark* seemed to delight its audiences, and its experimental deployment of world upon world brought out the best of a cast forced into a variety of greatly differing roles (Kern Falconer in particular proving a virtuoso in each one): its lack of critical approval was the natural result of anger against alienation coinciding with a coterie thinking sacrosanct its private view of the state of the art.

The Wallace induced other work also, including the long-delayed production of Professor R. S. Silver's *The Bruce*, finally realised in the late 1980s when its performance at St Bride's converted cynics by its strength and sincerity, and involuntarily convinced the *Financial Times* that Bruce lost Bannockburn. Similarly, a company not normally identified with Scottish Nationalism, the Glasgow Citizens' Theatre, found itself even more drastically reducing and reworking large-scale historical drama, in which Robert David MacDonald's post-Shakespearean translation of Schiller's *Don Carlos* unintentionally sent a Scottish internationalist home to roost: Schiller's main source was the Scottish historian Robert Watson's *Philip II*, and the delicacy and precision of the Citizens' Philip II as projected in sixteenth, eighteenth, and twentieth-century prisms by Giles Havergal was declared by one critic to have confirmed him as the greatest Scots actor of his generation. But the lesson is that Festival Scottish Theatre needs to think big. Nobody worked harder or more self-sacrificingly than John Drummond in trying to bring Fringework to Festival recognition, but prime Fringe favourites often seem to lose the bite of their challenge when apotheosed. Dunlop showed what could be done with classic James Bridie, when *Holy Isle* was revived in his regime, and a heavy adaptor's hand on its coyness gave it the discipline its over-powerful author had been in his lifetime too well-protected to experience. In fact, as Linda Mackenny demonstrates in her indispensable *'Straight-Backed Men and Women': The Search for a Scottish Popular Drama*, Bridie used his influence to frustrate opportunities for radical Scottish theatre, and did so in the young Edinburgh Festival as elsewhere. It was appropriate that populism in the seat of power at the EIF under Dunlop should posthumously discipline the foe who should have been its friend. Snobbery frequently eroded Bridie's natural dramatic genius, on the stage or in committee.

But if there was enough unrealised bigness in Bridie for a strong director (Charles Nowosielski) to add a cubit to his stature, Dunlop could not make a big-stage play out of a small-stage dream. It was a piece of his usual, captivating, *gamin*-like cheek to have brought to the EIF Sharman MacDonald's *When I Was a Girl I Used to Scream and Shout*, recently premiered in London by the Bush after it had been lost by the Traverse: the Traverse above all else liked to consider itself the home of *avant-garde*, and for the EIF to blossom into its *salon des réfusés* was both to outFringe and infringe the Fringe. It was a fine play, from a remarkable contemporary of fine Fringe actors such as David Rintoul and Ian Charleson in their student years (since when they had made triumphant EIF appearances): and the impishness of the joke was fine too. But it wanted studio work, and in the end the joke swamped the play. Iconoclasm could not become icon.

Drummond had faced the same problem, when he brought 7:84 to the Assembly Rooms in an EIF production, John McGrath's *Women in Power* (*Up the Acropolis!*) in 1983. The jester lampooning the King holds the house, but if the jester becomes King, what's happened to the jest? The idea involved bringing Aristophanes's anti-war *Knights* up to date, with Mrs Thatcher as Kleon and Roy Jenkins as the Sausage-seller, but in the end the old joke rejected a new skin. The whole principle of 7:84 was to deny the possibility of collaborationism with any establishment, however amiable its intentions. Nor was Drummond himself favourable to the idea of the EIF becoming some sort of award for meritorious Scottish theatre: he argued that the Festival simply would not be the right vehicle for some admirable forms of Fringe or other Scottish drama, and his readiness to set aside his misgivings proved ill-founded. One year he commissioned a Scottish play which simply could not guarantee it would be ready, and the consequent rescheduling pushed late-night material into peak hour prominence it could not justify. Brian McMaster similarly yearned for Scottish theatre success in his Festivals, and nostalgia for his teenage Traverse enthusiasm led him to revive on the EIF the work of C. P. Taylor. Some of it was far better than angry critics would allow, and at least one production of this 1990s revival, *Good*, in the hands of Michael Boyd of the Glasgow Tron Theatre, was a faultless, searing indictment of self-compromise in face of national evil, specifically a conciliation of the Nazis, exacerbating their genocidal treatment of the Jews. In our climate, where the arts miserably wonder if integrity does not condemn its practitioners to starvation by a vengeful government, *Good*'s EIF audiences saw intellectuals Nazify themselves while pleading that much could be gained by tactical yieldings. Taylor was a fine, if mixed, playwright: but what he really needs is serious production on the

Fringe in an atmosphere more revolting [sic] than the EIF can normally offer, Boyd excepted.

The Fringe misses most of the serious headlines, but Scottish theatre is far more alive there than is generally recognised. In 1995, 184 Scottish companies performed on it, racking up 29.68 per cent of the whole (second only to England with its 326 companies at 52.57 per cent). Theatre itself consisted of 484 shows out of a possible 1,237 (39.12 per cent), beating all other categories in which Music was next (316 shows, viz. 25.55 per cent), while the vaunted Comedy, even when including Revue, only reached 215 (17.38 per cent). But even here categorisation is misleading. Fringe-image is permitted too easily to be set by English (so-called 'national') critics, although Scottish (actual 'national') critics have greater and deeper knowledge of it, and sell more tickets (out of the minority of tickets sold by critiques). Fringe Comedy includes the eminent Scots playwright, Liz Lochhead, performing in person. The perennial demand 'is Comedy [stand-up comedians] driving out "serious Theatre"?' does more honour to the endurance of the questioners than to the appropriateness of the question in general; but certainly in Scotland as in Ireland the genres feed rather than starve one another (Irish stand-up comedians feeding themselves into plays include Sheridan's Mrs Malaprop, Goldsmith's Tony Lumpkin, Wilde's dowagers and dandies,[3] Shaw's Alfred Doolittle, Synge's Christy Mahon and Old Mahon, O'Casey's Fluther and Joxer, Beckett's Didi and Gogo: the Synge version actually includes casting, rehearsal, dressing and publicity in the play). All this derives in part from smaller country, fewer economic resources, fiercer struggle for identity, greater vulnerability of local icons: Christy Mahon has to kill his father to become a successful comedian. Stevenson makes this point for himself from a tragic perspective in his story 'The House of Eld', and in *Treasure Island* Silver (if well performed) is the anti-father as sinister comedian (cameo versions by Billy Bones, Black Dog, Blind Pew, Israel Hands; fall guys Job Anderson ('my Jo'?), George *Merry*). The bardic tradition meant a stand-up performer: Scottish comedians became national institutions and symbols (Harry Lauder, Billy Connolly) and Scottish poets became institutions by performance as well as production (Burns, Scott, Stevenson, MacDiarmid and many others). The nearest twentieth-century English equivalent seems to be Winston Churchill, and before that Dr Samuel Johnson (under Scottish management). Byron was 'born half a Scot and bred a whole one'. 'A Vision of Judgment' combines so much of the best of stand-up comedy as to impoverish all subsequent practitioners, while *Don Juan* perfectly unites the bardic-comic arts across the centuries from Homer to Lochhead. Its translation to Fringe First Award-winner of 1979 in John Retallack's adaptation meant staging, however minimalist the furniture, and the skill and passion of director-adaptor opened it up for a new generation: but ideally it's the longest one-person comedy in the language, with the comic's self-obsession, acrobatic tangentialism, audience-enlisting wit, and base-line of divine anger. Byron was a great playwright, save when he wrote plays.

Liz Lochhead's Byronism ranges between poetry, patter and plays, as neat an integration of anti-sexism and anti-snobbery as anyone could ask ('my boss thinks a *crèche* is a traffic accident in Kelvinside'): and in her case Festival means fire-power. Festival, for all its flaunting feminism, still means Men In Power (EIF Council is male by sixteen to five), although increasingly women are gaining control (EIF marketing and press, Fringe administration): Edinburgh and Glasgow still like to mime gentility *versus* genuineness; Scotland so often seems tokenised in its own Festival. All of these make excellent reasons for a Scotspeak Glasgow woman to declare a formidable presence, most particularly when 1987 meant Mary Queen of Scots 400 years dead. EIF put on Schiller (and, one year off, a Russian opera where John Knox and his Protestants delighted their audience by Orthodox Signs of the Cross after Sermon, and Mary yelled for her beloved 'Boswell!'); Communicado staged the Lochhead première *Mary Queen of Scots Got Her Head Chopped Off* integrating historical pageant/tragedy with finale in playground confrontation. The genius of it was that it made characteristically shrewd anatomisations of bigotry and rivalry, sexism and power-hunger, court intrigue and human psychology, all come to serve our contemporary understanding of history within ourselves. The EIF can produce countless miracles, but not the miracle of leaving us alone, isolated, in our own school playgrounds of however many years ago. Whatever else the Fringe motto may be, it can't be 'Think What God Might Have Done If Only He'd Had the Money!'

The Lochhead achievement requires a nerve to raise belly-laughs in the midst of tragedy and deepen audience identification with tragedy in the process. 7:84 made that work like laser-beams in *The Cheviot, the Stag and the Black, Black Oil* when the drunken stage-Anglified lairds capering with their shotguns suddenly cover the audience with an eye of awesome marksmanship to assert the permanence of their authority, and, all the more because it refused to enter the Fringe marketplace, 7:84 under John McGrath was probably the greatest single influence on ScotsFringe. But because high Scots Revolt would naturally despise kailyard and kitsch, tat and tattoo, intoning Tom Nairn's epodes on the Tartan Monster no less than his 'Festival of the Dead', its political theatre renewed Tartanry in the cause of satire, above all the lightspeed-skimming Merry Macs or the ham-handedly derisive 'Scotland the What?' (On the other hand, the most telling blow against Scotskitsch was struck on the EIF, when Drummond sponsored the Grigors' great 'Scotch Myths' exhibition, itself a theatre show of objects with life-size kitsch Walter Scott welcoming George IV in 1822 and a grand piano perpetually pumping water to the sound of Mendelssohn's 'Fingal's Cave'.)

Yet such strategic reversals of enemy guns could be less subversive than attack at much more unexpected quarters. One of the neatest assaults on establishment confidence I ever saw on the Fringe was when the Edinburgh Youth Theatre won a Fringe First for Gerard Lohan's *Maurice the Minotaur*, where the deeply conscientious Minotaur's rescue of a poltroonish Theseus is followed by an explanation that history is what it seems best to make people believe happened, so they imagine Theseus slew the minotaur. Children's theatre, when directed with dedication but without dictatorship so that it retains its aura of game, can prove more insidious than almost any other form of drama. Unfortunately, after some more outstanding original work, or original variations including such distinguished Scots characters as Frankenstein (who as first created by Mary Shelley resided in Orkney while building and dismantling Brides), and the Devil (whose theatre affiliations had long been saluted by the somewhat competitive ecclesiastical authorities), the Edinburgh Youth Theatre took to staging revivals of English musicals (*Agincourt*) and died. But it sired very remarkable actors of future Festivals, some via work of the Royal Scottish Academy of Music and Drama (although here again, despite the Fringe First scheme there was too little nerve for much of their own creative writing: yet they wrote excellent material on occasion). And it has had good successors including 1995's Realistic Theatre Company of Edinburgh visualising the '45 through *The Drummer Boy*, a little girl who rises and follows Charlie.

How Scottish could Fringeplays afford to be, linguistically? Theatre Alba, under Nowosielski, brought new techniques and old tongue to David Purves's sparkling version of an old tale, *The Puddock an' the Princess*, radiating love of a language that warmed the cockles of many a sceptical heart. In general, Fringe Scotspeak was dialect rather than language, with emphasis on the more accessible forms of alienation such as 'nae' meaning 'no' and 'no' meaning 'not', and thus usually within the grasp of the brighter visitors. If the play sought realism, obscenities could be made more gutteral to qualify as sufficiently native. Much Scots drama searched the past for its subjects and while few arched from then to now with the immediacy of Liz Lochhead's *Mary*, the Fringe was a natural place to celebrate a convenient centenary. Frederick Mohr's work on one-person theatre found its natural outlet when 1992 saw the bicentenary of the Scots recruit in the American Revolutionary naval cause, and Jimmy Chisholm, title-rolling *The Admiral Jones*, happily dawned to dusk his life-story with grace-notes in the Doric: his pre-mortem reminiscences to an imaginary audience would presumably have had to be in French for real authenticity since it was in Paris that John Paul Jones breathed his last, as the author deplorably demanded the corpse announce when the play had ended. It was the more annoying as Chisholm had worked the miracle, and we really could believe we were listening to the Scottish sailor who fought for the cause of his transatlantic Utopia.

But the master of Scots historical drama remains Donald Campbell, famed for his *The Jesuit*, a non-Festival play on St John Ogilvie, martyred in 1615. He turned the one-person show on its head with *Howard's Revenge*, where the founder of the Edinburgh Lyceum struggles to recall a speech he must deliver in his adaptation of Scott's *Rob Roy*, fights incessantly with his own lighting man, and wanders off into multi-dimensional reminiscence. Here all the biographical matter was justified by the plot instead of the usual mechanical I-was-born-until-I-died formula, and the audience had no knowledge of what bit of the protagonist's life he would slither through their perceptions next. It was the only production I have seen where the lighting very justly had its own round of applause on curtain, at the graceful salute of the actor, Finlay Welsh. J. B. Howard was in fact Irish, but Rob Roy needed a Scots accent of convincing inauthenticity, and so did another Campbell Festival *coup de théâtre*, *An Audience for McGonagall*, the latter directed by Campbell himself where *Howard* was the inspired achievement of Sandy Neilson. The McGonagall play is supposedly a conversation between McGonagall, Queen Victoria, and her attendant (and perhaps husband) John Brown: neither Victoria nor Brown seemed in the least authentic, and audiences were left to conclude Campbell's genius did not extend to direction, only to discover at the play's final lines that the worst poet in the world had forced his dreadful recitation unwittingly on two minor servants amusing themselves by playing Brown and Victoria. It was a bluff heightened by using apparent directorial inexperience as a stage device to triumphant effect. Campbell's idea of Scottish theatre makes some of its strongest gains by exploitation of our assumption we know more of Scotland's past than we do, profiting by the certainty we know something. A less history-conscious society would be unable to make much of him, but then it would hardly have given birth to him.

Festival work invites comparative stimulus from other cultures, and
Fringe economics offer a more rational scale of approximation. Various
impresarii have made their venues mini-festivals in international theatre,
the obvious leader being Richard Demarco, but the clear permanent focal
point for such work being the theatre he helped to found, the Traverse,
opened originally on 2 January 1963. Its work has become decidedly
more Scots in the past twenty years, following the Herculean efforts of
one English Artistic Director, Chris Parr, to make Scots shake off their
cringe and send in their playscripts. *The Jesuit,* presented under Neilson's
auspices, symbolised the new Scottish emphasis when it premiered at the
Traverse in May 1976. Parr had himself been an Award-winning Fringe
director (for Bradford University), and the theatre had from its beginning
asserted more than anything else in Edinburgh how the Fringe could be
kept in town all the year round. But Parr is the turning-point in its
Scots self-realisation. Among the highest points in its historical drama
was an international subject, *Losing Venice,* by the *Scotsman* critic John
Clifford, which in Fringe 1985 probed a war between Spain and Venice
at the end of the sixteenth century – a war that in reality almost happened
but did not. In those days the Traverse (then at its second, Grassmarket,
address) made a naval battle come to life with the assistance of two
chairs and energetic gestures: its more opulent surroundings beside the
Usher Hall today place less strain on the imagination but more on the
conviction. Clifford, at all events, conjured up his Mediterranean world
with the welcome lesson that the historical Scottish play should also
seek the international. It's a lesson that younger Traverse playwrights in
Fringetime, such as David Greig or Anthony Neilson, have hammered
home for present-day themes.

Modern Scottish nationalism complains of being eclipsed by England
from participation in the world beyond: to the Greigs and the Neilsons
Scotland needs to get on with its participation in the theatre if it
is going to prove its international credentials outside it. Greig's has
been an astonishing forest of plays for a writer still at school when
Clifford premiered; and Neilson has shown a horrifying mastery of
a hidden world of cruelty, violence and immense force. Neither are
Traverse-imprisoned: Neilson first premiered in the best of all Fringe
venues in good weather, the Pleasance, under a genial master of stage
design Christopher Richardson, and Greig has ranged through a whole
variety from the students' own Bedlam Theatre (site of the original
Edinburgh Bedlam where the poet Robert Fergusson died) to Roman
Eagle Lodge on Johnstone Terrace, where ancient Masonic ghosts
gracefully give way to newer rituals under the towering greenfall of
the Castle walls.

Joyce McMillan, in her invaluably innocent *The Traverse Theatre Story*, puts the birth of the Traverse in the context of Festival 1962:

> John Malcolm . . . has left Pitlochry Festival Theatre in high dudgeon in the middle of the 1962 summer season, and he is appearing – at his agent's suggestion – in a Festival Fringe production of Fionn MacColla's *Ane Tryall of Heretiks*, which is being staged in the basement of Jim Haynes' bookshop. The atmosphere of this Festival is peculiarly exciting; Jim Haynes and the publisher John Calder have mounted an International Writers' Conference which has attracted dozens of distinguished literati to Edinburgh. The show in Jim's basement naturally attracts more than its share of attention from this glittering crowd; it – and John Malcolm – receive a glowing review from Harold Hobson in the *Sunday Times*.

(He's gone, with his wheelchair: he would choose a Fringe show for lead coverage in his column at the expense of EIF lavish productions, when he so deemed, but much more often today lead critics take the EIF, stringers get the Fringe. Time was when the highest hope was to be Hobson's Choice.)

> And this is the crucial moment when the idea of some kind of arts club to keep the Fringe atmosphere alive in Edinburgh all the year round – kicked around in the Haynes-Demarco circle for years . . . suddenly takes root in the mind of an ambitious and radically-minded young theatre professional with the sheer physical energy and hard practical knowledge to push it through to fruition.[4]

Thirty years later, how Fringe is our Traverse? The Traverse came on the EIF in 1979, Drummond's first year, with Tom McGrath's incredible *Animal*, choreographed by Stuart Hopps and directed by Chris Parr, the dialogue being almost entirely ape movements and noises, and Billy Connolly's predictable *The Red Runner*, set in prison, the dialogue being almost entirely as banal as its stablemate was original. Connolly was a name; Drummond needed a gimmick; so did the Traverse; Peter Diamand, like Gallio, would have cared for none of these things, and revolutions require their *sans-culottes* no less than their *singes de qualités*. Connolly had brought a major success to the Traverse for Fringe 1976, *An' Me Wi' a Bad Leg Tae*. Fringe hero was EIF turkey, few dissenting. And neither EIF nor Traverse tried again until former Traverse playwright McMaster tried to revive his old love in a new form. Himself Drummond's protégé, McMaster did not risk commissioning new work possibly proving more akin to the stop-short *Red Runner* than to the phenomenal *Animal*, and the Traverse would not put on an old, not even their own C. P. Taylor. Thus there is a guarantee of openings for new work, and should it gain Traverse production in Festival, it is certain to gain London press coverage. For some distinguished journalists, no intelligent Fringelife exists beyond the Traverse. At least the Traverse is some years away from atrophy: David Greig is now reading its playscripts. And its new upmarket status may be haunted by its past, but it still can be haunted: it has not (yet) fully traded *avant-garde* for *nouveau riche*, it still wants to eat its cake and puke it.

So where does Scotfest theatre go from here? We may adjure the Traverse to let loose the madwoman in its own attic to whom it owes the rakish eminence enabling its present respectability, we may Scotch the Citz and display maps to the EIF showing what country (sirs) is this, we may jalouse that Scottish lairds may not win prize Portias by borrowing box-offices on the ears of the English (to adapt a Shakespearean line the Berliner Ensemble found too controversial for inclusion in their Edinburgh production of *The Merchant of Venice* in 1995), we may feminize Jock Tamson (who gave birth himself to nae bairns), we may rivettingly re-invent the *Oresteia* as did Bill Dunlop's Scots translation in Toby Gough's Darwinian progress on the top of Calton Hill, we may Tartanize *The Time Machine*. But then, sang Plato's ghost, what then? The most obvious answers may be the most important. There is no conventional wisdom by which to be ruled. The comedy argument is nonsense: it isn't excluding theatre, it's feeding it, Scotswise. The fears of conglomerate management driving serious theatre out is also absurd: successful impresarii in most cases really want the kudos of Fringe First plays and Scottish credentials. Scotophobic hijacking of Scottish university student theatre is a problem, albeit like most dangers to Scotfest Theatre much more publicized than it deserves to be: in any case, the only answer to this is for Scottish students with plays to perform to fight for their own theatre groups instead of decamping in virtuous hara-kiri at the first sound of a Yahccent. Rising costs are hell, but money can be raised, sponsors, busking, grants, emotional blackmail, etc. being far from exhausted in their possibilities.

But the whole essence of Scotland, festival, and theatre, is negated if the future is declared hidebound by Thatcherite or other materialistic constraints. By all means feel free to expose governmental or other official depravity in emasculation of the Scotarts, provided you do not sterilize yourselves in the process. The collapse of Scottish theatre enterprises has consistently been due, not to a failure of finance, but to a failure of nerve. They are not even alternatives: nerve makes finance possible. The Scottish cringe can yet collapse us all into its Dunciadic anticreation. Scottish festival theatre must die if it is incapable of thinking beyond English terms, logic, finance, crits, marketspeak, culturechatter, existence. We are either a fashionably removable appendix, a perpetually self-eliminating Dr Jekyll, a MacClone trying to be a YahClone, or we are real, and worthy in our own right of the attention of English and all other decent persons.

The Festival could not have happened had the Cringe ruled: and when it succumbs to the Cringe it proclaims the Death of which Tom Nairn long ago accused it. Festival Theatre means adventure, and above all finding space, technique, innovation where Convention proclaims No Highway. From Sadie Aitken handing Tyrone Guthrie the General Assembly of the Church of Scotland to the Welsh Actors' Company proclaiming the prowess of Cymbeline on Calton Hill, Toby Gough opening up the mind of Linnaeus through the Botanic Gardens, Faynia Williams throwing up three tiers backed by a naked crucified Christ in Richard Crane's *Satan's Ball* whence Edinburgh University's Old Chaplaincy and former town Bedlam became a theatre, Ben Harrison's seventeen hexameter-spouting ghosts driving audiences at the interval across the street into the adjoining Greyfriars' Kirk-yard for a second Act, even Brian McMaster sending his legions into the Corn Exchange whose major previous theatrical performance had been Gladstone's Midlothian Campaign in 1879–80 . . . Scots and invaders alike can strive, seek, find, not yield, and above all learn from one another. Neither London nor New York fashions are going to turn a barren Edinburgh hillside or condemned Close into a blazing new theatrical conception. Space itself forces new technique on the company, work is constrained and transformed by the ground you seize.

If Scottish Festival Theatre matters a single, solitary damn, it means a refusal to accept the logic of common sense as we know it. How else can you explain the theatrical tradition which flourished for centuries through the pulpit which condemned its existence as an abomination, or which even today sustains itself in mid-Festival above all by the condemnations which attend its progress? If Irish theatre won its supreme accolade by riot, Scottish claims its place by rite – the rite of exorcism. Even Scottish witches, poor, persecuted creatures, having been burned to further the politics of kings and desperate men, returned to force Scotland on English audience whether in *Macbeth* or in the most theatrical of all poems since the epic bards – Burns's *Tam o'Shanter* – after which neither Scottish nor English literature could ever be the same again. And that must also be our agenda.

NOTES

1. The EIF Artistic Directors were as follows: Rudolf Franz Josef Bing (1947–9); Ian Bruce Hope Hunter (1950–55); Robert Noel Ponsonby (1956–60); George Henry Hubert Lascelles seventh Earl of Harewood (1961–5); Peter Diamand (1966–78); John Richard Gray Drummond (1979–83); Frank Dunlop (1984–91); Brian McMaster (1992–). None were Scots: Drummond and Dunlop had Scots fathers. Eight theatre groups appeared at the first (1947) Festival in addition to those invited to perform; in the words of the Fringe's own 'Brief History', three 'defining features of the first Fringe . . . still hold true today – the performers were not invited to take part, they used unusual and unconventional theatre spaces and they took all of their own financial risks, surviving or sinking according to public demand'. The term 'Fringe' became used from 1948; Edinburgh University students opened a reception centre for Fringe groups in 1951; an Edinburgh printer produced a common programme in 1954; Edinburgh University students set up a central Box Office in 1955; the Festival Fringe Society was set up in 1958, with 19 companies performing; in 1969, 57 companies performed; John Milligan was appointed first professional Fringe Administrator in 1971; 45 new plays were presented at the 1972 Fringe, generally lacking financial success, whence the Fringe Board had the *Scotsman* offer Fringe First awards from 1973 for new theatre work, a scheme which under Arts Editor Allen Wright so strongly stimulated new work that 296 new plays were being premiered in the year of his retirement, 1994, when over 1000 companies from 36 different nations performed 1,432 shows in 188 performance spaces over 23 days.
2. David Hutchison, *The Modern Scottish Theatre* (Glasgow: The Molendinar Press, 1977), p.122.
3. Dandies are male and female, as well as being men and women; dowagers need not be widows but have husbands of no importance.
4. Joyce McMillan, *The Traverse Theatre Story* (London: Methuen, 1988), p.14.

Three

From Traverse to Tramway: Scottish Theatres Old and New

Mark Fisher

How much does the stock of theatre buildings in a country affect that country's theatrical output? Each time the debate about a Scottish national theatre comes around, one of the arguments used against a permanent building for such an organisation is that one generation's idea of a fine performing space is not always that of the next. Our uncertain, end-of-millennium culture, saddled with so many awkward legacies from the past, cannot bring itself to burden future cultures with any similarly immovable structure that would suit our own tastes and idiosyncrasies while conflicting with theirs.

This argument is most pressing when it comes to a national theatre, because a national theatre is primarily a symbol (of nationhood, of excellence, whatever) and would therefore risk embodying the values of today's society to an artistically stifling extent. But much the same argument is applicable to all theatre buildings. The very flexibility of the Traverse Theatre in Edinburgh's Cambridge Street and the very presence of multiple spaces at the Tramway in Glasgow's Albert Drive, for example, will speak to future generations of the rapid rate of change, the high level of uncertainty, perhaps even the insecurity of 1990s theatre culture, just as much as our kind consideration in not bequeathing another proscenium arch theatre to them. We erect buildings to match our needs, but we can't help values getting mixed in with the cement. At any one time, the theatrical landscape is delineated not only by the performance spaces that have been created or reclaimed specifically to satisfy current needs, but also by those that came into being ten, twenty or 200 years ago in accordance with the needs of earlier times. And while newly reclaimed spaces like the Tramway might tell us which way our theatre is heading, it is the established stock of buildings that hold the most dominant position in day-to-day theatrical life. My contention is that these have played a significant role in shaping our expectations of the Scottish repertoire in particular, and the wider theatrical canon in general.

Theatre architecture is something we take for granted. We go to the theatre to see a particular play, not because we like the building. It's not that people don't appreciate buildings and not that they don't build up a loyalty to them: a Perth Theatre subscriber once sat next to me and, only minutes before curtain up, peered down at his programme to find out what he was there to see. But I doubt if even that gentleman would ever have stopped to articulate what it was about the ambience of Perth Theatre – or more probably the ambience created by the company in that space – that kept him coming back. Even if he tried, he would probably have talked about his liking for the repertoire in general, long before he tried to explain what it was about the design of the building that made him feel comfortable.

Yet architecture is fundamental to our experience of theatre. The delicate physical and geographical balance in the relationship between actor and audience, spectator and spectator, the shape, materials and atmosphere of the building itself, are factors that crucially affect our appreciation of the theatrical event. If the same production ever appeared first in Glasgow's ghastly, civic-centre-style Mitchell Theatre and then in that city's exquisite Victorian Citizens' Theatre, it would come across as two different shows. Technically the play, the acting, the direction would have altered little, but where in the Citizens' the audience finds itself tucked tightly round the narrow proscenium arch, no single spectator very far from the performers, everyone cosily aware of the communal nature of the event, in the Mitchell that same audience is regimented into straight rows which confront the stage rather than gather round it: despite being in a smaller theatre, this creates a sense of space without intimacy.

Such is the general tenor of Iain Mackintosh's essential book on the subject, *Architecture, Actor and Audience* (Routledge, 1993), which initiates a line of thought that recurs in the commentaries of a number of practitioners (directors, actors, playwrights, critics) in the more recent *Making Space for Theatre: British Architecture and Theatre since 1958* by Ronnie Mulryne and Margaret Shewring (Stratford-upon-Avon: Mulryne and Shewring Ltd, 1995). In both books, the belief that the design of the auditorium is key to the impact of a performance is persuasively put. Looked at in technical terms, right down to the height of the stage and the volume of air dividing performer and audience, it helps explain why some venues never seem to generate the warmth or the sense of excitement of others. The critic's tendency is to blame the production for an unsuccessful performance: in reality the fault may lie in the very walls themselves.

We can argue, then, that individual buildings can affect individual plays, but by extension is it also possible to say that the wider provision of performance spaces across a whole country is capable of influencing the repertoire itself?

For playwrights are nothing if they don't have a place for their work to be performed. Take Shakespeare as an example. Today we admire the fluidity of his writing, the way it works perfectly, even preferably, without elaborate props or scenic devices. It has a spare, economical theatricality that we find refreshing. But for Shakespeare, the practical man of sixteenth- and seventeenth-century theatre, the possibility of using elaborate scenic devices simply did not exist and would never have crossed his mind. His 'theatrical' style was as much dictated as designed. He was, after all, quite happy to make use of those architectural quirks that did exist. Innovator he may have been, but not so innovative that he could operate outwith the technological standards of his time. By extension it must also be true that the playwrights and theatremakers of today carry with them a set of expectations about the capacity and capability of the spaces for which they are creating.

Since the appearance of the Traverse Theatre in a sixty-seater room of a former brothel off Edinburgh's Lawnmarket in 1963, the most distinctive feature in the provision of new theatre spaces in Britain has been the presence and ubiquity of the studio. The Traverse can be seen as an inspiration for Glasgow's short-lived Close Theatre, which furnished the Citizens' Theatre with an alternative experimental space from 1965-73, and also to Edinburgh's Pool Lunchtime Theatre, which lasted three years from 1971. But it was merely there at the start of a movement driven by compelling social factors, most prominently the abolition of theatre censorship in 1968 and the concomitant rise of politically-driven theatre companies such as John McGrath's 7:84 England and Scotland, which resolved to meet a non-theatre going audience on its own territory – church halls, shop floors, working men's clubs and community centres. As a result, by the early 1970s there had developed an awareness that theatre didn't have to take place exclusively in traditional proscenium houses, and a sense that the most interesting stuff was happening anywhere but.

Realising that theatrical energy had been deflected towards alternative spaces, the designers of new theatres invariably incorporated studios into their plans, imitating the 'found' spaces of the touring circuit with their

limited playing areas, flexible seating and blackened walls. The theatre
building boom of the 1970s benefited England more than Scotland, but
even so, a substantial number of major Scottish theatres have run studios
at some point in the last thirty years. Edinburgh's Royal Lyceum had
access to the Little Lyceum for a decade from 1975 and even now talks
about using its Grindlay Street rehearsal rooms as a theatre; Glasgow's
Citizens' annexed part of its foyer to install two studios which have been
running since 1992; Perth Theatre has one, albeit infrequently used;
and even the smaller theatres, like Glasgow's Arches, Tron and CCA
(formerly the Third Eye Centre), and Edinburgh's Theatre Workshop,
technically studio spaces in themselves, make use of a variety of
performance areas in addition to their principal stage.

Add this to the glut of multi-purpose arts centres that have sprung
up throughout the country, playing a particularly significant role in the
cultural life of rural areas, and you have a vast increase in the number,
if not the total capacity, of theatre spaces in Scotland over the past
thirty years.

And what is very apparent, writing in 1996, is that it is virtually
impossible for a new Scottish play to be produced on a main stage
without its first having proved a success on the studio circuit. Even
then, the chances of a transfer or a revival are low. Pitlochry Festival
Theatre, a big public space that would be ideal for heated political
dramas were it not for its situation in the heart of a genteel tourist
industry, is currently the only big theatre routinely staging a new play
in each summer season. The regimes at Dundee Rep and the Royal
Lyceum, Edinburgh, are harbouring plans to change this, but their
caution, no doubt financially justified, would have been intolerable
had playwrights had no other outlet. As it is, there has grown up,
particularly since the mid-1980s, a large number of small companies
– 7:84, Fifth Estate, Clyde Unity, Communicado – prepared to take
on new plays and perform them, by and large, in studio spaces.

The English playwright David Edgar, writing in *Making Space for
Theatre*, points out that as early as 1973 he was voicing the concern
that 'theatres with studios did less new work in their main houses than
theatres without' (p.86). For all the good intentions of the studio space,
it quickly came to represent a ghetto for new plays. Individual artistic
directors, such as Bill Bryden at the Royal Lyceum in the 1970s, might
buck the trend, but once that individual moves on, it doesn't take too
much pressure on box-office income for the big theatres to revert to a
programme of audience-friendly established texts.

The high profile in Scotland of the Traverse – a theatre dedicated to
new work from home and abroad – should have altered this situation. In

fact, it seems only to have reinforced it. Rather than being a stepping stone on the road to bigger productions, it has proved for many playwrights to be both the beginning and the end, at least within the context of Scottish theatre. Having been nurtured by the Traverse, they might have gone on to get work in film, radio or television, or theatre work outside Scotland, but few have forged a path from studio to main stage and stayed within the country.

It seems odd that a theatre which even by the mid-1970s had introduced 100 plays from around the world should have had so slight an impact on the Scottish national repertoire. This is not a reflection on the Traverse, which has played a part of inestimable significance in all areas of theatrical life: rather, it is a reflection on the structural inability of mainstream Scottish theatre to capitalise on the gains the Traverse and the other small studios have made. Think of any three mature, established Scottish playwrights – say John Byrne, Liz Lochhead and John Clifford – and ask yourself how many of their original plays (not translations, not adaptations) have been specifically commissioned by a mainstage Scottish repertory theatre. The answer will disturb you.

There could be a good reason for this. It could be that the very act of writing with a small space in mind produces small plays that work well up close, but fall apart in a more public arena. As with the example of Shakespeare and set design, the physical and practical conditions of the theatre must have some impact on the imagination. A playwright writing for a studio is most likely to be subject to two influences: firstly, that there will be neither the budget nor the space for a large cast (and a large cast is a big help when dealing with large, universal themes); secondly, that the audience is no longer the world in general, but a very specific constituency, whether this happens to be the avid theatregoers of the Traverse, or members of the working class or rural community who turn up to see a touring show. In theory at least, the studio playwright can be exclusive or elitist and not have to worry that references or attitudes will be misunderstood.

But it is harder to argue that such influences have affected the imaginations of playwrights so profoundly that they have come to occupy a marginal place in contemporary Scottish theatre culture. Even the big houses are falling back on small-cast plays in the name of economy, so shortage of characters should not be an obstacle. A mere glance through the catalogue of Traverse productions is enough to show that it is rich in big themes and broad perspectives. But for some reason, the main houses have been reluctant to draw on that same catalogue, and it was considered unusual when artistic director Andrew McKinnon introduced the Perth Theatre audience to Michel

Tremblay's *House Among the Stars,* Chris Hannan's *Elizabeth Gordon Quinn* and Alexander Gelman's *The Bench* and *A Man with Connections* in his seasons of 1993/94, all of which had received British premières at the Traverse.

Could it be that we have absorbed the notion that new plays belong in very small spaces and now accept it unquestioningly as a fact? Could that explain why when such plays cease to be 'new', they are not assimilated into the mainstream repertoire, along with the Wildes, the Cowards and the Shakespeares, but disappear altogether? Or could the fact that I list Coward, Wilde and Shakespeare, not Barrie, Bridie and Corrie, nor even Campbell, Conn and McGrath, suggest that the problem of excluding Scottish writers from the Scottish repertoire goes a lot further back than the arrival of studio theatre?

Without a long tradition of playwriting, perhaps Scotland is simply not used to lauding its dramatists (although, even if true, it's a pretty lame excuse) and at least the studios have prevented writers from being excluded altogether. The studios are there if you know where to find them, and if you do find them there is nothing like their up-front intimacy for cranking up the intensity. Iain Mackintosh wisely observes in *Architecture, Actor and Audience* that all the most revolutionary and creative points in theatre history, from the Globe of Shakespeare's day to the Royal Court of John Osborne's day, have been centred on relatively small theatres. The social impact extends beyond the number of people who see a production for themselves and reaches out into society at large. The proliferation of studio spaces and the proliferation of plays to fill them have brought a buoyancy and vibrancy to Scottish theatre unparalleled in earlier, leaner generations, even if more marginal than central.

So what impact have they had? Well, in one respect, the existence of a small-scale theatre circuit has made it possible for companies to survive with no fixed loyalty to one building above all others. There are obvious disadvantages in the touring system itself – high accommodation costs, variations in the size of the performance area and the unpredictability of technical facilities – but the availability of a wide range of potential theatre spaces can be a tremendous asset to the non-aligned company. Communicado is one of the best examples of a company exploiting this asset, seeking out the most appropriate space for each new project, whether it is a community arts centre for a children's show, a regular venue like Dundee Rep for a more conventional play or an undefined space in Glasgow's Tramway for an experimental adaptation. This is a flexibility that the building-based theatres cannot have (although paving over the stalls of the Royal Lyceum for a promenade production of *Oedipus Tyrannos* in 1994 was a shrewd attempt) and it opens the possibility for a freer form of creativity than might otherwise be expected.

The Edinburgh Festival and Fringe continue to surprise in the way they redefine the boundaries of theatrical space, but it is arguably Glasgow that has made the more lasting contribution in this area. In the late 1980s, as it prepared to take on the mantle of European City of Culture 1990, it began a process of reclaiming disused industrial sites and reinventing them as 'found' theatrical spaces. The Tramway, the former Museum of Transport and before that the factory where they built the city's fleet of trams, is the most prominent example: the building Peter Brook selected to stage *The Mahabharata* in 1988, and since used to house one of the most exciting international line-ups in Britain, from New York's Wooster Group to St Petersburg's Maly Theatre. The Tramway is now just one of a number of bare-bricked buildings that Glasgow has as its disposal: the Arches Theatre, hidden in the rumbling vaults beneath Central Station; the Harland and Wolff Engine Shed, home to Bill Bryden's vainglorious epics *The Ship* and *The Big Picnic*; and the Fruitmarket, a still under-used city-centre warehouse. Add to these the sites that the large-scale NVA Organisation (formerly Test Dept) has brought into use – the Cottier Church in the West End, now developed into a venue in its own right; the massive St Rollox Locomotive Works in Springburn; and a piece of industrial wasteland on the banks of the Clyde – and you can see a very clear movement toward spaces which carry none of the cultural weight of traditional theatres (whether this is perceived as bourgeois and elitist or just dull) and which demand that the theatremakers respond imaginatively to the environment (which in the case of NVA's 1995 production *Stormy Waters*, meant going as far as choreographing the cranes on the opposite bank of the river).

As the most consistently programmed venue, the Tramway has made the single biggest impact on recent Scottish theatremaking, seeming to demand that all those who perform in it attempt to excel themselves. Whether that is because of the precedent immediately established with the nine-hour *Mahabharata*, or whether it is because of the ambience of the building itself is impossible to determine. 'The pre-performance sensation,' writes former programme director Neil Wallace in *Making Space for Theatre*, about Tramway and other Brook-inspired theatres 'suggests that, before a single actor has appeared, or a note of music has been sounded, or a house light dimmed, the theatrical adventure, the story, has already begun' (p.62).

The kind of work that has flourished there, however, has tended to be non-text based or, at least, theatre which places substantial emphasis on the physical, visual or directorial aspects of performance. This was epitomised by Communicado's memorable contribution to Glasgow's Year of Culture, *Jock Tamson's Bairns*, a beguiling, visual feast of a show, but one from which the credited 'playwright', Liz Lochhead, all but dissociated herself because of its slim textual content.

Looked at impartially, there is nothing wrong with this – even if you prefer text-based theatre, it's hard to argue that it is implicitly better than any other form – but the combined consequence of the studio ghetto on the one hand and Tramway on the other does mean that, after a period in which the Scottish theatre is considered to have flourished largely on account of its playwrights, those same Scottish playwrights find themselves associated neither with the theatrical avant-garde nor with the theatrical mainstream. And the worry is that many of the achievements that have been made over the last thirty years will be lost because of the very conditions that helped produce them in the first place.

Four

Glasgow and its Citizens'

David Hutchison

To the average Glasgow theatregoer in his or her early forties or younger, the Citizens' is the company presided over for the last quarter century by Giles Havergal and his co-directors, Robert David MacDonald and Philip Prowse. To older members of the audience the Havergal regime, although it represents a very sharp break with the earlier traditions of the theatre, displays a staying power and a continuity which have no parallel in the history of rep in the city.

The Citizens' was founded in 1943 by the distinguished Scottish dramatist James Bridie, who assembled a board of directors and a company which began operations in the Athenaeum Theatre in Buchanan Street, and two years later moved to the Royal Princess's Theatre at Gorbals Cross, a venue which had until then been associated with pantomime rather than serious drama. Under a succession of directors, the company presented seasons of world, English and Scottish plays and anchored itself firmly in the post-war British repertory movement. Its fortunes varied, but much excellent work was done in building up audiences for drama, nurturing Scottish acting talent and encouraging indigenous writers to develop their skills. The decade preceding the appointment of Giles Havergal as artistic director in 1969 was latterly not a happy one, but it had seen the opening in 1965 of a club theatre, the Close, next to the main house, and some notable productions, including the première of John Arden's *Armstrong's Last Goodnight* in 1964, with Iain Cuthbertson giving a commanding performance in the leading role, the première in 1967 of Peter Nichols's *A Day in the Death of Joe Egg*, and in the same year a production of Brecht's *The Resistible Rise of Arturo Ui* which featured a dazzling performance as the Hitlerite hero by Leonard Rossiter, then little known. Both of these productions were directed by Michael Blakemore, who at that time was co-director of the theatre with Michael Meacham. In its earliest days a production of *Dr Faustus* at the Close directed by Charles Marowitz caused a brief exciting scandal because of alleged offensiveness to the Queen. These presentations were among the highlights, but alongside them a lot of good repertory work was being done, and although there was rather less Scottish drama than there had been in earlier days, the career of Tom Gallacher in his native country was launched in 1969 with a production of *Our Kindness to Five Persons*, originally presented at a Sunday afternoon reading in the Close before being given a main house production.

However, despite the quality of much that was being offered, audiences were declining and relations between the board and successive artistic directors had become increasingly fraught. When Giles Havergal arrived from Watford Palace Playhouse in the autumn of 1969, he initially offered a fairly conventional programme, but when that failed to boost audiences significantly, he and Philip Prowse, who had originally joined Havergal as a designer, decided 'if nobody likes what we do, we can do what we like'.[1] What followed was the transformation of the Citizens' into a theatre quite unlike any other to be seen in Britain, let alone Glasgow at that time. This radical change was not achieved without a great deal of controversy which in the early years could be extremely bilious, and although much of the uproar was probably not unwelcome to the theatre's management, there were occasions when relations between the Citizens' and the various constituencies with which it had to deal – audiences, reviewers and funding bodies – were tense. That all is calm in the mid-1990s is due to a number of factors which will be discussed below.

The first and most striking aspect of a Citizens' production is the emphasis on the visual: theatre must stimulate the eye and, beyond the eye the emotions, before it engages with the intellect. That is not to say that words are of no importance, but a concern with the literariness of a dramatic text is not characteristic of the Citizens', and Philip Prowse in particular has on a number of occasions made plain his distaste for what he regards as the dead weight of the text-bound English theatrical tradition, which gets in the way of the physical and visual excitement which he wishes to offer.

Actors are expected to look interesting, to be confident and to move well; they are less likely to be valued for their ability to structure a speech.

> what we're after from actors isn't what other people are after. We don't place much emphasis on a detailed naturalistic form of characterisation. We aim for what the Americans call 'presentational' kind of acting – a style that requires the actors to turn towards the audience, and to remember all the time that they *are* acting.[2]

Performers, then, are part of a realisation in which often dazzling visual metaphors, sustained by set, lighting and costume, are the basis of the interpretation of the text. The text itself is far from sacred, but is there to be reworked in order to create an exciting contemporary theatrical experience: *Painter's Palace of Pleasure* (1978), for example, amalgamated three different Jacobean plays; a production of *Pygmalion* in 1979 inserted lines from the Preface, and scenes from the film version, which to anyone familiar with the instructions on a Shaw performing licence to the effect that not a syllable can be altered, displayed an extraordinary *lèse majesté*.

The repertoire which the Citizens' draws on is wide and eclectic. It has offered its audiences English drama – Jacobean plays and the works of Noël Coward have enjoyed particular prominence – but above all it has explored the European tradition, regularly presenting work by writers as diverse as Brecht, Goldoni and Schiller. Brecht's name does sit uneasily with the other two, for it is clear that the Citizens' directorate is more comfortable with Goldoni – 'the virtuoso of the superficial', as MacDonald describes him[3] – and Schiller, but Glasgow audiences are sympathetic to Brecht's social critique and successive managements have presented his work; some older theatregoers can still remember the first production of a Brecht play at the Citizens, a very moving presentation of *The Good Woman of Setzuan* in 1962. Political engagement is not a conspicuous Citizens' strength, despite the ongoing commitment to Brecht, but occasionally a European play which deals head-on with political action has been presented, for example Rolf Hochhuth's *Judith* (1984), a piece which rather startlingly appears to suggest that there are circumstances in which it is legitimate to assassinate an American president.

One of the most striking achievements of the Citizens' has been its ability to take European works that most companies would regard as unstageable and to turn them into effective theatre. Robert David MacDonald, who joined Havergal and Prowse in 1972, and has worked as dramaturg, translator and director, is primarily responsible for this

aspect of the company's repertoire. In 1985 he pared Goethe's text of
Faust to three and a half hours and turned it into compelling and witty
theatre. In 1983 he adapted Karl Kraus's epic *Last Days of Mankind*
and, by setting it in a Viennese *Kaffeehaus*, emphasised the underlying
frivolity of the Austrian bourgeoisie as their world crumbled about their
heads. Most memorably, in 1980 he took Proust's *A la recherche du
temps perdu* and produced from it a piece of theatre which succeeded
in engaging its audiences in the characters' search through memory for
meaning and purpose. The vast majority of those who saw *A Waste of
Time* probably had not read Proust, and most of those who saw *The
Last Days of Mankind* had never heard of Kraus, but that in itself is
justification enough for attempting these kinds of adaptation, always
provided that it is effective theatre which results.

MacDonald has also written original work for the company, including
Summit Conference (1978), an exploration of the nature of fascism which
did not entirely take fire, largely because it developed into a discussion at
something of a remove from the thuggery and tyranny with which it was
concerned, and the much more successful *Chinchilla* (1977). *Chinchilla*
is supposedly about Diaghilev, the impresario who presided over the
Ballets Russes, but in fact anyone watching the play, with its emphasis
on the value of art for its own sake and art's basis in passion and sex, soon
realised that *Chinchilla* was a manifesto in which the Citizens', nearing the
end of its first decade under the Havergal/MacDonald/Prowse regime,
self-confidently asserted its belief in what it was doing.

Sex – hetero and homo – violence and excess were often seen as basic
characteristics of the Citizens' company in the 1970s. The sex is still
there – 'all plays are about politics, sex and death. If they are not, they
tend to be jolly boring'[4] – but there is less violence, to some extent
because of the nature of the current repertoire, but also to a degree
because in the early years there was clearly a desire to shock and to
push at the frontiers of taste. Sooner or later the horizon is reached
and what once seemed risqué becomes passé: in any event, in an age
of films such as *Reservoir Dogs*, it is quite hard to startle an audience
with blood and gore. For those who prefer the classical approach, in
which the gruesome takes place offstage and its significance is explored
onstage, the change is no doubt welcome. As to sexual excess, that is very
much a matter of taste, but for some spectators it can become a little
wearing. Michael Coveney, in his enthusiastic and illuminating study
of the company refers to the 'divinely decadent stage compositions'
which have often been presented.[5] What Coveney seems reluctant to
acknowledge is that is is possible to admire the work of the Citizens'
but to remain wary about the 'divinely decadent' for perfectly sound

non-puritanical reasons, which centre on the moral stance towards the
subject matter being adopted in such spectacles.

In many ways this is yesterday's argument, for the Citizens' has
evolved over the years and few voices would be heard articulating
such a concern nowadays. However the issue of the place of new
Scottish work in the repertoire remains a live one. The 1970s was
a period of upsurge in indigenous playwriting and a renewal of the
historically erratic commitment of theatres to encouraging Scottish
drama. As the possibility of devolution approached, all theatres but
one felt obliged to present Scottish plays: sometimes they did so out
of a genuine commitment, sometimes for more opportunistic reasons.
Scottish playwrights, who have never been able to make much of a living
in their homeland, felt that their collective fortunes were permanently
on the mend. The post-referendum 1980s were to cast some doubt on
the wisdom of such optimism, but at the time it seemed justifiable.
Alone among Scottish theatres, the Citizens' held out against presenting
indigenous work, other than plays written by its house dramatist who,
it was often repeated, was born in Elgin of a long-established Glasgow
business family. This stance angered many Scottish writers, and led to
an antagonism between them and the theatre which has yet to be finally
dissipated. The fact that most Scottish writing was naturalistic in form
and socially realistic in content and therefore would have been almost
impossible to mount in the Citizens' house style tended to get lost in
the discussion, or was used as an argument against the whole post-1970
Citizens' project. Michael Coveney, eager to support the position taken
by the company, overdoes his attacks on Scottish dramatists, and shows
no understanding of the difficulties posed by the fact that the only rep
theatre in the country's most populous city – the Close had been
destroyed by fire in 1973 – refused or was unable to find space for
Scottish plays.[6]

The situation has improved since the 1970s for a number of reasons. In
the first place the Tron Theatre opened its doors in 1982, and, although
it has never had the commitment to indigenous work of the Chris Parr
period at the Traverse in the 1970s, it has consistently found a place in
its programming for new Scottish plays and revivals, as well as pieces
by American writers such as Sam Shepard and David Mamet, whose
understandable absence from the Citizens' programmes was a loss to
Glasgow audiences. The Tron has encouraged new playwrights such as
Peter Arnott and Chris Hannan and revived work by writers such as
Hector MacMillan and C.P. Taylor. It has made a particular feature
of the plays of the Quebecois writer, Michel Tremblay, usually in Scots
translations undertaken by Martin Bowman and Bill Findlay.

The opening of the Tramway in 1988 gave Glasgow a new flexible venue. That theatre has specialised in bringing foreign productions to Glasgow, and has established a particularly strong link with Peter Brook's Paris-based ensemble, which launched the Tramway with *The Mahabharata*. Several of Robert Lepage's creations have been presented – cementing the Glasgow/Quebec link – and companies as varied as the Wooster Group and the Maly Theatre of St Petersburg have performed there, as have some of the Scottish touring ensembles which have established themselves in the last twenty years, and other British companies.

The Mahabharata was presented as part of the 1988 Mayfest season. Mayfest was launched in 1983, not so much as a competitor to the Edinburgh Festival as an alternative. It drew much of its initial drive from the trade union movement and retains a commitment to involving working-class people throughout the city via community productions and in more conventional ways. In recent years its distinctiveness and *raison d'être* have sometimes been a little difficult to discern, but in practice it has added to the amount of theatrical and cultural activity in Glasgow. The theatrical side of Mayfest has benefited from, and contributed to, the growth of new companies such as Annexe and Wiseguise which do not have venues of their own but tour arts centres and the like; Annexe in particular is committed to the presentation of new Scottish work. The municipalised King's Theatre in the city continues to offer a mixture of amateur musical productions, pantomime and touring companies of various kinds, while the Pavilion provides lighter fare. The Theatre Royal, home of Scottish Opera, also plays host to touring drama productions mounted by the National Theatre and other companies.

As a result of all these developments, theatregoers in the West of Scotland are offered a much wider range of fare than has ever been the case in the past. It is now well nigh impossible to see all of the shows that are worth seeing and also to keep up with music, opera and ballet, let alone film. The menu today is now an international one, where the eclectic Europeanism of the Citizens' is complemented by the European and American companies at the Tramway and Canadian and Irish work at the Tron, which, in addition to being a production house, plays host to visiting companies.

It is no longer the case that the refusal or inability of the Citizens' to mount Scottish work is a matter of vitriolic controversy, since there are now other opportunities for indigenous dramatists (although rather too many productions of new plays involve unemployed actors and directors working in the often forlorn hope of a share in the profits). If changing circumstances have helped diminish antagonism between the Citizens' and Scottish writers, so too have some astute moves by the Citizens' management, which in the early 1980s began to develop a policy of offering the theatre to touring companies mounting Scottish work. 7:84's 'Clydebuilt' season in 1982 was presented in the Gorbals and at other venues throughout Scotland. Clydebuilt comprised revivals of socially committed plays originally presented by Unity Theatre in the 1940s, and proved to be a very mixed bag, but Giles Havergal's own production of Ena Lamont Stewart's *Men Should Weep* brought out deeper resonances in the play than a straightforward naturalistic one would have done, and in a sense marked a truce between the Citizens' and indigenous dramatists.

One further development within the Citizens' itself has enabled the company to extend the range of what it does, and that was the opening of the small Stalls and Studio performing spaces in 1993. This has meant that at any one time a range of work and styles – including presentations by visiting companies – has been available under one roof, although the mounting of new Scottish work from outside the company's own resources has only just become a feature of programming, and its future is uncertain.

A crucial factor in the survival of the Citizens' has been the political nous of Havergal and his colleagues. By good fortune or design they have had a supportive board of directors, under Labour lawyer and municipal politician, Bill Taylor, from 1970 until 1991, and thereafter under Professor Jan McDonald in the chair of Drama at Glasgow University. Furthermore, there has been a consistently rigorous approach to financial management, which, combined with populist measures such as a cheap seats policy, has ensured that the public funding bodies on which the theatre relies for its survival have been generous as far as both revenue and capital expenditure are concerned. It was equally astute to retain the education-oriented TAG (Theatre About Glasgow) company, and to encourage it to find a place for Scottish material in its programming. Likewise, the continuation of the Christmas panto tradition has had both financial and cultural benefits. Since its inception in the 1940s, the Citizens' company has joined in Glasgow's pantomime mania: it would have been difficult not to do so, given the Gorbals theatre's own history pre-1945. In the 1960s, however, the tradition was faltering, with some rather indifferent shows, and Havergal's decision to opt for pantos with strong narrative lines meant that the Citizens' was offering an experience complementary to city-centre productions. Drawing on the Howard and Wyndham tradition, for the most part these have been built around spectacular stage presentation and the presence of stars such as Rikki Fulton, Jimmy Logan and the most distinguished of post-World War Two dames, Stanley Baxter, who began his own career as a 'straight' actor at the Citizens' in the late 1940s.

The Glasgow theatrical scene of the mid-1990s, in which the Citizens' continues to play a central role, is much richer than it has ever been, but there are still gaps in provision. The contemporary English repertoire, for example, is only fitfully presented, and the non-operatic musical theatre tends to be the province of local amateur companies, backed up by touring professional presentations of the more popular shows: as a result, there is little chance to see professional productions of the work of a writer like Stephen Sondheim in the city. Scottish dramatists will continue to argue, with justice, that they are under-represented, to an extent that has made them almost an endangered species. There have been periods when their work has been extensively presented, but they have never enjoyed the consistent long-term support from the Scottish theatre that is offered by the English theatre to English writers.

As far as the future of the Citizens' is concerned, a quarter of a century after the present policy was embarked on, it will be surprising if the quiet evolution which has been noted here does not continue. A point may be reached when the current triumvirate decide to move on, although that does not seem likely, or simply to retire – two of them are in their late fifties, one in his mid-sixties. It is highly improbable that such an unusual combination of talents can be replicated, so when a new artistic director (or directorate) takes over, policy and style must inevitably change. But it is crucial that the achievements of the previous regime are neither rejected out of hand nor fossilised in endlessly revived productions, as has happened in some continental ensembles. It would be very depressing if the Citizens' were to become indistinguishable from the duller English provincial rep. Fortunately that is an unlikely outcome, since the the audiences which have been exposed to the range of material offered in Messrs Havergal, Prowse and MacDonald's 'palace of delights' are most unlikely to settle for such an unappetising bill of fare.

NOTES

1. Quoted in Michael Coveney, *The Citz* (London: Nick Hern Books, 1990), p.37.
2. Quoted in interview with Joyce McMillan, *Scottish Theatre News*, 5, 4 (1981), pp.4–9.
3. Coveney, p.143.
4. Coveney, p.149.
5. Coveney, p.65.
6. Coveney returns to this theme in an article in the *Observer* of 20 August 1995, in which he attacks Scottish dramatists who criticise the Citizens' as 'unperformed and untalented'.

Five

The People's Story: 7:84 Scotland

Linda Mackenney

7:84 Scotland has a unique position in the history of Scottish drama in the twentieth century, in so far as anything in the world of theatre can claim to be unique. What follows is an outline of 7:84's story – including its high points and its low points – and an attempt to assess the company's significance by placing it in the context of other contemporary developments in Scottish drama.

7:84 took its name from a statistic in the *Economist* which claimed that 7 per cent of the population of Britain owned 84 per cent of the wealth. The company made a massive impact on Scottish consciousness, touching nerves hidden deep in the national psyche. John McGrath, its founder, had begun to stir the waters in Scotland with two plays: *Trees in the Wind*, which was performed by 7:84's sister company at the Edinburgh Festival in 1971; and *Random Happenings in the Hebrides*, which was performed at the Royal Lyceum in Edinburgh in 1970. He returned to Scotland in 1973 to write *The Cheviot, the Stag and the Black, Black Oil*, which linked the modern day exploitation of the oil found off Scottish shores with the Scottish landowners' exploitation of the Highland crofting community in the nineteenth century, and explored these experiences using a new theatrical form based on the traditional ceilidh. The play broke new ground in terms of its subject (McGrath used new research being done at the University of Edinburgh), form and style. It appealed to audiences throughout Scotland because it stirred memories and sensibilities concerning injustices both past and present, using the format of the traditional ceilidh in a manner that struck a vital chord with the people's sense of their own cultural identity.

John McGrath had gathered round him at this time a company of highly talented individuals: these included Elizabeth and David MacLennan, founder members of 7:84 England; Dolina MacLennan, a Gaelic singer from Lewis; Allan Ross, whom McGrath described as a 'fiddler extraordinaire'; John Bett, Alex Norton and Bill Paterson, who had previously appeared together in Billy Connolly's *The Great Northern Welly Boot Show* and between them possessed a wide variety of skills as live performers; and Chris Martin and Ferelith Lean, who helped with publicity and front of house. These people worked as a collective in a co-operative manner. John McGrath wrote the play by sections, following workshops in which the actors went through piles of printed material concerning past and present events in Highland history, exploring their potential for a song, a political speech or scene. During the run which followed, additions were made as new material concerning Scotland's oil became available. John Byrne designed the set, a highly original pop-up book, which allowed the company to change the set with a turn of each enormous page. The whole company mucked in with regard to finding or making, washing and repairing costumes and getting in and out of theatres and halls. Allan Ross, Doli MacLennan and the other members of the company who could sing or play a musical instrument came together and formed the Force Ten Gaels in order to provide music for the ceilidh which followed every performance of the show.[1]

Such moments of spontaneous, corporate creativity are extremely rare and cause immense, immediate excitement. Everyone who took part in producing *The Cheviot, the Stag and the Black, Black Oil* or who saw it live in the theatre knew without doubt that they were witnessing an important moment in Scottish theatre history. The play had an extraordinary appeal: it attracted people from every age group, every social class, from the Highlands and the Lowlands of Scotland. Its subject was local in the true tradition of popular drama, but its appeal was national, and even universal.

It wasn't just the subject matter, the form, the mode of creation and the celebratory spirit of the *Cheviot* that was new. 7:84 broke what was seen then to be new ground by touring their production, taking their play to audiences, seeking them out in village halls throughout the country, rather than waiting for their audiences to seek them out in the big theatres of Edinburgh and Glasgow. In fact, 7:84 was reviving a tradition established by theatre companies in the early twentieth century, companies like the Scottish National Players (1921–48), or Joe Corrie's Fife Miner Players, who toured village concert halls, cinemas and music-hall theatres in the 1920s, or Glasgow Unity, who toured throughout Scotland in the 1940s. It is important to add at this point that, like Joe Corrie and Glasgow Unity, 7:84 Scotland went in search of a working-class audience, whose needs and likes and dislikes remained uncatered for, a point McGrath emphasised in his account of the tour which was published with the play. He recalled 'an ancient, near-blind, Gaelic poet, the Bard of Melbost' who came up to him after one show in the Outer Hebrides and said, 'I have heard the story of my people told with truth. If I die tonight, I die as a happier man.' McGrath observed that this man had been paying his taxes to support the Arts Council. He concluded: 'For the first time he was getting something back. I hope it won't be the last.'[2]

7:84, then, by the end of the *Cheviot* tour could congratulate themselves for three main achievements: they had produced a new kind of Scottish play, which made use of a new dramatic form, based upon a traditional cultural form much loved by its audience; they had also found a new, previously dispossessed audience; and, last but not least, their success had won them a Scottish Arts Council grant, which would enable them to continue their work. The SAC had been dubious about the *Cheviot* at first and turned down 7:84's application for financial support. But, after a meeting between McGrath and Chris Martin, they changed their minds and awarded the company a £2,000 guarantee against losses.[3]

During the next five years, the company produced a range of new plays that explored different aspects of Scottish working-class history and contemporary experience, drawing on a range of popular cultural forms, touring them to clubs, halls and theatres around the country. John McGrath's *The Game's a Bogey* (1974) and *Little Red Hen* (1975) both explored the history of Red Clydeside with a view to reminding their audiences about their socialist past: the former celebrated the life of John Maclean, while the latter took a critical look at the activities of Scottish socialists in the 1930s and encouraged its audiences to take an equally critical look at the activities of the Scottish Nationalist Party in the 1970s. Thus 7:84's political stance concerning Scottish nationalism and socialism was confirmed.

During this time, the composition and organisation of the company underwent a number of changes. Members of the original company left: some to follow new opportunities, others because they became unhappy about the choice of material or changes in the way the company was run. 7:84 was also joined by several new people: these included David Anderson, who with David MacLennan, wrote a musical interrogating the music business, *His Master's Voice* (1978).

John McGrath included music in a list of nine necessary ingredients in a popular piece of drama.[4] From the beginning, music had made a significant contribution to the appeal and success of 7:84 productions. However, different opinions began to form about what kind of music they should be using, and the way they were using it. McGrath liked using folk music, as well as contemporary pop and rock, and argued that the main purpose of the songs was to support the meaning of a scene by reinforcing ideas and feelings. But the two Davids favoured the use of pop and rock as a means of appealing to a young audience, believing that songs could be used to shape and sustain dramatic narrative. It was decided that rather than squabble over the allocation of one Scottish Arts Council grant, the company would split in two. The SAC allowed 7:84 to stop working for a short period, so that Wildcat Stage Productions could come into being. By the end of the year, it was clear that the new company was a viable proposition. When 7:84 regrouped, the SAC agreed to finance the two companies as separate entities.

7:84 itself entered a new phase of its development. During the years he had spent touring, John McGrath had heard about the other companies that had toured Scotland with their plays about Scottish working class life and experience in the 1920s, 1930s and 1940s. He commissioned some research into the activities of these companies and used this material to mount a new season of past plays. The 'Clydebuilt' Season was presented at the Mitchell Theatre in Glasgow between January and May 1982. It included five plays: Joe Corrie's *In Time o' Strife*, a play about the General Strike in Scotland, which was first produced by the Fife Miner Players in 1927; Ewan MacColl's *Johnny Noble* and Harry Trott's *UAB Scotland*, documentary dramas about life in the 1930s, first produced by the Theatre Workshop and Glasgow Workers' Theatre Group respectively; George Munro's *Gold in His Boots* and Ena Lamont Stewart's *Men Should Weep*, first produced by Glasgow Unity Theatre in 1947.[5]

'Clydebuilt' had important repercussions as far as the future of 7:84 was concerned. The season was an outstanding artistic success. Its plays appealed directly to Scottish audiences in much the same way that the *Cheviot* had nine years earlier. In particular, the last play in the series, Ena Lamont Stewart's *Men Should Weep*, elicited strong sympathies across a wide range of social groupings for its historical awareness and the playwright's innovatory attention to the predicament of working-class women: features reinforced by the sensitive use of easily identifiable popular cultural forms deployed in Giles Havergal's production.[6]

During the 1970s the company had toured with small-scale productions, which explored a wide variety of topics, using a range of popular techniques and devices. John McGrath was justifiably proud of the new theatrical form that had been developed, but also gradually became frustrated by the fact that the company's fixed budget, and commitment to providing a set number of touring days, limited him to two or three productions per annum, each of which had to contain 'five actors and a piano'. As he pointed out, there was a limit to how inventive you could be with these resources. He knew that his work was being criticised for becoming increasingly formulaic. He hoped that 'Clydebuilt' would help to provide new artistic opportunities. In order to present the season, the company had raised a substantial sum of money from the Scottish Arts Council and Strathclyde Regional Council. This enabled the company to employ an unusually large number of actors for a longer period of time. It was hoped that 'Clydebuilt' would open up opportunities in terms of the kind of work and the scale of the productions 7:84 was able to produce, allowing the company to continue its small-scale touring productions, while also presenting large-scale tours of new plays, adaptations of the classics and revivals of other Scottish works. 7:84's aspirations here were entirely consistent with those of its precursors: Glasgow Unity had also sought to present a mixed programme of new Scottish works dealing with local historical and contemporary issues, and adaptations of the classics; they felt the latter had been unjustifiably appropriated by the repertory theatres of their day and could be revived in a way that would appeal to their own working-class audiences.

'Clydebuilt' certainly enabled 7:84 to add a new string to its artistic bow, in the form of large-scale touring productions of other Scottish plays recovered from the past. These productions opened once a year at Mayfest in Glasgow, then toured the larger theatres in Scotland. They were directed by David Hayman, who became an Associate Director with the company. They included a new production of Joe Corrie's *In Time o' Strife* (1984) and Robert McLeish's *The Gorbals Story* (1985), which like *Men Should Weep* were published by 7:84 Publications.[7]

'Clydebuilt' might have provided 7:84 with more opportunity to expand, but for the two catastrophes which followed. Although 'Clydebuilt' had been an artistic and popular success, drawing large audiences, it was a financial disaster. It had been carefully budgeted and funding had been raised from outside sources. None the less, the season ran up a huge, unpredicted deficit, which the tiny administrative team were unable to keep abreast of at the time. The consequences of this were that 7:84 lost the confidence of the Scottish Arts Council and other funding bodies. From this moment onwards, the SAC became reluctant to give 7:84 more money, and became increasingly fussy about how 7:84 conducted its administrative affairs and spent its small-scale touring grant.

7:84's chances of extending its artistic range were also damaged by the artistic failure of John McGrath's *Women in Power*, an adaptation of two plays by Aristophanes, presented at the Edinburgh Festival in 1983. It is not necessary to go into the causes of this disaster: McGrath has covered them fully in his book *The Bone Won't Break*. But the consequences cannot be underestimated. It led to the immediate dispersal of the company that had come together in 'Clydebuilt' and, in the long term, further damaged the disintegrating confidence of its funding bodies.

During the next few years 7:84 produced a great deal of high quality work that continued to draw large, appreciative audiences in the Highlands, in the clubs and halls in local communities and in larger venues in the cities. During the late 1980s, it also began a battle for survival, which commenced shortly after 7:84 England's grant was cut in March 1984. It is difficult to come to absolute conclusions about what posed the biggest threat to 7:84's continuation as a popular drama group. There were a number of factors that came into play, and there are many striking parallels between what happened to 7:84 and what had happened to its precursors in the late 1940s and early 1950s.

It is important to see 7:84 in the context of Scottish theatre history, for there is a discernible cyclical pattern. During the twentieth century, several popular dramatists and drama groups have come into being and made a contribution, but few have been able to establish themselves with the kind of permanence that is seen to be the norm for many repertory theatre companies. It could be argued that 7:84 came closest to establishing itself as a permanent institution. It had a life span of fifteen years. Its name survives today and the work that the current day 7:84 theatre company does is highly commendable, though it is not the work of a popular drama group. Since the late 1980s, the work of the original 7:84 company has been continued by Wildcat Stage Productions, which staged, among other shows, John McGrath's *Border Warfare* at the Tramway in Glasgow in 1989, undoubtedly the single most significant and inventive piece of theatre he had produced since the *Cheviot*.

7:84's demise was the result of many on-going problems – some personal, others political, some artistic, others organisational. During the 1980s, McGrath was criticised for refusing to let go of the company's reins. For those that knew him well this was curiously ironic. He was certainly anxious that 7:84 pass into the hands of someone or some group of people who would develop the traditions he had established, and because no such person or persons appeared, he hung on longer than he wanted. He spent much of the 1980s frustrated by the constraints of writing for 'five actors and a piano'. He fought long and hard for the right to maintain and develop the three strands in 7:84's work, but increasingly found much of his own artistic stimulus outside the company, writing films, librettos and so forth.

McGrath must at times have felt like King Canute. During the early years, between 1973 and 1979, 7:84 was able to function confidently in the knowledge that trade union power had proved strong enough to bring down a Conservative Government and put a supportive Labour Government in its place. During the 1980s, 7:84 was always in a precarious position. It was only a matter of time before the Thatcher Government would begin to call the socialist theatre companies of the 1970s to account. This situation parallels what had happened forty years earlier when Glasgow Unity's career blossomed in the wake of the Labour victory in 1945, began to wane as the Labour Government lost its sense of direction in 1948, and foundered in the year the Conservatives were restored to power.

When one looks back at the mid- to late 1980s, what seems strange is that 7:84 survived so long, and this reflects well on the company's resilience and sheer street-fighting determination. When the Scottish Arts Council announced that it intended to withdraw 7:84's annual grant, its spokespersons declared that this decision had nothing to do with 7:84's artistic policy, but was the consequence of concern regarding 7:84's ability to administer its income. This is an uncannily clear echo of the late 1940s, when James Bridie, as the Chairman of the Scottish Committee of the Arts Council, argued that Glasgow Unity's guarantee against loss had been withdrawn because of concern about administrative competence.[8] In both cases there were grounds for concern regarding financial errors, but there can be little doubt that there was another hidden agenda. James Bridie regarded Glasgow Unity's working-class audiences with contempt.[9] He described the political content of the plays of 'left-wing writers' as an 'infectious disease'.[10] When the Scottish Arts Council inadvertently released their records of anonymous internal reviews of 7:84 productions, it was clear that much of 7:84's work aroused similar feelings.[11]

During the 1980s, 7:84 came under increasing pressure to organise its activities in an increasingly bureaucratic manner. It had begun life as a 'collective', in which everyone was paid the same, and decisions were taken at company meetings, called as they were required. One of the conditions of an SAC grant was the introduction of a management team and a Board of Directors. The management team comprised the artistic director, an administrator and a publicist, who were all paid the same weekly wage as performers. However, as the decade continued and money became short (as it did for so many organisations in these years) there was constant pressure to become competitive and raise money from alternative sources. For years there were bitter disputes about the amount of money that was spent on administration. When, towards the end, the decision was made to pay an administrator more money than other members of the company – in the hope that this would attract the sort of person

that would appease the SAC and generate money from new sources –
there was a funereal atmosphere round the table.

What 7:84 had achieved in fifteen years was immense. It had produced
plays that explored and challenged perspectives on Scottish history and
contemporary culture. It had created a vibrant new theatrical form that
was uniquely Scottish, drawing on forms of entertainment that were
familiar and therefore appealed to Scottish people's minds and hearts, and
which spoke directly to their own cultural identity. 7:84 had also found a
new audience for theatre in Scotland by taking its work to its audiences in
halls in their own communities without, as Neil Kinnock put it, the 'mys-
tique' or the 'expense' of traditional theatre.[12] Its innovations have made
an indelible mark on the work of other theatre companies in Scotland and
around the world. Its influence can also be seen in much of the work that
appears on Scottish television and film. As the presenter of a retrospective
documentary said, the *Cheviot* was a 'modest little show',[13] presented on a
shoestring, but its influence was such that 'much of what we now think of
as Scottish theatre', much of what we now take for granted, 'owes its existence' to that moment in time when a group of committed popular artists
came together to create a show about the history of the Highlands, and in
the process gave birth to a new theatrical form, and to a new tradition.

NOTES

1. For more detail concerning the *Cheviot*, see John McGrath, 'The Year of the
   Cheviot', *The Cheviot, the Stag and the Black, Black Oil*, (London: Methuen,
   1981), pp.v–xxviii.
2. Ibid, p.xiv.
3. See Elizabeth MacLennan, *The Moon Belongs to Everyone: Making Theatre with
   7:84* (London: Methuen, 1990), pp.45–7.
4. John McGrath, *A Good Night Out: Popular Theatre: Audience, Class and Form*
   (London: Methuen, 1981), pp.55–6.
5. See Clydebuilt materials in the Scottish Theatre Archive, Special Collections,
   Glasgow University Library.
6. See Linda Mackenney's critical introduction to Ena Lamont Stewart's *Men Should
   Weep* (Edinburgh: 7:84 Publications, 1986), pp.iv–ix.
7. See Joe Corrie, *Plays, Poems and Theatre Writings* (Edinburgh: 7:84 Publications,
   1984) and Robert McLeish, *The Gorbals Story* (Edinburgh: 7:84 Publications, 1985).
8. See James Bridie, 'Dramaturgy in Scotland', *Proceedings of the Royal Philosophical
   Society*, LXXXIV (1949–50).
9. Ibid.
10. Letter from Bridie to Corrie, 21 December 1944, Papers of Joe Corrie, National
    Library of Scotland, MSS 26551 (9).
11. See Scottish Arts Council review of John McGrath's *Mairi Mhor* in John McGrath,
    The Bone Won't Break, pp.128–9.
12. See interview in 7:84: *Keep Right On*, presented by Ex–S on BBC Scotland, 1
    February 1993.
13. Ibid.

Part II

PLAYS AND PLAYWRIGHTS

Six

Language and Identity on the Stage

Lindsay Paterson

In the Introduction to his 1992 Scots translation of Rostand's *Cyrano de Bergerac*, Edwin Morgan comments on the potential of urban Glaswegian in the theatre: '[I]t is widely spoken, can accommodate contemporary reference . . . and comes unburdened by the baggage of the older Scots which used to be thought suitable for historical plays'.[1] That comment could be a linguistic manifesto of Scottish playwrights over the last three decades: authenticity has been located in the working-class dialects of the Glasgow area. Indeed, so pervasive has this belief become that it has spread even to television drama produced for a UK audience. Mark McManus as Taggart and Robbie Coltrane as the psychologist Fitz in *Cracker* have come to stand for a directness and honesty that is allegedly lacking in the repressed culture of decadent Britain.

But that is not in fact all that Morgan said: he added that urban Glaswegian was also 'by no means incapable of the lyrical and the poetic', and his translation itself bears that out magnificently. This new way of looking at that speech form is a sign of an exciting development in Scottish writing, and reflects a new maturity in the examination of national identity.

First, though – before we look at Scots as poetic – we must acknowledge the great achievement of writers in demotic Scots. It is easy to forget just how stultified Scots-language writing had become by the 1960s. Historical plays used a highly artificial form of older Scots (as Morgan observes); contemporary writing used at most a Scottish accent. When dramatists such as Hector MacMillan, Tom McGrath, and Donald Campbell started writing in a Scots that could be felt to be real, they were contributing to that awakening of national self-confidence in the 1960s and 1970s which has now thoroughly reinvented the national identity.

The first thing these writers did was to harness the sheer energy of working-class Scots into a vigorous theatricality in which issues of wide social significance could be debated incisively. Take this exchange from near the beginning of MacMillan's *The Sash* (1974), a play about religious sectarianism. Bill is trying to persuade his son Cameron to take part in the annual Orange Walk; Cameron – product of the 1960s – is choosing to reject his father's culture, but with difficulty:

> *Cameron:*   You'd think the world would come tae a stop, if Ah didnae go on The Walk!
> *Bill:*   Your world could just stop! An if it does, it'll be because idle bastards like yoursel are too lazy t'get up aff your arses an dae somethin aboot it!
> *Cameron:*   It's no a case o bein idle!
> *Bill:*   You've got t'fight tae keep whit you've got!
> *Cameron:*   Maybe Ah don't want whit you've got![2]

As well as the conflict of generations between Bill and Cameron, we also have the partly linguistic conflict between Bill and his neighbour Bridget O'Shaughnessy, whose language is working-class Ulster Catholic. The language is what makes this play, and the power of the rhetorical contrasts was evident in its dubious popularity in parts of central Scotland in the 1970s, where rival factions of the audience used to cheer on the protagonists.

The same kind of aggressive energy can be found in numerous other plays of the 1970s and early 1980s. Another famous and influential example is *The Hard Man* (1977), by Tom McGrath and Jimmy Boyle, about the latter's life as a Glasgow gangster and his subsequent imprisonment. The dialogue is staccato and brash, with a violence that reflects the brutal action. Here is the central character Johnny Byrne and his friends explaining why they took to robbery:

> *Byrne:*   Ah hud a joab wance but it wus a waste o time, cooped up aw day wae somebody watching yir every move when yae could be oot oan the streets enjoyin yirsel.
> *Danny:*   Aye. So whit else can ye dae but turn tae thievin. Yir hands are forced.
> *Bandit:*   Nae option.
> *Danny:*   A man's goat tae dae something tae keep himsel alive.[3]

Similarly, in John Byrne's *The Slab Boys* (1978), it is working-class Scots that gives the dialogue its energy. And in *The Widows of Clyth* (1979), Donald Campbell particularly asks for the speech not to be in a 'conventional "Highland" accent' (Introduction), and he uses it to deflate any grand ideas that the characters might have: one of them, having returned to Caithness from a spell in the Merchant Navy, travelling as far as Australia, dismisses this experience with 'och, it's a bit like Thurso if ye want to know!'[4]

Now, not much in Scottish culture happens without reference to England, and the implicit contrast running through all this is with English. The convention that has grown up along with this aggressive Scots is that an 'English' accent signifies social detachment. In *The Hard Man*, to be English is to be 'very cordial' (p.35) – the opposite of the values asserted by Byrne and his associates. For John McGrath in *The Cheviot, the Stag and the Black, Black Oil* (1973), an 'English' accent denotes the effete aristocracy.

But the linguistic contrast with English has not mainly been with England itself so much as with those Scottish social groups that can be claimed to have betrayed their country. Thus the language of the law courts in *The Hard Man* is English, a contrast made pointedly at the end where a prison officer mimics in English the judge who convicted Byrne, and then switches to Scots to mock Byrne's fate (p.65).

The most sustained example of this type of contrast between Scots and English is in Campbell's *The Jesuit* (1976). The play is about an early seventeenth-century Scottish priest, John Ogilvie, who refuses to recant his Catholicism in the face of imprisonment and torture imposed by the Protestant Archbishop Spottiswoode. The reason Spottiswoode wants Ogilvie to yield is pragmatic: he foresees religious conflict if the Catholics gain a martyr. Thus from one point of view Ogilvie is a fanatic; from another he is a hero.

Ogilvie has spent most of his life abroad, and speaks with a modern educated English accent; his principled arguments are presented elegantly as if in a theological debate. Spottiswoode speaks a modern Scots, as do the soldiers who guard Ogilvie. The soldiers' speech has the same demotic energy as could be found in *The Hard Man* and *The Sash*, and this points up Ogilvie's distance from the people he claims to serve: that is the sense in which he is a fanatic. Spottiswoode eventually despairs of persuading Ogilvie to give up his beliefs, and exclaims in frustration: 'what garred you return [to Scotland] after all these years? Ye canna even speak the language!'[5]

The convention that betrayal of Scotland can be symbolised in a linguistic betrayal has become now utterly standard in Scottish drama, as in Scottish culture generally. But an interesting shift has taken place, reflecting greater subtlety by means of a wider range of linguistic registers. This subtlety was always present in the best writers. For example in Campbell's *Somerville the Soldier* (1978) Scots and English are contrasted, but not neatly aligned with social class or with national identity. .The educated English accents of the revolutionary plotters indicate their indifference to the human concerns of the working class on whose behalf they claim to be fighting. This is contrased with the vigorous Scots of Somerville himself, but also with the Cockney of Sally Barbour and the other staff of the inn in which Somerville stays.

In Liz Lochhead's *Mary Queen of Scots Got Her Head Chopped Off* (1987), the Scots of Queen Mary is counterposed to the English of Queen Elizabeth. The English Court ridicules Mary's writing of verse in Scots. But Lochhead is far too fine and ironic a writer to adopt unproblematically the Scottish–English conventions of earlier writers. Mary's Scots, after all, is heavily accented with French, and some of the most vigorous Scots in the play comes from John Knox, whose religious fanaticism would align him as a dramatic character (though not theologically) with Campbell's John Ogilvie. He also admires Elizabeth as a 'Good Protestant' (p.50). Who then speaks for Scotland?

Identity, for Lochhead, is not a straightforward matter anyway. Mary and Elizabeth each switch roles (and languages) to become the other's maid, indicating a private bonding between them as women which their public conflict precludes. Lochhead's irony has its most incisive expression through the commentary of La Corbie, a character detached from the action who comments on it throughout. She opens the play, for example, by commenting

> Ah dinna ken whit like *your* Scotland is. Here's mines.
> National flower: the thistle.
> National pastime: nostalgia.
> National weather: smirr, haar, drizzle, snow.
> National bird: the crow, the corbie, le corbeau, moi![6]

Her comment on the linguistic contrast is: 'there are two queens in one island, both o the wan language – mair or less' (p.15). The contrast is not so stark after all, and its shading into a mere cultural nuance presages the Union which was the ultimate resolution of the political conflict that the play explores. La Corbie sings 'The Twa Corbies' (pp.60–1), a reminder of the incessant bloodshed which accompanied the old military versions of the conflicts between Scotland and England. Linguistic or political antagonism may be painful, but at least we are alive at the end of it.

Lochhead is, in general, fascinated with questions of identity, especially of gender and nation, and of how these are expressed in language. Such issues were explored in her Communicado Theatre Company *Jock Tamson's Bairns* (1990), in which the central character is a symbolic Drunk Man descending into hell to become the haggis at a demonic

Burns supper. This character embodied (androgynously) the whole of Scottish identity in 'his' head: one central dimension of the tensions which this entails is a contrast between harsh social conditions and the beautiful (but maybe specious) lyrics of Burns.

She makes linguistic duplicity a feature of all the characters apart from Dorine in her translation of *Tartuffe* (1986), thus adding a special Scottish aspect to the theme of hypocrisy. Tartuffe, for example, speaks Scots when he is girning about his health or trying to pursue his affair with Elmire, but speaks a Scots-accented English when he is playing the Holy Willie at prayer. Lochhead has her own distinctive way with this, though: in the middle of trying to find out about Elmire's feelings for him, Tartuffe asks 'you want a wee boiling tae sook, or a bit o lickerish?' (p.49) – a moment that exploits the deflating potential of Scots that emerged from the 1970s on. Dorine, likewise, speaking Scots throughout, inherits the earlier association of Scots with honesty. In Lochhead, the honest character is usually female – Dorine and La Corbie in these plays; or the female voice which figures in much of her poetry.

So the use of Scots to point up social contrasts has become more subtle in the last two decades, and in that it reflects a wider debate about Scottish identity – a rejection of the image of Scotland as residing in the male industrial worker of the 1950s and earlier (or his unemployed son of the 1970s and later), and an exploration of the different identities available to women or to people from various ethnic backgrounds.[7]

But even this use of language could still be said to be about social realism, of however subtle a kind. The most innovative development in Scots in the theatre has been its use for purposes that are not realistic at all. In this respect, we have a fusing of the realist tradition in Scottish literature with the fantastic.[8]

There has always been an element of fantasy in Scots. The dialogue in *The Sash* is hyperbolic, arising from the depth of feeling which the characters put into it. The Orangeman Bill can become quite lyrical in praise of Protestantism and King William:

> Oor forefaithers fought for the Prodisant ascendancy. We're still up against that. We cannae . . . let stupit things divide us. That's aw they're waitin on, y'know. Divide and conquer. (*snaps fingers*) They'll be ower us like that! Back tae Papish tyranny! The Scarlet Harlot! The Mark of the Beast! The end o everything oor ancestors fought an died for. (p.27)

That this speech is set in an ironic context – Bill is as ludicrous as he is passionate – does not detract from its rhetorical power for a certain audience, especially when set in the play's use of song, flags, and colourful Orange Order uniforms.

A more sustained use of fantasy Scots can be found in John Byrne's *The Slab Boys*, *Cuttin' a Rug* (1979) and *Still Life* (1982). Byrne has an excellent ear for the exotic metaphors that characterise working-class speech in west-central Scotland. For example, Lucille in *The Slab Boys* responds dismissively to male teasing about who she is going to the staff dance with by refusing to take them seriously, pretending that their archness is just obscurity stemming from stupidity: 'Honest to God, see when you come in here it's like trying to find your way through the middle of Gene Vincent's wardrobe with a glow worm on the end of a stick. Quit talking in riddles.'[9] This would not work in English (although it might in the accents of New York).

These plays are full of wordplay. Thus Phil and Spanky respond to an ironic 'comprendez' from a fellow-worker with a pointless (because he has left) but enjoyably fantastic duet:

> *Phil:* What is this . . . the bloody Berlitz Academy? Comprendez!
> Capeeshez . . . cahoochey . . . Capucci . . .
> *Phil and Spanky (together as they chop and grind at their [paint] slabs):* Comprendez? Capeeshez? Cahoochy? Capucci? Comprendez? Capeeshez? Cahoochy? Capucci? (p.29)

These examples are both fantastic and deflating. But there is also lyricism. In *Cuttin' a Rug*, Hector expresses his passion for Lucille: 'God, whenever I think of her reaching up to get that jar of chrome yellow and the sun just caught the bloom on her arm . . . like the golden fuzz on a peach skin' (p.7). This might have been smutty, but quite clearly is not. Indeed, we find something of the same kind of style from the feminist Lochhead. For example, here is Mary making ready for love with Darnley:

> And I shall loose my lang rid hair,
> Ungimp ma girdles o' the plaited silk
> Slip frae ma sark and in the dark
> Ma bodie will gleam as white as milk
>
> And I shall be dressed in nakedness,
> My briests twa aiples o' desire
> And you shall hae the brichtest jewel
> That nestles in my brooch o' red-gowd wire. (pp.37–8)

Alongside the development of this fantasy language, there has been a growing use of Scots for serious, intellectual topics. One of the first examples in this period was as far back as 1971, in Stewart Conn's *The Burning*. The achievement there was to modernise Scots for affairs of state, moving away from the old styles that – as Morgan commented – dominated earlier writing. But Conn stopped short of using full Scots for Royal Proclamations and such like.

A more confident intellectual Scots is found in Campbell's *Archbishop Spottiswoode*, but he modulates the degree of Scottishness to suit the occasion. Thus when he is talking to Ogilvie, he uses a less broad Scots than he does with the soldiers. More confident still is Lochhead's writing for Mary and Knox, and indeed in that play there is no feeling at all that the language cannot bear the theological and political weight that is asked of it. For example, Mary has been castigating Knox for sedition:

> *Knox:*　My heart is God's. But I shall be as weill content to live under ye as Paul was tae live under Nero.
> *Mary:*　Sae ye will gie to Caesarina whit is Caesarina's?
> *Knox:*　I see madam kens her scriptures.
> *Mary:*　I ken ma scriptures. I hae baith heard and read. (*pause*) Maister Knox, because I am by nature douce, and queyet, dinna think I hae nae convictions or beliefs locked in ma silent heart – though I dae not *trumpet* them abroad. (p.21)

The supreme recent example of the high use of Scots is Edwin Morgan's. It would be difficult to think of a vehicle better able to display the scope of Scots than *Cyrano de Bergerac*, and Morgan showed that Scots could amply fulfil the potential which he identified in the quotation with which I started. The translation contains a great variety of rhetorical registers – action, politics, religion, but above all love and death. Cyrano himself addresses the question of rhetoric explicitly, advising Valvert – who has been taunting him about his big nose – on twenty styles he could have used for these insults (pp.24–5). The classification itself is Scots ('saft-hertit', for example, or 'bummin'). But then Cyrano finishes Valvert off with the flourish:

> But even if ye'd hud the nous tae throw
> Sic pure deid brilliant whigmaleeries oot
> Intae this deid brilliant audience, Ah doot
> Ye'd no could stammer the first syllable
> Before Ah'd shawn it tae be killable:
> Thae juicy jests are mine, Ah love them, but
> When ithers try tae mooth them, Ah cry, 'Cut!'

There is sensuousness to match Lochhead's quoted above, either in elaborate similes for love –

Jist as someone gies a lang stare at the sun
And sees a rid-spot wurld fae roof tae grun,
Ivry time your flames go onto hold,
Ma dazzled eyes see flecks and coils a gold! (p.92)

– or in the evocation of baking:

Take some eggs and whisk them well,
Tae froth and mell;
Wance it's foamy, tip in neat
A spurt a yer best citron juice;
Then a sluice
A milky aumond pashed and sweet. (p.46)

At the end, Cyrano dies with a rhetoric that places literary creation (but also his preposterous nose) at the centre of his being:

Cyrano: . . . But there's somethin at the close
Ah kin still take tonight, and at heaven's gate
Ah'll swish the big blue threshold wae, a great
Memento, unbumfled, fresh as a bloom,
Ah'll take despite ye . . .
and that's . . .
Roxane: Yes?
Cyrano: Ma plume. (p.163)

Morgan demonstrates in this translation that fantasy, intellectual seriousness and the demotic can all be as well expressed through Scots as through any other language (implicitly, here, French and English at least). He could not have done this without the developing Scots idiom of the last two or three decades, and neither could Lochhead have delivered the equally fine dexterity of *Mary Queen of Scots*. But the achievement of these two writers has raised writing in Scots for the stage to a new level. Scottish identity and culture are no longer assumed to be mainly working-class, mainly male, or mainly about left-wing social realism. These experiences are important, but the culture embraces others too. Lochhead and Morgan have shown that the language can rise to expressing that diversity.

NOTES

1. Edwin Morgan, trans., *Edmond Rostand's Cyrano de Bergerac* (Manchester: Carcanet, 1992), p.xi.
2. Hector MacMillan, *The Sash* (Glasgow: The Molendinar Press, 1974), p.5.
3. Tom McGrath and Jimmy Boyle, *The Hard Man* (Edinburgh: Canongate, 1977), p.18.
4. Donald Campbell, *The Widows of Clyth* (Edinburgh: Paul Harris, 1979), p.52.

5. Donald Campbell, *The Jesuit* (Edinburgh: Paul Harris, 1976), p.85.
6. Liz Lochhead, *Mary Queen of Scots Got Her Head Chopped Off* (Harmondsworth: Penguin, 1989), p.11.
7. For some of this debate, see D. McCrone. *Understanding Scotland: The Sociology of a Stateless Nation* (London: Routledge, 1992), chapter 7; A. Howson, 'No gods and precious few women: gender and cultural identity in Scotland'. *Scottish Affairs*, 2 (Winter 1993), pp.37–49; J. Idle, 'McIlvanney, masculinity and Scottish literature', *Scottish Affairs*, 2 (Winter 1993), pp.50–57; T. C. Smout, 'Perspectives on the Scottish Identity', *Scottish Affairs*, 6 (Winter 1994), pp.101–13; C. Whyte, ed., *Gendering the Nation: Studies in Modern Scottish Literature* (Edinburgh: Edinburgh University Press, 1995); and A. Brown, D. McCrone and L. Paterson *Politics and Society in Scotland* (London: Macmillan, 1996), chapter 9.
8. See Colin Manlove, *Scottish Fantasy: A Critical Survey* (Edinburgh: Canongate, 1994).
9. John Byrne, *The Slab Boys* (Edinburgh: The Salamander Press, 1982), p.14.

Seven

Plugged into History:
the Sense of the Past in Scottish Theatre

Ian Brown

Themes and topics drawn from history recur in theatre. Euripides, Shakespeare and Brecht are only three of the playwrights who have used historic material to deal with contemporary issues or to rewrite history to endorse current perceptions of society or human relations. Shaw's presentation of St Joan as a 'Protestant' and 'Nationalist' lets him adapt her story to his view of the processes of political change. He is particularly adept at this technique, Michael Holroyd noting of *Caesar and Cleopatra* that Shaw

> makes the ancient Briton, Britannus, so exactly like a modern Englishman. Shaw never wrote costume drama for its own sake: his plays were always addressed to the present. The figure of Britannus keeps the audience imaginatively half in the present – which was one of the ways Shaw became a model for Brecht.[1]

In theatre, as Peter Ustinov's President of 'the Smallest Country in Europe' in *Romanoff and Juliet* says, 'the great virtue of history is that it is adaptable'.[2]

Playwrights in the three immediate post-war decades generally showed a strong interest in this 'adaptability'. Arthur Miller's *The Crucible* is a prime American example, balanced by the work in England of Robert Bolt, Peter Shaffer and John Arden. Much of this work, especially on the English stage, tended to follow a pattern, that of epic theatre, perhaps somewhat naturalised to the commercial or national company stage, but concerned to tell a story, often of the heroic individual standing out against a flawed society. Other playwrights have explored a wider and more subversive variety of techniques in presenting history on stage:

Peter Weiss's *Marat/Sade* had a particular impact, especially through Peter Brook's seminal RSC production, widely seen in the 1964 film version, while the deconstructionist and broadly comic work of Paul Foster on historical topics, such as his *Tom Paine*, for New York's various La Mama companies was seen at several Edinburgh Festivals in the late 1960s. The adaptation by Barbara Garson of *Macbeth* to *Macbird* (1966), satirising Lyndon Johnson's conduct of the Vietnam War, had great impact in its time and illustrated the refocusing of recent events through serious parody and sub-Shakespearean pastiche for ideological purpose.

One of the great achievements of the Scottish stage in the last twenty-five years, following those post-war experiments, has been the variety and complexity of the ways in which it has dealt with history and the particular significance of this use of the past for the present stage of Scottish culture and history. An English playwright whose varied techniques at times parallel those of recent Scottish writers, David Hare, usefully remarks:

> For five years I have been writing history plays. I try to show the English their history. I write tribal pieces . . . Reading Angus Calder's *The People's War* changed all my thinking as a writer; an account of the Second World War through the eyes of ordinary people, it attempts a complete alternative history to the phoney and corrupting history I was taught at school.[3]

There can be no doubt that the historiography of the 1960s and 1970s – the work, for example, of Angus Calder, or, pre-eminently, Christopher Hill and E. P. Thompson – built on the achievements of an earlier generation to explore what is sometimes called 'hidden history'. Meantime, the impact of the work of A. J. P. Taylor in the 1950s and 1960s had alerted a wider public to the significance of historical understanding.

This process of revealing 'hidden history' has, in Scotland, been given added significance by the post-war revisiting of Scottish history under such figures as Professors Gordon Donaldson and Geoffrey Barrow. It is significant, for example, that one of the seminal texts of modern Scottish history, Christopher Smout's *A History of the Scottish People*, was published in 1969, at the start of the period under review. The excavation, rediscovery and re-examination of Scottish history coincided with the surge in Scottish self-awareness and developing self-confidence, typified culturally by a range of phenomena in the decade between 1963 and 1973, including the opening of the Traverse Theatre, the foundation of Scottish Opera and Scottish Ballet, the introduction of the influential Perry and Havergal reigns at the Royal Lyceum, Edinburgh, and Glasgow Citizens', and the establishment of the Scottish Society of Playwrights. The rewriting of the history of Scotland according to modern historiographical principles formed part of a wider cultural process which provided, both directly and indirectly, material for Scottish playwrights that was not simply historical, but also, in Hare's term, 'tribal'.

This is not to say that all playwrights working in this area were at first primarily drawn to the idea of writing historical drama. Stewart Conn says of his *The Burning* (1971): '*The Burning* did not spring from any predisposition on my part towards Scots historical drama; but from what struck me as the theatrical potential of the theme, and its relevance today.'[4] Indeed in a programme note on the 1975 revival of his *The Rising*, Hector MacMillan remarks that:

> The year 1970 was the 150th anniversary of the Scottish insurrection of 1820. Some time prior to this an attempt was made to raise interest in a proposed stage play about the event. There was no interest. Scottish theatres were quite definitely not in the market for plays about Scottish history.[5]

Some of Conn's distancing of himself from the idea of writing historical drama and the reluctance of the theatres MacMillan identifies may arise from the fact that until their own impact was felt, alongside that of others to be discussed, much historical drama in Scotland had been inclined to the sentimental and fey. The reasons for this were not ignoble. Katja Lenz has noted of the work of Robert McLellan:

> Above all McLellan attempted to set up a standard Scots as a separate language from English. He therefore needed a form of Scots which a) is very different from English, and b) does not strike the audience as 'vulgar' or obscure.
>
> McLellan's choice of 'ideal' Scots, in conjunction with naturalist conventions, rules out a contemporary urban setting. The plays are therefore usually set *either* in remote times and places, where and when such usage may at least *seem* authentic – with all the problems this creates because of its contemporary base. *Or* they are located in a fairy-tale world, where socio-historical linguistic facts do not apply and audiences have to take it for granted that this type of Scots is spoken. Robert Kemp and Alexander Reid employ a similar kind of Scots when writing a similar type of play.[6]

The general point is well made, though one recognises exceptions where earlier historical drama had a serious contemporary relevance, as in McLellan's *The Flouers o' Edinburgh* (1948), or an ideologically inflammatory purpose, as in Sydney Goodsir Smith's *The Wallace* (1960). McLellan himself remarked, of course, that he was trying to write the kind of historical drama that should have existed in earlier centuries but did not: he was seeking to develop a sense of tradition where none existed.

Another stigmatisation of fictive treatment of historical material arose from the situation of the historical novel. While this has a vibrant history in Scottish literature since the time of Scott, there has been a tendency for the genre to be seen as children's literature, as the novelist Margaret Elphinstone observes. She suggests that since the time of Scott, Galt and Hogg

> when the historical novel was new, popular and serious, there seems . . . to have been a curious emphasis on gender and maturity (or lack of it) in the *readership* of historical novels, which has become a way of marginalising the texts . . . Boys' books and women's books – doesn't sound very important, does it?[7]

It may indeed be that one cause of the marginalisation to which she refers is the sentimentalising and kilted costume-dressing of many Scottish historical novels, something also pioneered by Scott. The general point surely holds, notwithstanding the serious work of such writers as Naomi Mitchison, Nigel Tranter and Allan Massie.

The playwrights discussed in this chapter broke quite consciously after 1970 with the sentimental tradition, aiming to treat historical themes as serious creative and dramatic discourse, addressing both interpretation of historical event and the meaning of contemporary Scottishness. Their material almost entirely relates to previous generations, from before the end of the Second World War, and this working definition of 'historical' I adopt here. Drawing on their wide experience of world theatre, they revisited lively Scottish topics in a fresh way.

Hector MacMillan's outstanding historical plays are *The Rising* (1973) and *The Royal Visit* (1974). Both began as radio scripts despite MacMillan's initial desire to write them for the stage. As we have seen, MacMillan felt his work was stifled at first by the prevailing attitudes of managements of Scottish theatres. He nevertheless persevered and through the interest of Stephen MacDonald, newly arrived in 1973 as Artistic Director at Dundee, he was at last able to develop his plays for the theatre. MacMillan explores aspects of history not widely known and apparently suppressed and misrepresented. His work frees and clarifies the historical record in theatrical form, revealing to audiences aspects of their history they may never have heard of, or known only in a 'phoney' form, to use Hare's term. MacMillan uses song, especially period song, to advance and comment on the action and so reinforces the ways in which he addresses folk history and reveals it afresh. In dealing with the Scottish Insurrection of 1820, *The Rising* presents the betrayal of Scottish radicals by government provocation and spies. *The Royal Visit*, a more humorous play, deals with Sir Walter Scott's political stage management of the royal visit of George IV to Edinburgh in 1822. As part of the process of maintaining his power base, for example, Scott is seen helping invent the tartan industry. MacMillan revisits history in order to reveal what is hidden within it, and, through questioning the ways in which it has been hidden, to examine the nature of contemporary power, political propaganda and manipulation of opinion.

Although the radio version of *The Rising* had been broadcast in 1970 and *The Royal Visit* soon after, MacMillan's work was not seen in theatrical form until two other highly influential plays had been presented at the Royal Lyceum, Conn's *The Burning* and Bill Bryden's *Willie Rough* (1972). The former had a particular impact. In dealing with witchcraft trials and political machinations in the court of James VI, it can be seen to draw on Miller's *The Crucible* and Robert McLellan's *Jamie the Saxt*, but it also had specific fresh qualities of its own: it explored the theme of manipulation of political power more directly than either, while its use of Scottish historical material, freshly reviewed, showed a spiritual link to *The Rising*. It was presented at the Royal Lyceum after the arrival of Bill Bryden in 1970, an appointment by Clive Perry marking a new determination to present fresh work by Scottish writers.

Through the twenty-five years under review, Bryden himself has conducted a long wrestling match with the complexities of recent Scottish history, particularly that of his native Greenock and its nearby big cousin, Glasgow. *Willie Rough* occupies another dimension of historical drama as represented on the Scottish stage. While plays already referred to have used public historical material – action involving public figures and drawing substantially on the public record, however personalised through the addition of occasional fictional characters – Bryden sees large historical events through the eyes of individuals, some based on older members of his own family, though transformed by his imagination. His capacity to create a lively sense of community and the felt reality of characters is something he brought to the developing Scottish historical drama of the 1970s. His *Benny Lynch* (1975) not only details the rise and fall of the world champion boxer, but does so by placing him in an imaginatively realised social context which makes sense of his downfall in historical, social and emotional terms. In these plays, Bryden sought to enter imaginatively the everyday reality of a given historic period, something which MacMillan and Conn had done in less detail, given their emphasis on the larger historical perspective. His later play, *Civilians* (1981), however, loses this sense of a fully realised context, settling for spectacular effect, the opening Clydebank blitz scene foreshadowing his later techniques, and presenting rather sketchy, even sentimental, characterisation, reducing plotting at times to staged anecdote.

The present author's plays of the period moved in a different direction. *Carnegie* (1973) sought to address the myth of the benevolent millionaire philanthropist, the lad o' pairts. This view of the story of Carnegie arose from research into the murderous Homestead strike-breaking, where Carnegie carefully removed himself from the scene, having previously set all in place. It explored the gaps between the ways Carnegie spent his riches and the manipulative, oppressive and lethal ways by which he acquired them. The play concerns Carnegie's story, but also the ways in which the writing of history and the shaping of public perceptions could modify, as to a large extent they still do, the Scottish perception of Carnegie, recognised in America as one of the nineteenth-century 'Robber Barons'. The play used song and choric figures to distance and explore the history and myth of Carnegie. *Mary* (1977) addressed, arguably more successfully, another Scots historico-mythical figure, Mary, Queen of Scots. Randall Stevenson has observed:

> In *Mary*, the even more multifaceted figure of the queen is appro-priately dramatised through a multiplicity of styles, tones, and historical points of view. Their variety communicates unusually successfully the extent of the problem Mary's much-dramatised life has posed for Scottish history and the Scottish imagination.[8]

Mary Queen and the Loch Tower (1979), a children's play, aimed at exploring the same issues and techniques, but in a mode accessible to a younger audience, while *Beatrice* (1989), marks a naturalistic flirtation in dealing with the French topic of Catharism at Montaillou.

A more influential figure in exploring history and political myth has been John McGrath. His most prominent work, *The Cheviot, the Stag and the Black, Black Oil* (1973), draws on historical material over three centuries, using song, dramatic scenes and agit-prop and front-of-cloth techniques to explore the exploitation of the Highlands from the Clearances onwards. He powerfully develops his themes, theatricalising the Highland ceilidh format, while drawing on the work of Brecht as developed by such followers as Joan Littlewood at Theatre Workshop. The play combines poignant details with satiric creations

such as the Glaswegian entrepreneur, a 'Property-operator's man', Andy
McChuckemup, with his vision of Highlands development:

> So – picture it, if yous will, right there at the top of the glen,
> beautiful vista – the Crammem Inn, High Rise Motorcroft –
> all finished in natural, washable, plastic granitette. Right next
> door, the 'Frying Scotsman' All Night Chipperama – with a wee
> ethnic bit, Fingal's Caff – serving seaweed-suppers-in-the-basket,
> and draught Drambuie. And to cater for the younger set, yous've
> got your Grouse-a-go-go.[9]

McGrath's work is closely related to the work of the company he helped
found, 7:84 (Scotland), and he produced three more plays for it in rapid
succession, developing and modifying his use of historical material:
The Game's a Bogey (1975), *Little Red Hen* (1975), and *Joe's Drum*
(1979). In all these, McGrath presents historical material in dynamic
dialectic with contemporary events, so that history is used to explicate
the contemporary, often presenting current attitudes as a falling away
from ideological clarity and vigour. *The Game's a Bogey* sets the life
of the Red Clydesider, John Maclean, against modern temporising and
compromise. This theme is taken further in *Little Red Hen* where the
older Hen, Henrietta, takes to task her granddaughter, Henrietta, for
falling away from the integrity of the Red Clyreside campaigners into
what is seen as the evasiveness of contemporary politics. *Joe's Drum*,
a review of key events and popular protest in Scottish political action
since the Union of 1707 was written in direct response to the failure
of the devolution vote in 1979, more directly than ever using historical
material to argue for direct popular action as a model of democratic
rectitude. His last history play of the period is *Border Warfare* (1989),
presented by Wildcat. This ambitious play seeks to cover Scottish
life and politics from pre-history onwards. Its theme is the national
identity of the Scots, first defined when the territorial ambitions of
their southern neighbour provide an incentive for the unity of the
several nations which formed Scotland, and it shows two millennia
of Scottish experience in the light of necessary reaction to English
expansionism. It is a spectacular and theatrically highly self-conscious
piece, drawing on promenade conventions, intimate detail and broad
caricature to achieve its range of effects, and making use of song and direct
quotation from sources such as the Declaration of Arbroath, Barbour
and Burns, and from McGrath himself. The self-referent theatricality
of his examination of 'Scottishness' is reinforced by the incorporation
of text from both *Little Red Hen* and *Joe's Drum*; the speech of Robert
Dundas, for example, on the eighteenth-century riots in Edinburgh's

George Square is substantially taken from the latter. The purposeful, sly and often witty theatrical cross-reference is highlighted too by the representation of a law tyrannically imposed by Charles I:

> Number 168, Law Anent the suppression of the Profession of Bard in our wilder territories, such Bards having the temerity to put the population in mind of unfortunate events which occurred in years gone by, thus inciting them to angry reflection and to precipitate action in their own time, such Bards shall be either forced to take up some less harmful profession or be banished from this land.[10]

McGrath's historical material, while absolutely central to the dramatic action, is not used chiefly to understand the complexities of the history, so much as to apply a vision of history, which may itself be somewhat mythologised, to support McGrath's contemporary vision, rather like that of the banned Bards of Charles I. He deconstructs history and theatre through dramatic exploration. In this, the central interest is his perception that economic and social desiderata have been eroded by historical and political pressures he wishes to expose as contingent, not inevitable. He challenges the 'facts' of history, wishing to reconstruct historical myths as motive for future action.

Stewart Conn also explored further in the 1970s the ways in which theatricality and theatrical deconstruction could be employed to express and illustrate the ways in which historical events are presented and understood. *Thistlewood* (1975) is concerned with the fate of Arthur Thistlewood and other participants in the 1820 Cato Street Conspiracy, the ways in which they were manipulated and betrayed by government spies. Where others using material from this period, MacMillan, and later Donald Campbell and James Kelman, have tended to work naturalistically, Conn manipulates original song, the choric figure of John Bull and a number of post-Brechtian techniques to mark the manipulation of the characters by the authorities, and the ways in which the manufacture of historical events is itself a process of manipulation of knowledge. Significantly, in relation to this, the repressive Home Secretary whose officials entrap Thistlewood, Lord Sidmouth, is shown reading Mary Shelley's *Frankenstein* throughout the action of the play.

Donald Campbell is another key figure in the development of Scottish historical drama. His approach may be seen to parallel that of MacMillan and early Conn, concerned to explore specific broader issues through focusing on personal quandaries, emphasising parallels with contemporary behaviour patterns. In this, he goes further than either. *The Jesuit* (1976) explores large issues of religious faith and repression within the framework of the Jacobean religious settlement. He presents his characters in sympathetic detail, in the end leaving the audience with a sense of the complexity of the moral issues faced. While he is clearly alert to the larger ideological issues surrounding his characters, his focus is very much on the individual. This allows a deeper characterisation than is found in most texts so far discussed and lays the groundwork for the craft of Campbell's later historical plays. *Somerville the Soldier* (1978) centres on a radical Royal Scots Grey who, after protesting in the Press at the use of soldiers to suppress civil rights activity, is legally victimised by his officers. His is a *cause célèbre* and a group of London radicals, protesting against the sentence of the Tolpuddle Martyrs, seek to use him for their own varied purposes. The play is, in a sense, a detective story in which we gradually discover the double dealing, hidden agendas, naïveties and corruptions of the group's members. The final vision is of the liberal humanity of Somerville, seeking progress, set against the extreme ideological puritanism of Gillies, a radical who believes the cause more important than any individual. *The Widows of Clyth* (1979) clearly shows the growth of Campbell's interest in imaginatively understanding, and representing, human interaction in given historical contexts and draws on his own family background. It explores the cost to a family, and its community, of a fishing disaster in which most of its men are lost at sea, the grief of the womenfolk, the guilt of the brother, George, who did not fish that day, and the ways in which both the women and the survivors cope with their suffering. The play reasserts love and forgiveness in its final scene when, ten years later, another survivor, Hector, apparently drowned, is revived by the bereaved women, who warm his chilled body with their own so that he may survive and marry. Campbell's interest in specifics of human emotion explored within imagined experience of historical events continues in his work in the 1980s: *Blackfriars Wynd* (1980), the musical play, *Till all the Seas Run Dry,* telling the story of Burns from Jean Armour's perspective, and *Howard's Revenge* (1985), a one-person play exploring the pre-performance emotional state of the early Royal Lyceum actor-manager, J. B. Howard. Campbell continues his exploration of Caithness life, begun with *The Widows of Clyth,* with *The Auld Fella* (1993).

The range of experimentation and achievement in the rest of our period can be seen to flow from the foundations established in the 1970s. Indeed the outline provided sells short the great variety of work found in that decade. C. P. Taylor's *Columba* (1973) presented a revisionist view of the saint incorporating a startling use of dance, while his remarkable study of the gradual corruption of a good man in Nazi Germany, *Good* (1981), was an international success for the RSC. Tom Kinninmont wrote with fresh theatricality, debunking the myth of the founders of the great encyclopedia, in *Britannica* (1978), while W. Gordon Smith had reviewed the John Knox/Mary, Queen of Scots conflict in *Knox* (1975). Perhaps more importantly, Smith wrote the seminal one-person play *Jock* (1972), played memorably for many years by Russell Hunter. Smith's work, as with his later *Mister Carnegie's Lantern Lecture* (1985), extended and significantly developed the range of the one-person form, while questioning assumptions underlying the myths of recent Scottish history. Such developments were foreshadowed in Jack Ronder's *Cocky* (1969), about Lord Cockburn, and Smith's own *Vincent* (1970), about Van Gogh. With its capacity to explore the individual psyche, facing the ethos and values of a specific society, the one-person form has provided inspiration both for David MacKail, writing as Frederic Mohr, with his *Bozzy* (1981) and *Hogg* (1985), both on literary figures, and his plays on John Paul Jones and Florence Nightingale; and for John Cargill Thompson, whose many plays since the mid-1980s include, for example, his 1994 play on the life of James I, *An English Education.*

A number of key figures developed the experiments and themes of playwrights emerging in the 1970s. Sue Glover's *An Island in Largo* (1980) deals with the history of Alexander Selkirk, his youth in Largo, his lonely life as a marooned sailor, the consequences of his return to Fife and the subsequent use of his history by Daniel Defoe. Through the latter figure, she hints at the role of the playwright in using, adapting and reinterpreting history though her own imagination:

> *Defoe*: And you have already talked to many, many people! (*Surveys Alex*) I have a feeling that now – what is it – two years later – you might not talk so freely.
> *Silence*
> *Alex*: (*with difficulty*) I found that, though they listened, they were not listening to me – but to something in themselves. Speaking to them damaged what I'd found.
> *Defoe*: Oh, I only want facts, Mr Selkirk. I want to pin my adventures against facts. . . .
> *Defoe*: . . . I have interviewed people all my writing life – in the taverns, the streets – in Newgate, often the very night before the wretches were to hang. I have stolen the facts from their lives. But this time – for the very *first* time – I will write my own invention.[11]

In this play, Glover's invention shifts theatrically both in place and time, intercutting scenes ironically to convey the differences between the stay-at-home family and the rebellious Selkirk, whose very name is his own variation of the family's preferred historical spelling, 'Selcraig'.

Her work successfully focuses on both Selkirk's sense of alienation
from his family and community and his physical isolation on Juan
Fernandez Island. The text achieves a sense of the very texture of life
which Glover develops further in her two subsequent historical plays,
The Straw Chair (1988) and *Bondagers* (1991). The former deals with
questions of male power and political corruption in eighteenth-century
Scotland as an Edinburgh minister and his new wife arrive on St Kilda
to find Lady Rachel in effect exiled there by order of her husband,
the Lord Advocate, to prevent her revealing his political duplicity and
treason. Glover provides a sense of the texture of beliefs at the time and
of the mutual incomprehension and confrontation of cultures, whether
between the middle-class minister and his wife and the noble lady, or
between the world-view of the Edinburgh folk and the Gaelic universe
of Oona, whose astonishment at the existence of trees seen on her one
visit to Skye, her happy union of animism and Christianity, and her very
language, mark her as of another world. Glover's capacity to combine the
realisation of difference, female versus male and class versus class, comes
to high fruition in *Bondagers* which follows the cycle of the agricultural
year from one February Hiring Fair to the next. We observe a group of
women working in a Borders farm as they labour, love and face personal
crises. The play is a highly successful embodiment of the travails and
ironies of labour and class for women in rural nineteenth-century
Scotland, and by extension everywhere now. It addresses directly the
ways in which male systems of power, whether economic, political
or sexual, oppress women and deprive them of a freedom of action
and untrammelled integrity. Glover's invention combines historical
re-creation and contemporary comment with remarkable directness
and skilful understatement.

Peter Arnott has also continued the quizzical examination of the
hidden history of Scotland. *The Boxer Benny Lynch* (1984) concentrates
more than Bryden's Lynch play on the specific personal relations of
Lynch's life, exposing his inadequacy against the economic forces which
used and abused him. Arnott's view of Lynch shows individual aspiration
manipulated and corrupted by those with economic power. This theme is
complemented by his *Thomas Muir's Voyage to Australia* (1986) and the
related community play *Thomas Muir's Transportation Show* (1986). The
former, in particular, deals with political oppression and the attempted
destruction of the integrity and hope represented by the reforming zeal of
Thomas Muir and his colleagues. As with many of the texts of the 1970s
and Glover's *The Straw Chair*, Arnott finds in hidden history material
which allows him to address, through the quandary of an individual,
larger questions of power and autonomy, of democracy and authority,

and of personal and political identity within both Scotland and the framework of the United Kingdom. His play shifts, rather as in *An Island in Largo*, between past and present, moving back and forth across the world and presenting, with remarkable succinctness considering the range of material covered, the wide scope not only of the reforming activities of Muir, but the state of Scottish justice in the 1790s, the French Revolution and life in the prison colonies of Australia.

Liz Lochhead, in *Mary Queen of Scots Got Her Head Chopped Off* (1987), created a poetic vitality and force which grasped the myths of Mary and Elizabeth and developed them in a wildly theatrical exploration of the nature of Scottishness, its oppositions, contradictions and (dis)satisfactions. The theatrical flexibility referred to already in the case of *An Island in Largo* and *Thomas Muir's Voyage to Australia* is here allied to the fluency and flexibility of earlier plays such as *The Cheviot, the Stag and the Black, Black Oil* to create a gallimaufry which in its very variety embodies the complexity of the historical representations of Mary and Elizabeth. The play explores the dialectics of creativity and oppression, puritanism and pleasure and does so using forward-looking techniques. It represents one of the greatest achievements so far of the deconstructionist approach and has been particularly important in having received probably the widest range of productions of any of the plays discussed in this chapter.

Other playwrights have continued to address the theatrical re-creation of the texture of individual crises presented and re-focused in the lens of historical events. In *Hardie and Baird: The Last Days* (1990); James Kelman returns with an increased psychological focus to a theme dealt with by MacMillan from a more socio-political perspective: the 1820 Scottish Insurrection. Following Campbell's experiments in treating history, Kelman finds a personal style focused on the predicament and conscience of the idiosyncratic individual. George Rosie's work, too, has had a particular impact in the 1990s. *The Blasphemer* (1990) and *Carlucco and the Queen of Hearts* (1991) develop the theatrical investigation of the conflicts between authoritarianism and freedom and between romantic myth and political reality in his lucid and emotionally powerful examinations of characters reacting to personal religious and political pressures. Both reflect some of the strengths of the traditions developed by Conn in *The Burning* and Campbell in *The Jesuit*, while exploiting Rosie's own sardonic force and theatrical directness.

In the meantime a new spectacular strand of theatrical work has been developed by Bill Bryden, providing such *coups de théâtre* as the launching in *The Ship* (1990) or the hydraulic movement of the audience sideways as it follows soldiers going over the top into tracer fire, simulated by lasers, in *The Big Picnic* (1994).[12] The former, examining the building of the QE2, was generally well-received, although some felt it had sacrificed character development for sensation, perhaps an inevitable problem in the epic scale Bryden chose, but one reflecting a criticism of his earlier *Civilians*. The latter, however, interestingly divided critics. It dealt with mythically and ideologically fraught topics, of which the First World War, Scots maleness, Caledonian militarism and Glaswegian comradeship were only four. Bryden's concern with the individual emotional journey is seen in both plays as is his concern to address major events in the folk history of Scotland. His spectacular effects seemed to some to camouflage a sentimental and macho treatment of his topics, when their complexity needed the greater attention to details of character and motivation seen in his earliest work. Nevertheless, *The Big Picnic* was perhaps the greatest popular success of all.

The process of exploration continues. The variety of Stewart Conn's experimentation and creativity in dealing with history on stage continues with his more naturalistic *The Dominion of Fancy* (1992), representing the 1825 Glasgow theatrical wars between Alexander and Seymour, rival actor-managers, and containing scenes using the stage techniques of the time. The play centres on their aesthetic, as much as their economic, conflict. Above all, it focuses on the objection of the anglicised Irish Seymour to Alexander's 'tartanry'. Towards the end of the play, when Alexander has triumphed over Seymour, his stage manager, McGlynn, raises the anxiety that historical drama may result in escapist romance:

> You cry yersel the People's Choice: how then are you no doing plays aboot them, and their condeetion, which in this city is waur nur savage – instead of charades frae the past? You'd rather reinvent an antique nation, than fecht fur a new wan. (*pause*) Nae doot, you're waiting to craw?

Alexander responds, 'That's the last thing I have in mind.' In the play's final scene, he states his own position on theatrical experiment and 'naturalness in any Art' and addresses the nature of the Scottish consciousness:

> But not at the expense of that element of the fantastical that is part of our being. And helps distinguish us from those in the south. The dilemma is how to stay true to our heritage, yet break from too narrow a covenant with the past. Our being an island makes it the more essential we do not end up in a prison of our devising, but constitute an imaginative *escape*.[13]

The dilemma continues to exercise contemporary Scottish playwrights. The potential of history is explored and developed by more writers even than can be dealt with adequately in the scope of this chapter. Such writers as John Clifford, George Gunn, George Byatt and Raymond Ross have all found inspiration in working with historical material in their different ways. The process of exploration continues to find renewed vigour in fresh experiment. Ike Isakson's *An Gaisgeach – The Hero* (1995) for example, deals in new ways with the historical figure of Macbeth. Written in Gaelic and Scots, using music and powerful visual imagery, it seeks a new synthesis of languages and theatricality as it explores the historic pressures on the Celtic culture and society embodied by the impact of Malcolm Canmore on Macbeth's peaceful polity.

The imaginative approach to history revealed by contemporary Scottish playwrights is remarkably varied, ranging from concern with naturalistic, almost documentary, work to re-examination of the very concept and nature of both Scotland and history. Their treatment of their complex topics and the variety of their approaches inspires the thought that their work can be seen to work across a range of possible types or categories of historical drama: the deconstructive, about how historical myths are made, why, and how they deceive; the implicative, showing risings, for example, in the hope of another; the pictorial, recreating historical events, as Bryden's recent work does, often spectacularly; the consolidatory, revisiting the past to coalesce a sense of nationhood or common humanity; the consolatory, revisiting the past to comfort the audience that a state of nationhood might exist or, conversely and paradoxically, no longer matters; the progressive, focusing the past as an incentive for present political action; the psychological and the socio-political, both viewing historical material as a source of exemplars to explore past and present human psychological, social and economic-political attitudes.[14] Few individual plays I have considered would belong exclusively to any one category, though most overlap some. One striking point, however, is that very few indeed fit into the consolatory category, perhaps the most nostalgic and potentially regressive and conservative of all, while almost all tend towards lively and forward-looking perspectives.

At a recent Conference on the adaptation of *Lanark*, Tony Graham, Director of TAG Theatre Company, remarked that he was 'conscious that a lot of Scottish stage has been backward-looking or historical, trying to deal with the struggle of Scotland to create a nation. I wanted to look at the world now.'[15] What I hope to have shown is that, however much the treatment of history may have been generally backward-looking, even consolatory, before 1970, its developing use over the last twenty-five years has been concerned not only with the 'now' of Scotland, its society, identity and future, but also with the potential of theatre as an expressive and exploratory art. Scots dramatists have developed and augmented the work of their novelist colleagues in exploring and marking out a Matter of Scotland, which is concerned with its contemporary and future shape. History for them is immanent in the present and influential on the future and must be rediscovered, revisited, revealed, questioned and, however faultily, understood, in order that it be created again alive in the minds, imagination and consciousness of audience members.

In this they are close to the philosopher of history, R. G. Collingwood, when he says: 'The past which a historian studies is not a dead past, but a past which in some sense is still living in the present . . . all history is the history of thought . . . history is the re-enactment in the historian's mind of the thought whose history he is studying.'[16] Christopher Hill has made a similar point recently:

> History means two things: first the past as we believe it to have existed, and second, the past as we attempt to reconstruct it in our writings. Cynics say that when historians claim to be describing the past they are really writing contemporary history – or autobiography. This is true to the extent that the new questions which each generation of historians asks inevitably reflect the interests of that generation.[17]

One does not need to be a cynic to see the parallel between such historians and contemporary Scottish playwrights. The concern with history shown by contemporary Scottish playwrights is absolutely rooted in their concern with the present and developing state of their nation. As they examine, explore and create the new Matter of Scotland their true interest lies in the matter with Scotland now.

NOTES

1. Michael Holroyd, *Bernard Shaw, vol.2 (1898–1918) The Pursuit of Power*, (London: Chatto and Windus, 1989), p.19.
2. Peter Ustinov, *Romanoff and Juliet*, in *Five Plays*, (London: Heinemann, 1965), p.55.
3. David Hare, 'A Lecture given at King's College, Cambridge, 5 March 1978', in *Licking Hitler* (London: Faber, 1978), p.66.
4. Stewart Conn, Author's Note, *The Burning*, (London: John Calder, 1973), p.8.
5. Hector MacMillan, Programme Note, *The Rising*, Glasgow 800 Theatre Company Production, Citizens' Theatre, 1975. (The programme note as printed is anonymous; but I have confirmed with Hector MacMillan that he is its author.)
6. Katja Lenz, 'Modern Scottish Drama: Snakes in Iceland – Drama in Scotland', paper presented at ESSE Conference, Glasgow, 11 September 1995, p.6. (I am indebted to Ms Lenz for her helpful comments on the draft of this chapter.)
7. Margaret Elphinstone, 'Women's Writing and Historical Novel', Paper presented at ESSE Conference, Glasgow, 9 September 1995.

8. Randall Stevenson, 'Scottish Theatre 1950–80' in Cairns Craig, ed., *The History of Scottish Literature, Volume 4, Twentieth Century* (Aberdeen: Aberdeen University Press, 1987), p.359.
9. John McGrath, *The Cheviot, the Stag and the Black, Black Oil* (London: Methuen, 1981), pp.48–9.
10. John McGrath, *Border Warfare*, unpublished typescript (1989), p.60.
11. Sue Glover, *An Island in Largo*, unpublished typescript, pp.83, 84.
12. *The Ship* is the one play set later than the period considered here to define 'historical material'. It so clearly falls within Bryden's interests in dealing with twentieth-century Scottish historical topics, however, that it seemed unduly pedantic to exclude it.
13. Stewart Conn, *The Dominion of Fancy*, unpublished typescript.
14. This attempted taxonomy arises from helpful discussion with Randall Stevenson, for whose suggestions I am most grateful.
15. Reported in 'Festival Conference: From Page to Stage', *The Scotsman*, 18 August 1995, p.16.
16. Quoted in E. H. Carr, *What is History?* (Harmondsworth: Penguin, 1972), p.23.
17. Christopher Hill, 'Lies about crimes', *The Guardian*, 29 May 1989, p.9.

Eight

In the Jungle of the Cities

Randall Stevenson

Glasgow, the sort of industrial city where most people live nowadays but nobody imagines living . . .

if a city hasn't been used by an artist not even the inhabitants live there imaginatively. What is Glasgow to most of us? A house, the place we work, a football park or golf course, some pubs and connecting streets. That's all . . . Imaginatively, Glasgow exists as a music-hall song and a few bad novels. That's all we've given to the world outside. It's all we've given to ourselves.[1]

The first comment comes from The Oracle in Alasdair Gray's *Lanark*, the second from his protagonist Duncan Thaw, surveying the city from a hilltop above Cowcaddens in the 1950s. Critics seem to have found both views conveniently oracular, frequently using them to sum up the supposedly dreary state of affairs in Glasgow – a city apparently impoverished as much artistically as economically – before its literary imagination was revived by Gray and the novelists who followed him in the 1980s. Conveniently for such a view (and leaving aside for the moment that music-hall song), *Lanark* overlooks the theatre, which had in fact been 'using' Glasgow, surely imaginatively enough, for at least a decade before *Lanark* was published in 1981. Moreover, 1970s drama had often 'used' the city in ways owed, or comparable, to a tradition of urban realism going back a further quarter of a century, and fairly firmly in existence in the 1950s: something Duncan Thaw might well have taken into account before dismissing so thoroughly the imaginative life of the city he surveys.

Any regular theatre-goer in Glasgow in the 1950s should have been familiar with the vision of its life established by Glasgow Unity Theatre in the previous decade, and continued for some time after the company's demise in 1951 by authors it had encouraged. After all, Unity's greatest success, *The Gorbals Story*, was seen by over a hundred thousand people in six months after its first performance in 1946. Much in Robert McLeish's play appealed immediately to audiences throughout industrial Scotland: accurate depiction of working-class tenement life; humour familiar from music-hall comedy; a sharp edge of political commentary, particularly directed at the post-war housing crisis. Such interests and idioms were quickly carried forward by other Unity writers. In *Men Should Weep* (1947), Ena Lamont Stewart focused specifically through women's experience a vision of urban poverty and squalor similar to McLeish's. Much the same conditions figured in another Unity success in 1947, *Gold in his Boots*, though George Munro's play did also examine a rare way of escaping them, by means of success as a professional footballer.

Even such limited optimism is rare in Munro's plays. Several use Robert Burns's phrase 'From scenes like these old Scotia's grandeur springs' as an ironic commentary on 'Destruction. Dirt. Despair.' which Munro surveys 'from Falls of Clyde to Tail o' the Bank', presenting this dire landscape with a talent for realistic detail perhaps acquired during his career as a Glasgow journalist.[2] For obvious reasons – principally for the immediacy and imaginativeness of his vision of city life – Sean O'Casey is the playwright the modern Scottish theatre has always most longed to find some version of for itself. Munro's vivid realism and tenement settings made him a likely candidate in the late 1940s and 1950s, the comparison also extending to the kind of conflict between Catholic and Protestant which figures centrally in *Vineyard Street* (1949) as well as *Gold in his Boots*. Though more melodramatic than O'Casey, and clumsier in construction, Munro is nevertheless an unjustly neglected Unity playwright, the successful rehearsed reading of *Gay Landscape* (1958) in 1994 suggesting his work still has a resonance for audiences at the end of the century.

Munro's main significance, however, is as an intermediary, carrying forward into later years the urban landscapes – of minimal gaiety and maximum grimness – established by Unity in the post-war years. By the time Munro's career was drawing to its close with *Mark but this Flea* in 1970, cityscapes and attention to the life of the industrial working class had begun to appear in the plays of a new generation. C. P. Taylor's *Bread and Butter* (1966), for example, offers a history of life in the Gorbals from the 1930s to the 1960s, an appropriate context for Taylor's concerns with the nature of idealism and principles of social reform. Stewart Conn's early play *I Didn't Always Live Here* (1967) is more firmly centred in Unity's tenement territory, also offering in the memories of its ageing heroine a picture of Glasgow life and poverty dating back to the 1930s. Like Munro's *Mark But This Flea*, Hector MacMillan's *The Sash* (1974) examines religious conflict in the west of Scotland, powerfully and sometimes poignantly combining folk-song with the play's vivid dialogue and stark portrayal of conflict. Like Munro, McMillan portrays religious bigotry as a distraction from a properly political commitment to improving the conditions of urban squalor and deprivation on which it feeds. *The Sash* opens to the sounds of a 12th of July Orange march in the streets of Glasgow, but closes with singing of the chorus

> Tell them to Hell with Orange and Green!
> Our banner like our common blood
> Should be Red – not Orange, not Green!

Another McMillan, Roddy McMillan, links the theatre of the 1970s still more directly with strengths and interests established by Glasgow Unity. Early in a distinguished career as an actor, McMillan played Hector, the old Highlander in *The Gorbals Story*, and McLeish's influence remains visible in the concern with desperate poverty and dismal housing in his own first play, *All in Good Faith* (1954). Much the same focus on a destructive, claustrophobic environment shapes his second, *The Bevellers* (1973), which shows the harshness of Scottish working life splintering the soul of a young apprentice during his first day's work in a mirror factory. Critics have often supposed that McMillan's example contributed substantially to another portrayal of a day in working life, John Byrne's *The Slab Boys* (1978). But the play's brilliant verbal wit – which Byrne extends into later parts of his trilogy, *Cuttin' a Rug* (1979) and *Still Life* (1982), as well as his later work for television – makes it apparently a much lighter experience than *The Bevellers*. A likelier beneficiary of McMillan's influence is Bill Bryden, who directed *The Bevellers* as part of the Royal Lyceum Theatre's renewed interest in Scottish drama in the early 1970s, and used McMillan to play the dour foreman in his own first play *Willie Rough* (1972).

Like McMillan and Byrne, Bryden concentrates on working life, setting his play in the shipyards of his home town, Greenock, during the Red Clydeside period of the First World War. The industrial conflicts of the time are presented through the kind of sharp dialogue and economic scene-construction which enhance Bryden's later plays, though sometimes without doing enough to create a firm overall narrative. In giving an episodic account of Greenock life in the Clydebank Blitz during the Second World War, *Civilians* (1981) is less successful in this way than *Benny Lynch* (1974). The story of the Glasgow boxer – at first brilliantly successful, later pathetically drunk and abandoned – offers a kind of paradigm for the vision, in many of the plays so far discussed, of the destruction even of the most worthy or talented, sooner or later, by the dirt and despair which surrounds them. Significantly, Peter Arnott concentrates on the same figure in *The Boxer Benny Lynch* (1984), and Tom McGrath on a comparable one in *Buchanan* (1993). Collaborating with Jimmy Boyle, Tom McGrath had provided in *The Hard Man* (1977) another version of this paradigm of talent and energy corrupted into self-destruction within the jungle of the cities – this time through violent crime and the seductive mythology of 'the hard man'. Later, in *Animal* (1981), McGrath made the metaphor of the jungle almost literal, examining the roots of aggression in a nearly wordless ritual of primate behaviour.

In one way, the plays mentioned surely offer enough evidence that even by the 1950s – and certainly by 1980 – Glasgow was neither altogether imaginatively unused nor theatrically barren. Yet in other ways, doubts remain. A tradition of Scottish urban drama, largely centred on Glasgow, can easily enough be shown to exist: but how surely can it be shown to amount to anything more worthwhile than the music-hall song and handful of bad novels mentioned in *Lanark*? The question becomes more pressing in the context of some recent criticism, or even of some of the earliest opinions of *The Gorbals Story*. While most contemporary reviewers welcomed McLeish's play, at least one compared it with Alexander MacArthur and H. Kingsley Long's notoriously sensationalist portrayal of Glasgow's ganglands, *No Mean City* (1935) – thus equating one of the very sources of the urban tradition with just the sort of bad novel Duncan Thaw might have had in mind.[3] Later commentators have similarly found fault with other plays in the urban tradition. If they have not accused them of sensationalism, they have at least pointed to a kind of perverse selectiveness: to a distorting, simplifying concentration on negative aspects of life in Scottish cities – such as poverty, drunkenness, violence, bigotry, or wage slavery – which cannot, after all, be held to affect *all* their inhabitants all the time. Even when plays seem free of such pessimism, it often only leaves them open to the charge of sentimentality – of presenting tumbledown tenements with silver linings stacked at every stairhead, or as homes for cheery hardmen wearing hearts of gold on their sleeves. Worse still, in the view of some critics such sentimentality often comes in a form especially toxic to the Scottish imagination: nostalgia, the 'national pastime' Liz Lochhead warns against in the first lines of *Mary Queen of Scots Got Her Head Chopped Off* (1987) – a readiness to live in or celebrate the past evident in a number of plays and in a way summed up in the title of Stewart Conn's *I Didn't Always Live Here*.

Sensationalism, selectiveness, sentiment, simplification, nostalgia – several recent commentators have summed up such apparent shortcomings by applying almost unquestioningly the phrase 'urban Kailyard' or 'industrial Kailyard' to plays set in Scottish cities.[4] The phrase carries the suggestion that, far from adding to the imaginative life of the cities, the urban tradition limits Scottish imagination and self-perception as damagingly as did the sentimental treatment of rural life in the fiction of J. M. Barrie, S. R. Crockett and other novelists at the end of the nineteenth century to whom the term 'Kailyard' was first applied. Given David Hutchison's conclusion that 'urban naturalism has become the dominant mode' of Scottish plays, and that 'if there is a Scottish dramatic tradition then it can be traced back to writers who worked for Unity',[5] such charges against city drama spread a whiff of the Kailyard disturbingly far across the field of recent Scottish drama in general.

Fortunately, there are ways in which it can be largely dispelled, first of all by looking harder at the implications of that term 'Kailyard' itself. One of the achievements of Glasgow Unity was to escape from the kind of heathery rural world – in a way, a late version of the Kailyard – which had figured largely in Scottish theatre between the wars, particularly in the work of the Scottish National Players. Glens and heather are immediately shunned in *The Gorbals Story*, one of McLeish's characters remarking early in the play on the irrelevance to city dwellers of 'miles and miles o' long grass and no' a tram caur in sight' and of 'yon pictures they print on boxes o' shortbread – big blue hills and coos that need a hair cut'.[6] Simply moving the setting of plays from country to city does not, of course, of itself make them immune to the kind of doubts mentioned above, except in one obvious way. The Celtic-twilit, pastoral landscape favoured by Kailyard authors – and sometimes the Scottish National Players – offered urban audiences an *escape* from the gritty actualities of their industrialised cities, whereas plays in the urban tradition confront them with those same actualities, in forms whose accuracy they can verify from their own experience. Such drama may stray into sentimentality at times, but in general it thrives not on the allure of escapism but of identification – the kind of excitement, enough to make Duncan Thaw jump up and down with glee, which occurs when a city *does* at last start to live imaginatively; to find, heightened and made significant within dramatic form, the kind of speech, humour, outlook and general experience audiences know intimately from their own daily lives. The vision and energy which results may not be the most subtle the theatre can offer, but it is nevertheless fundamental to its powers, enabling audiences to engage more fully, even outwith the theatre, with experience they have found so deeply implicated in its spectacle. Sometimes this potential is sufficient to sustain the drama almost on its own – in Tom McGrath's community-based *City* (1989), for example, using many ordinary Glaswegians to perform their own drama, or in Billy Kay's *They Fairly Mak Ye Work* (1986). Though the latter offered little more than a sketch of working life in and around Dundee's jute mills, this was enough to pack Dundee Rep, throughout the run, with local audiences enthralled by the relative novelty of finding anything of their own life and experience represented on a stage at all.

'Kailyard', then, is a term which rather distracts from recent theatre's power to make spectators engage with rather than evade the realities of their lives. Recognition of this engagement, and its function, also helps construe the charges of sensationalism made against the urban tradition. For audiences to identify easily with what they see on stage, plays require an element of realism; of convincing, naturalistic representation of the lives they know themselves. This helps explain why, as critics such as David Hutchison and Alasdair Cameron have concluded, 'an overwhelming number' of Scottish plays fall into the naturalist mode.[7] The predominance of this mode also shows Scottish theatre – tagging for so long behind developments elsewhere – catching up at last with the styles which dominated the continental (and often the English) stage at the end of the nineteenth century; styles which moved away from melodrama and the well-made play in favour of accurate reflection of everyday life. The work of writers such as Emile Zola, Maxim Gorki, or the early August Strindberg, however, was concerned not only with allowing audiences to consider *how* they lived, but with showing them *why* they lived and were forced to live as they did: with depicting the conditions – economic, familial, political – surrounding and determining the life of the individual and of society as a whole. Recognising the recent predominance of naturalism on the Scottish stage helps clarify, by analogy, that its concern with 'Destruction. Dirt. Despair.' is no more (nor less) sensationalist than Zola's drama, or Gorki's appropriately-entitled *The Lower Depths* (1903). Instead, it is a way of challenging audiences into recognising the nature and determining influence of conditions – very often depths of poverty and urban deprivation – endured throughout the twentieth century by large sections of the Scottish population. Such conditions *are* shocking: making them so on stage may help them to be understood, and empower audiences with a will for change.

The more sensational of recent Scottish plays have sometimes been careful to justify their methods in these terms. For example, in staging

the life of one of Scotland's most famous criminals, Jimmy Boyle, *The
Hard Man* is quite explicit about its need to find 'a way of telling' the
story 'that will finally get you to see the bitterness and indifference . . .
inherited from whatever the system was the series of priorities that
created the world into which [he] was born.' The Boyle-figure, Byrne,
is regularly shown as 'a product of this shit-heap system', and concludes
himself that 'Ma roads mapped oot fur me . . . What can ah change? Fuck
all'.[8] By beginning with a verse from 'The Song of the Clyde', and using
a chorus of 'windae-hingers' who describe their own desperate poverty
throughout, the play expands the significance of Byrne's individual
experience to encompass much of the depressed urban landscape of
the west of Scotland. It also demonstrates the dramatic usefulness of
the doomed hard men, such as Byrne or Benny Lynch, who turn up so
often within this landscape: such figures can illustrate fully the dismal,
inexorable effects of city poverty on the self. The hard man can be
shown being hardened by his bitter environment, yet however hard he
becomes, it's never hard enough to beat it: his temporary triumph and
ultimate defeat are each exemplary of the forces that prey upon him.
Significantly, the characters who do manage to avoid complete defeat
and somehow survive in the city slums are usually women – in *Men
Should Weep, I Didn't Always Live Here,* John McGrath's *Little Red Hen*
(1975), or Tony Roper's *The Steamie* (1987), for example. Often, they
do so through compromise – an alternative to the hard man's conflict
and confrontation – though one whose high price in frayed resilience,
self-denial and self-abnegation is an issue Scottish dramatists have still
to consider fully.

Plays which comment less explicitly or less shockingly than *The Hard
Man* on the urban environment can nevertheless contribute equally
powerfully to an understanding of its effects. While *The Bevellers,* for
example, may seem no more than a painfully accurate portrayal of a
day in working life, its vividly presented grinding and bevelling work is
emblematic of the habitual cruelties of Scottish working life; of soulless
conditions and denials of emotion which grind men into hardness. The
play's basement setting, beneath the feet of idle passers-by, is likewise
metaphoric of the class and social hierarchies, and the depths of wage
slavery, in which most of the characters are trapped. These hierarchies
are further emphasised at many points throughout – for example when
music from the band of the 'the Academy boys', on their way to a
summer holiday, wafts evocatively into the basement, reminding the
young apprentice that 'they're up there, an' you're doon here . . .
grinding yur guts tae get up therr amongst it'.[9]

The Slab Boys likewise offers much more than an unchallenging picture of working life. The wit which makes it apparently a much lighter play than *The Bevellers* also has its darker side, functioning for the characters themselves as a necessary, sometimes desperate response to personal crisis and the grinding tedium of factory work. Like much of Byrne's later drama, *The Slab Boys* exploits as entertainment the humour which is a distinctive feature of Scottish urban life, in Glasgow especially, while also showing its origins in a need to escape from the oppressive monotony of daily life. Like their taste for sharp, fashionable clothes, the Slab Boys' comic invention and dextrous rhetoric and repartee create a bright, stylish surface for lives whose drab actuality they cannot fundamentally change. The city of Glasgow itself might be seen as having used a similar strategy of disguise in 1990, its year as cultural capital of Europe a sophisticated distraction from continuing urban crisis and post-industrial decline.

The nature of this decline suggests a more worthwhile function for what has often seemed like nostalgia in recent theatre. Of course Scottish plays do frequently revisit the past, but often with less interest in escaping a disagreeable present than in finding ways of understanding it and the historical forces that brought it into being. *The Steamie*, for example, does offer a warm, idealised version of vanished Glasgow life in much of its action, and in Mrs Culfeathers's genuinely nostalgic picture of still earlier times when 'Glesca Green was like a sea of colour' and 'there was never any loneliness . . . *naebody* seemed tae be lonely'. But the play also points out what has left people 'no aw-the-gither as they used to be'[10] – an age of television and status-conferring domestic appliances which have made city life easier, but in doing so undermined a sense of community which was one of its few real assets. More subtly, setting the play at a time when it was still possible to think of Drumchapel as a leafy, utopian alternative to life in city-centre tenements is an irony which clarifies how far Glasgow was betrayed and blighted by post-war urban planning.

Playwrights in the 1970s who turned back to the Red Clydeside period of John Maclean likewise did so not to escape present circumstances but to find analogues – or ideologues – to comment upon them. Performed so soon after the workforce's occupation of the Upper Clyde Shipbuilders (UCS) Yard in 1971, *Willie Rough* offered John Maclean's agitation as an obvious, if implicit, comparison with contemporary radicalism. Such comparisons are entirely explicit in John McGrath's *The Game's a Bogey* (1974), which uses Maclean's speeches and 'lessons in how capitalism works' to direct his audiences' understanding of a 'new age' of 'sewage' and of 'brand new twenty storey slums'.[11]

The UCS dispute, incidentally, might be seen as an influence not so much on McGrath's politics as on the entertaining, didactic style he developed to communicate them. Several of the performers who joined him in founding 7:84 Scotland and appeared in its first, hugely successful production – *The Cheviot, the Stag and the Black, Black Oil* (1973) – had immediately previously worked on *The Great Northern Welly Boot Show*. This used sketches, pantomime or music-hall routines, and songs by that recent great legatee of music-hall, Billy Connolly (a city playwright himself) to tell the story of UCS, thinly disguised as a boot factory. Hugely popular in Glasgow in 1972, and later during the Edinburgh Festival, *The Great Northern Welly Boot Show* offers further evidence for the case Femi Folorunso makes later in this volume: that the music-hall and its derivatives form a strong strand of Scottish theatrical tradition, though a subordinate one, too often ignored. Perhaps *Lanark* should not have dismissed that music-hall song so readily. The Song of the Clyde and others like it are part of a theatrical idiom which, adapted and politicised in the influential work of 7:84, returned to centre stage in Scotland in the 1970s, continuing to contribute to the development of later Scottish theatre.

City drama since the 1970s has itself had the opportunity, and a need, to develop in new directions. By the 1980s, stage representation of urban and industrial life, and the resulting power of audience identification, discussed above, had ceased to be novelties and become established resources which could be shaped towards new interests and possibilities. Urban environments and their problems could be used more freely as significant contexts for action, and less as centres of attention in themselves. Though *Elizabeth Gordon Quinn* (1985), for example, remains concerned with tenement life during the rent strikes of the Red Clydeside period, this remains partly in the background; part of the oppressive context in which Chris Hannan analyses a self-deluding, embattled individual, half-admirable, half-absurd. Like many figures in the drama discussed above, this heroine is shown fighting against her environment (often in all the wrong ways), but it is the nature of the heroine, rather than the environment, which is eventually of most concern. Scottish theatre should probably have ceased long ago to be haunted by Sean O'Casey: though he is in many ways a very different writer, on the evidence of *Elizabeth Gordon Quinn* Hannan might be the man finally to lay this ghost to rest. Like O'Casey's, his play shows the rigours of tenement life, and the urge to escape it, deeply ingrained in the consciousness and action of his characters, yet this is never his only subject, nor even a main one. Other recent playwrights – Ann Marie di Mambro in *Tally's Blood* (1990), for example – have likewise shown the city environment as an inescapable influence on the lives of their characters, without making it an inescapable subject of their plays.

Simon Donald shows Scottish city drama moving forward in another way, in terms of the kind of city envisaged. Plays such as *The Bevellers* or *Willie Rough* have been only partly successful in recent revivals, probably less as a result of diminished novelty than because the kind of working-class struggle they examine has been superseded or, disastrously, just lost. Successful labour action of the kind associated with UCS – even the availability of remunerative labour – sometimes seems almost as much a thing of the past as UCS itself. The evisceration of Scotland's industry by successive Tory governments has left its cities with a set of problems – crime, drug-abuse, unemployment and urban hopelessness – different in scale and nature to those most dramatists envisaged twenty years ago. Much of this new urban desolation is reflected in zany form in the lives of the 'unemployable' drug-groupies and incompetent criminals who appear in Donald's *The Life of Stuff* (1992). As Peter Zenzinger suggests when discussing recent drama later in this volume, plays such as *The Life of Stuff* or the adaptation of Irvine Welsh's novel *Trainspotting* (1994) show the effectiveness of a new generation of Scottish writers in commenting on the rigours of the cities – jungles as dark, complex, and deeply implicated in Scottish experience as ever.

Scottish theatre's shifting interests have also been matched by substantial changes in style. While generally remaining within the naturalist idiom which Hutchison and Cameron rightly see as its dominant mode, city drama has long ago abandoned the fully-furnished box-sets of *The Gorbals Story*. Stylised dialogue, imposing lighting and a sometimes dream-like intensity of action took performances of *Elizabeth Gordon Quinn* close to a form of expressionism, while the loosely connected scenes and minimal set of *The Life of Stuff* likewise often moved beyond plausible, realistic action. Further and more confident movement in such directions might be worthwhile. When Bertolt Brecht examined city life in his early drama (*In The Jungle of the Cities*, 1924, for example), it was in a freely expressionist style, ready whenever necessary to move from realism to dream in order to accentuate the issues involved. Among recent Scottish authors, only John McGrath has comparably combined or experimented with non-naturalistic genres, culminating in his comprehensive, Constructivist history of Scottish labour, *John Brown's Body* (1990). Partly as a result – and despite the effective political commentary made by many of the naturalist plays discussed above – 7:84 Scotland and its successor Wildcat have probably done most to expose the economic forces and policies shaping the life of Scotland's cities in the late twentieth century.

So in terms of those views of Glasgow in *Lanark*, it might still be suggested that Scottish dramatists have not yet used the city imaginatively enough, however much they have succeeded in avoiding Kailyards, clichés, sentiment or nostalgia. What really sets *Lanark* apart from the Glasgow novels that preceded it – bad or otherwise – is the originality in Gray's use of an extended dystopian fantasy as an analogy for the condition of the city, and the powerful forms of commentary on its life that this allows. Audacious steps of this kind, into fantasy and political allegory, are ones Scottish theatre has yet to take: perhaps authors were encouraged to do so by the 1995 Edinburgh Festival adaptation of *Lanark* itself, regardless of the actual quality of this production. Other steps might be taken more easily – away from Glasgow, a little more often, for example. Even allowing for the presence of the majority of the urban population in the west of Scotland, there is much dramatic potential in domestic and working life elsewhere, as Duncan McLean has recently shown in *Julie Allardyce* (1993), exploring the impact of the oil industry on Aberdeen and the North-East.

Yet even thus far, the drama of the cities has ensured that there is much less cause for the kind of complaint Edwin Morgan made in 1967, when he suggested the theatre allowed 'Huge areas of Scottish life [to] fly past uncommented on'.[12] Theatrical vision in the last thirty years has at last reached the kind of areas where most Scottish life takes place, making it possible to inhabit them a good deal more imaginatively – to give, as Alasdair Gray might have wished, more to ourselves, as well as more account of ourselves to the world outside.

NOTES

1. Alasdair Gray, *Lanark* (1981; rpt. London: Granada, 1984), pp.105, 243. The playwright David Greig offers some interestingly comparable reflections, based on views very similar to Gray's by V. S. Naipaul in 'Internal Exile', *Theatre Scoland*, 3, 11 (Autumn 1994), pp.8–10.
2. 'From Scenes Like These' is the title of a one-act play: the phrase also appears in *Mark But This Flea*. The quotations are taken from the unpublished typescript of *Gay Landscape*, Act II.
3. Edward Gaitens, *Scots Theatre*, no.3, November 1946, quoted in Linda Mackenney's Introduction to Robert McLeish, *The Gorbals Story* (Edinburgh: 7:84 Publications, 1985), p.13.
4. Linda Mackenney mentions the risk of lapsing into an 'industrial Kailyard' in her section on 'Scotland' in *The Cambridge Guide to Theatre*, ed. Martin Banham (Cambridge: Cambridge University Press, 1992), p.876; Alasdair Cameron talks of 'urban Kailyardry' in his Introduction to *Scot-Free: New Scottish Plays* (London: Nick Hern, 1990), p.x.
5. David Hutchison, 'Scottish Drama 1900–1950' in Cairns Craig, ed., *The History of Scottish Literature, volume 4: Twentieth Century* (Aberdeen: Aberdeen University Press, 1987), p.176.
6. *The Gorbals Story* (see note 3), pp.21–2.
7. As quoted earlier, Hutchison sees 'urban naturalism' as 'the dominant mode' of modern Scottish theatre; Alasdair Cameron's Introduction (see note 4) suggests of twentieth-century Scottish plays that 'an overwhelming number . . . seem to belong to a genre that could best be described as 'serio-comic naturalism', p.ix.

8. Tom McGrath and Jimmy Boyle, *The Hard Man* (Edinburgh: Canongate, 1977), p.33.
9. Roddy McMillan, *The Bevellers* (Edinburgh: Southside, 1974), p.63.
10. Tony Roper, *The Steamie*, in Alasdair Cameron, ed., *Scot-Free: New Scottish Plays* (London: Nick Hern, 1990), pp.228–9.
11. John McGrath, *The Game's a Bogey: 7:84's John MacLean Show* (Edinburgh: EUSPB, 1975), p.6.
12. Edwin Morgan, 'Scottish Writing Today II: The Novel and the Drama', *English* (Autumn 1967), p.229.

Nine

Fantasists and Philosophers

Sarah C. Rutherford

Hang up philosophy.
Unless philosophy can make a Juliet . . .
(*Romeo and Juliet*, III. iii. 56–7)[1]

What is the use of philosophy in the theatre? As Romeo knew,
philosophy has a terrible tendency to evaporate into contemplation
of the universal and the abstract, rather than bringing us closer to
the blood-and-bone centre of our lives. Ask Romeo for his picture of
the typical philosopher, and he would probably come up with some
stoical bearded fellow untouched by human relationships, removed
from immediate practicalities, musing alone in his study in search of
some nebulous higher experience. What place does such a figure have
in the theatre?

For certain playwrights of the Scottish stage, the isolated philosopher
holds a vast amount of charm. Understandably so, in some ways. A
playwright may be naturally drawn to characters set apart from the
rest – which makes the brooding thinker an obvious choice. But the
theatre is not merely a forum for thought. And the danger comes when
the philosopher's limitations become the playwright's own, when writers
are attracted to characters as some kind of subconscious 'projection' of
their own personalities. Aspiring to a higher experience through the
power of the imagination is all well and good. That's fiction; at its
most heightened, it's fantasy. But what business is it of playwrights,
creators of the most communal, democratic art, to be aloof? What
business is it of theirs to dismiss the concerns of the audience, to refuse
commitment to their creations? At its most extreme, the stance of the
philosopher playwright is downright dangerous. But as the philosopher
recluse retreats from the stage and a more communicative form of fantasy

takes over, a more responsible – and indeed more entertaining – form of theatre is created. It is this development which emerges from the plays of Stanley Eveling, Tom Gallacher, Tom McGrath and John Clifford.

STANLEY EVELING

An early example of the philosopher recluse on the Scottish stage is Algernon Charles Fortescue, protagonist of Stanley Eveling's short play *Oh Starlings!* (1971). Algernon's plan is to withdraw from the world and devote seven years of his life to meditation. He lays in provisions, settles down in 'the intimate security of [his] self-imposed prison,'[2] and begins to operate his chosen method of 'free association', a kind of stream-of-consciousness technique with no particular goal. So far, so futile. Then inconvenient reality intervenes. Somehow, in the midst of all his meticulous preparations, Algernon forgot to put a shilling in the meter, and is in danger of freezing. From here the play takes off into a free association of its own. A character called George materialises to save Algernon (although this also involves making sexual advances to him), and after a round of 'Somewhere Over the Rainbow' with the audience, Algernon reveals to us that George is in fact an *ant*. The remainder of the action involves Algernon apparently killing George with DDT, and George taking revenge by transforming Algernon into a grub to feed his numerous babies. The starlings? One suspects they were little more than an excuse for a clever title; like Eveling's singing rocks in *The Balachites* (1963) their presence, as occasional sound effects, merely mystifies or irritates, as the audience chooses.

And this is where Eveling wins. Like Algernon, he enjoys a bit of 'randomising'; the difference is that Eveling gets away with it and has never yet become ant-fodder. While Algernon meets his grotesque fate as a waving mass of bandages, his methods live on, and his breathtakingly unironic Emperor's-New-Clothes justification could easily come from the mouth of Eveling himself:

> Mind you, mind you, you mustn't expect to be understood. It'll take years. Centuries even. You'll be dead and then you'll be understood. After all, people expect a clear and precise meaning. They need it. The little people, they call out for it. Give us meaning, cry the people, and he gave us free-association. (p.76)

It is as if Eveling, pre-empting criticism, has fastened onto some tag-line from the Aesthetic movement of the turn of the century – its tendency to ignore or even despise its audience, the bourgeois little people – and combined its pessimism with that of the so-called Absurdists of the 1950s. Both influences are entirely superficial, lacking both Aesthetic intensity and Absurdist exhilaration. But what about now? Surely in the 1990s we require something a little more substantial, a little more communicative? Not according to Mr Eveling.

In his latest play, *The Albright Fellow* (1995), the philosopher figure reappears, although this time isolated only in terms of his self-absorption and his inability to communicate successfully with those around him. The trouble with such an emotionally sterile protagonist is that he gives us an emotionally sterile play, a triumph of the intellectual over the emotional, confirming Eveling's distaste for 'accessibility'. Eveling admits having decided, when writing this play, not 'ever to think about whether the audience would know what the information was'.³ Accordingly, the action is punctuated with laboured extracts from the lectures of Geoffrey – a philosophy don like Eveling himself – delivered on tape from a dark, unpeopled stage. Here the obscurity comes not from arbitrary symbolism but from academic narrow-thinking. Of course, Eveling is attempting to examine the nature of the tragic by placing a great intellectual mind in a great emotional dilemma ('it's an ethical problem and I'm lousy at ethics', says Geoffrey⁴); the trouble is that this only serves to highlight Eveling's own reliance on the intellect, preferring educational sophistication to emotional commitment. Why else make these people speak incessantly in terms of broad generalisations rather than concern themselves with their specific situation? When Aileen justifies her actions with, 'I just wanted you to know that pure bloody cruelty is not a male prerogative' (p.80), it is as if all she had been doing was attempting to demonstrate a fundamental truth about gender. And like his symbols, his endings are largely arbitrary; in *Dear Janet Rosenberg, Dear Mr Kooning* (1969) we are offered alternative conclusions, while in *The Albright Fellow* Eveling seems constantly to draw back from possible consequences. Was Geoffrey offered the crucial professorship? Did Aileen burn the only copy of her secretly written book on Richardson? Is Geoffrey dead? After the second or third reversal, we get wise to the game and cease to care. We even begin to wonder if Eveling cares, either for his story or for his characters – or for us, for that matter.

Eveling is as out of touch with his audience as he is with his characters, his portrayal of cut-off philosophers a definite projection of his own insularity and detachment. Even Hayden Murphy, a self-professed 'fan' of Eveling's work (in spite of an initial 'befuddlement'⁵), makes an implied comparison between the playwright and his aloof fellow-philosopher Ludwig Wittgenstein, following a description of Eveling's lofty home in the towers of Fettes College from whence he 'writes and ventures out as Teaching Fellow in Philosophy' with a reference to Wittgenstein's retreat to his rooms, from whence he 'dictated his notes to a select few and they made copies to be handed out to "the rest"'.[6] Eveling's plan for a new play that treats rape 'lightly' ('Everyone takes rape terribly seriously, so I thought I'd write about it in a comical way'[7]) is illustrative of his crucial failure of empathy and involvement – and the dangers of that failure. While neglecting to commit himself to his imaginative world, Eveling is – like the fictional philosopher recluse – insufficiently engaged with the real one.

TOM GALLACHER

In the plays of Tom Gallacher, the attraction of the philosopher recluse lies in his status as 'exception', a type who appears in most of his plays:

> Sometimes the exceptions are artists; sometimes it is another kind of outsider, a genius, a catalyst, or a singular man. All of them are in some way seeking to extend the meaning of their lives or the boundaries of reality.[8]

Gallacher is not a philosopher by profession like Eveling, but his plays are in fact more firmly and explicitly grounded in that discipline than those of his contemporary. Danish philosopher and theologian Søren Kierkegaard appears in more than one of Gallacher's plays, first as a critical influence on Bernard in *Revival!* (1972), and later in person, characterised in *The Parole of Don Juan* (1981). Gallacher was also influenced by the metaphysics of Hegel – in which the mind of man is the highest expression of the Absolute – and those of Arthur Koestler, who believed in the individual human being as the centre of an ordered, systematic design. If Gallacher's heroes turn out to be egoists, then, it's hardly surprising.

Bernard Kevin, the philosopher recluse of *Revival!*, has retired from acting to the attic of a theatre in order to study the theories of Kierkegaard and prepare for death. As he enters his 'last act' and becomes involved, against his better judgement, in a production of Ibsen's *The Master Builder*, his search for another realm of reality seeps into the play itself, where the boundaries between reality and fiction shift and change. At times this merely results in a whimsical toying with illusion; eventually it becomes a weapon with which Bernard defends himself against a series of doctors (all played by the same actor) who attempt to 'cure' his mental state. Disconcertingly for both doctor and audience, Bernard threatens one of them with proof that he is an actor, and the doctor is rescued only by Bernard's wife Delia jumping her cue. But by the time the actor appears for the third time he is ready for Bernard, using his own trick to force him into a corner:

> If we were alone it would not matter. But you have found it necessary to engage the attention of an audience for your victory. You depend upon them. Is that the behaviour of a philosopher, or an actor? You must choose.[9]

Bernard is finally persuaded to return permanently to the stage – and hence, paradoxically, to real life – when the doctor confronts him with a passage from Kierkegaard which he has till then chosen to ignore. A happy outcome for all.

These theatrical games may be enjoyed on two levels: as erudite entertainment or as a paradigm for the questions posed by metaphysics. Heavily concealed beneath the comedy is a serious consideration of the problems of Duality (as illustrated by Bernard's encounter with Clear), Perception, Appearance and Reality, Time, and Survival of Spirit. One could be forgiven for missing every one of these. On neither level, however, is there any great exploration of Bernard's intriguing relationships; in the creation of a philosophical model, once again some humanity is lost. Tantalising episodes are presented: the cancellation of his daughter's engagement when she is asked to play his cast-off mistress in *The Master Builder*; the prevention of his suicide by another young actress (at great risk to her own life); the final decision that his next role will be Prospero with his estranged wife as the sea ('How else am I to stay afloat?' [p.53]). But the lack of fine detail, of attention to the idiosyncrasies, the mannerisms, the *smells* of these people, leaves them as mere sketches rather than finished portraits or even vivid daubs of colour.

Pure naturalism is an unpopular mode amongst all of these dramatists; and understandably so for those who began by pushing against the limiting 'kitchen sink' trend of the late 1950s. And yet it is from the naturalistic form that Gallacher's talents really emerge. *Mr Joyce is Leaving Paris* (1970) deals with another brilliant but utterly self-absorbed individual, cut off from the world not in the physical sense but – like Gallacher's own Don Juan – by taking no responsibility for the effects of his actions upon others. The impossible combination of dependency, exploitation, admiration, contempt and simple love in the relationship between James Joyce and his brother Stanislaus is achingly explored in the first pared-down two-man part of the play. The idiom of the two brothers is acutely observed and the trivia that constantly undermine Stan's attempts to be authoritative and firm are ludicrously painful, as when he ruins his grand walk-out by getting tangled in the packing and forgetting his shoes. Here are the failings and foibles we were missing in *Revival!*: they make all the difference between a moving play and a merely entertaining one. Here, too, the relationship between life and fiction really captures something of importance, rather than being an end in itself. When Stan and Jim explore an exciting metaphor, the basis of a new play, Stan suddenly stops short:

> STAN (*slapping his brow*). Oh God help me! I keep forgettin'. No matter who or what we're talking about, *we* are really talking about *you*.[10]

The consequences of Joyce's careless shuffling together of life and art are explored in part two, which shifts into a different mode altogether. Still we have the all-revealing minutiae – like the money Joyce spent on postcards of himself instead of on new teeth for his mother – but we have moved from the vividly physical, claustrophobic world of Stan and Jim into a place inhabited by eerie, anonymous voices who address Joyce from the shadows. The ghosts – still suffering, in death, from Joyce's power over them – confirm his fatal distance from reality:

> STAN Wouldn't it be simple if people were just words.
> JOYCE (*turning to him*). I have been concerned with feeling too . . . I've been affected by the people I've used – and put them to a purpose when they had none of their own. (p.62)

Unlike Bernard, Joyce remains doggedly defiant, justifying his actions to the very end. And as in *Don Juan*, the great man is finally left unjudged. The balance is fine and intriguing.

TOM MCGRATH

In Gallacher's *Revival!*, a good deal of contempt is aired towards experimental theatre as represented by the ludicrous Victor Bray, an avant-garde theatrical director. It is always tempting to put a name to the 'nudity, the crudity, the cruelty and the absurdity' (p.3) Victor has been directing for the past few years, but Bernard's accusation in particular may drag the early work of Tom McGrath to the ungenerous mind:

> Dazzling lights where the language failed, real brick walls instead of story, then when neither lights nor walls could hide the emptiness – off with the clothes and we're back to the only entertainment the stone age possessed . . . You have set two thousand years of human mind and spirit at nothing, and your next step can only be to grunts and silence. (p.12)

Certainly McGrath has had a tendency to rely on technical effects and an enormous amount of input from actors and directors, and one has

only to look at the script of *Animal* (1979) – consisting largely of long
and detailed passages of stage directions to actors playing speechless apes
–, to see that the descent to 'grunts and silence' was never far away. And
yet McGrath's theatrical experiments occur for the opposite reason from
those of Stanley Eveling. They arise not out of isolation from the world
beyond the typewriter but from an extraordinarily strong involvement
with it; not from an exclusively cerebral approach but from an unusually
visceral one.

McGrath's attitude towards scripts has always been an open one;
just as he believes in the priority of communication between play
and audience, the composition process is something of a collaboration
between playwright, actors and director. A trip to the United States in
the early 1980s crystallised these ideas. Influenced by the avant-garde
thinking of Robert Wilson, Richard Foreman and Joseph Chaikin,
among others, he came to think of the play as a barrier between
actors and audience, and moved away from conventional forms of
storytelling towards a more improvisational approach. The result was
the trilogy *1 2 3* (1981), a bewildering exploration of male identity.
Certain aspects of the plays are directly traceable to Chaikin's Open
Theatre group of the 1960s and early 1970s: the emphasis on a form of
Collective Creation by means of improvisation and a close relationship
between actors and audience, the 'collage' technique whereby actors
are transformed from one role to another, and the move away from
Method acting's emphasis on the integrity of psychology. From Wilson
and Foreman come the disorienting streams of images, the lack of
conventional plot and characters, and the surreal, disjointed snatches
of dialogue. The result involves extracts from letters, stand-up routines
and television commentaries; we are jolted from scene to scene without
explanation, then returned for repeat sequences. At its best it has the
manic hilarity of Monty Python; at its worst it degenerates into the
pretentious meaninglessness of German choreographer Pina Bausch, a
kind of self-conscious anti-theatre – and with lines like 'A jug with a
handle is not who I am',[11] it is certainly in danger of straining the
patience. The idea was to allow the actors a great deal of freedom;
McGrath had in mind the variations and improvisations of jazz and
the unpredictability and 'round-by-round quality' of a spectator sport
such as judo. It was a 'relativistic' technique, aiming 'to give an accurate
reflection of the world I live in . . . and to somehow catch and hold the
various self-contradictory aspects of the male psyche'.[12] To McGrath's
disappointment, however, the actors learned his lines instead of using
them as a basis for improvisation, and the examination of masculinity
was somewhat obscured by the distracting array of novel techniques. It

was a valid experiment – and by definition, an experiment has room for failure.

Philosophy in its most academic sense is not a concept one would tend to associate with McGrath. In fact, the figure of the philosopher recluse all but fades from the scene in his plays, while the fantasy develops. In *The Android Circuit* (1978), 'a science-fiction farce with a tragic launching ramp',[13] we have a research scientist, Astro, marooned in space with his butler after a nuclear holocaust has made the earth uninhabitable. Although Astro's isolation from the world is not by choice, his mistake is to believe in his futile scientific research (symbolised through his literal impotence) as the only hope in resisting 'entropy', the steadily encroaching enemy. In retrospect, the plot turns out to be a pretty conventional sci-fi fable with a pretty conventional moral: 'that human and technological virtues must be harnessed if their mutual self-destruction is to be averted'.[14] But the development, after the tale of *Laurel and Hardy* (1976) and the hard-hitting collaboration with convict Jimmy Boyle, *The Hard Man* (1977), was a surprising one from McGrath. One thing held the plays together: McGrath's attachment to music. McGrath was a jazz musician before he became a playwright, and music has continued to be a crucial part of his work since, with the exception of his disillusioned, propagandist days during the 1980s. He once solved a problem with the production of *Animal* by listening to the Elgar cello concerto, and he plays the piano a great deal when in the early stages of composing a play. It is all part of the pre-rational element of McGrath's writing, the element that comes direct from the gut, or the soul, or whatever you care to call it. In the first production of *The Hard Man* percussionists emphasised the primitive and ritualistic aspect of the violence, while the ape-drama *Animal* was an explicit exploration of that primitive nature. It is not the first time music has been joined with literature in this way. T. S. Eliot, who believed that the most intense moments of dramatic poetry 'touch the border of those feelings which only music can express',[15] referred in his examination of the effects of poetry to a 'pre-logical mentality' which 'persists in civilised man;'[16] it is a concept based on the idea of the 'group unconscious' which allows human minds to communicate below the levels of consciousness because of some 'vestiges of the primordial mind from which . . . our minds have evolved'.[17]

And perhaps that is why McGrath's work, though often just as puzzling and infuriating as Eveling's, does seem to communicate at some indefinable level, particularly when at its most primitive. 'You want some kind of "ping"', is how he puts it. 'Some kind of chemistry between play and audience'.[18] And, at times, somehow, that is just what he gets. McGrath quotes with approval the description of playwrights by the Quebecois Daniel Danis, whose *Stones and Ashes* he has recently translated for the Traverse, as 'doorkeepers of the unconscious'. Once again, Eliot comes to mind; like Eliot, McGrath is attempting to touch that 'fringe . . . of feeling which we can only detect, so to speak, out of the corner of the eye' ('Poetry and Drama', p.145). Eliot wrote of poetry that 'we do not know until the shell breaks what kind of egg we have been sitting on' ('Use of Poetry', p.89); likewise McGrath says, 'In the best plays I don't know what I'm expressing.' And it is on this level – a kind of primitive, subconscious communication – that McGrath occasionally hits the right vibration. It is no small feat.

JOHN CLIFFORD

The collective unconscious is a factor, too, in the plays of John Clifford, who bases many of his works around ancient myths and legends and their age-old symbolism. A generation younger than the previous three playwrights, he has most in common with Tom McGrath, whose sense of moral responsibility, of connection with his characters and with his audience, he has inherited. Unlike McGrath, however, Clifford bases his work firmly in the storytelling tradition. His characters, like McGrath's, may be flexible, capable of transformation and able to address the audience directly, and they may move instantly and effortlessly from place to place, but structure is all. This gives Clifford's work considerably more optimism than that of either McGrath or Eveling. Stories imply that the world can make sense, a concept that is the antithesis of the Absurd. 'The world is mad,' says Quevedo in *Losing Venice* (1985). 'Madness incarnate. Total chaos. Or so it seems. But underneath is the web'.[19]

Much of Clifford's style can be understood through his attachment to seventeenth-century Spanish drama, on which he completed a PhD thesis just as he was beginning to be recognised as a playwright. His first performed plays, in fact, were translations of Calderón, and his work in that area continues. The model provided by Spanish theatre of that period brings to Clifford's work its reliance on the spectator's imagination, the strength of its storytelling, its rich combination of tragedy and comedy and its democratic accessibility. Latin America has also had its impact on Clifford. The sense of addressing a vast continent has an obvious appeal for a writer dealing with such universal themes, but his writing also has certain affinities with the work of the Magic Realists in its freedom of imagination and its dreamlike ability to introduce the fantastic without comment into scenes of everyday realism. In *Light in the Village* (1991), the result of Clifford's travels to India, an all-too-real public rape is followed by the appearance of the goddess Kali to comfort and promise revenge. It is a scene that illustrates Clifford's sense of responsibility – neither shying away from the pain of the situation nor abandoning the audience in the darkness he has led them into – as well as the boldness of his imagination. It is the logical step forward from the more contrived combination of naturalism and the supernatural in Gallacher's *Mr Joyce* and the pessimistic use of real detail (the aftermath of the Vietnam war, for instance[20]) in McGrath's *The Android Circuit. Light in the Village* also shares the Magic Realist view of the truth as a collaborative creation, in its telling of the story through multiple narrators. Again this was prefigured by Gallacher in his preoccupation with 'the dual nature of the remembered past – omnipresent in influence and irretrievable in fact'.[21]

Clifford describes his use of the past as 'a kind of science fiction backwards':[22] as in good science fiction, the audience is transported to another place and time to look at the world from a different angle. Many of Clifford's plays use these imaginative games to present fundamental truths in an undogmatic way; as with McGrath, the message may permeate the subconscious without ever being explicitly articulated. Unlike Eveling with his weak justification of his 'free association' technique, nothing is justified in Clifford's plays, nothing explained or commented on, whether it is a female character in a surprising role or a fantastic occurrence at an unexpected moment. Some of this unselfconscious freedom stems from the childlike, game-playing aspect of Clifford's writing. Clifford has revealed that one of his best-known plays, *Losing Venice*, was inspired by watching the fantasy games of his young daughter;[23] the admission is hardly surprising. It is entirely consonant with the purity and clarity of his writing, its magical quality and indeed its sense of fun. 'Crying is easy', the Priest tells Quevedo. 'Laughter requires a little more strength' (p.95). Pablo and Maria, with their silly jokes and rude noises, are the poorest characters in *Losing Venice* but also the strongest and most fruitful. Admittedly Clifford's childish streak can, on occasion, border on a rather alienating bathos; the war involving poisoned tapioca, flour bombs, custard pies and buckets of goo in *Lucy's Play* (1986), while no doubt expressing the absurdity of war, makes the subsequent deaths and resurrections impossible to take seriously. Likewise, one slip with the exquisite, poetic simplicity of Clifford's language and it tumbles into banality. At his best, though – in the little-known *Playing with Fire* (1987) especially – Clifford can take an age-old story, a selection of familiar figures, gloriously clear language, ancient symbolism and universal themes, and transform them into the most startlingly rich and moving theatrical experience. Whether or not

Clifford's virtues have arisen partly from a need to fight for an audience in these days of reduced subsidy is another issue. He is a shining reminder of the theatre's ability to be, as Noël Coward put it, 'a house of strange enchantment, a temple of dreams'.[24] And, as Coward would have agreed, entertainment is not a dirty word.

What has become of the philosopher recluse in all this? He has not been forgotten, even by Clifford. Significantly, though, he no longer dominates the stage. In *Losing Venice* he appears as Quevedo, the cynical poet who reviles human relationships and has given up on the world:

> . . . Power is madness.
> The world is corrupt. Action is futile.
> Love is a farce. Happiness, impossible.
> Poetry the only meagre consolation. (p.60)

The humourless, actionless Quevedo, however, is as unproductive as the war-mongering Duke, devoted to action at the expense of thought. All Clifford's philosopher recluses are undermined in this way; after Quevedo they do not even appear on the stage. In *Lucy's Play* we have Maria's father, the man who hides away in a hut 'way up beyond the valley'. His hopelessness may be justified in the short term, but his work is as futile as it is marginal:

> . . . He was going to found a city.
> Something to do with geometry . . .
> He showed me the plans. It was to be round.
> He said it was to imitate the order in the sky.
> Or that roundness made for harmony.
> Or something, I couldn't follow it really.
> He paced up and down and drew diagrams. He said he'd found
>   the site, this was it he said,
> The perfect place but he couldn't bring himself to do it.
> It was too beautiful, he said,
> Humans would spoil it.[25]

The most constructive character in the play is Mary mother of Jesus, who performs a similar *deus ex machina* function to that of Kali in *Light in the Village*. Clearing up after the battle and waking the dead, she sums up the defeatism of the ultimate philosopher recluse, God:

> I knew it would end in tears.
> I knew it. I went to the Lord and I said to him 'Listen,' I said –
> and you have to shout to him these days to get through, he's that
> preoccupied – 'Listen,' I said, 'Them humans.' 'They're going

to end up in serious trouble' I said 'Unless you do something.' He just shook his head. Men. So I just came back to see what I could do.[26]

Put at its simplest, the journey from Stanley Eveling to John Clifford is a journey from the mind-games of the philosopher to the warm-blooded dreamings of the fantasist. It is a journey symbolised by the gradual marginalisation of the philosopher recluse, and his fading away is a sign of hope for the Scottish stage, which has itself at times shown that figure's tendency towards cosy introspection. Like Bernard in *Revival!*, the Scottish theatre must be prepared to step out and be judged under the glaring lights of international theatre, set against the standards of the best drama everywhere. It is a process of demystification which may at times be disillusioning. What if we compare Eveling's *The Albright Fellow* with Edward Albee's *Who's Afraid of Virginia Woolf?* (1962), another play by a writer loosely associated with the Theatre of the Absurd, which also deals in an academic setting with 'the way married people can be so cruel to each other' (*Albright*, p.67)? Beside Albee's play of conflict and exorcism, *The Albright Fellow* looks impossibly slight and dilute: a scattering of thought-provoking perceptions in a sea of self-indulgent generalisation. And ironically, while a performance of Albee's play can still be a hilarious, harrowing and cathartic experience more than thirty years after the first, Eveling's was already out of date and unmoving at its première. More comfortingly, the assimilation of international influences by McGrath and Clifford signal a refreshingly outward-looking future. And the difference in effect between a play by Eveling and a play by Clifford confirms Keats's claim that 'axioms in philosophy are not axioms until they are proved upon our pulses'.[27] Whether that proof comes through the identifiable foibles of Gallacher's Joyce, the erratic spark of McGrath's rhythms or the infectious suffering and laughter of Clifford's dreams, it is our pulses which must finally decide.

NOTES

1. *Romeo and Juliet* (London: Methuen, The Arden Shakespeare, 1980), p.177.
2. 'An Evening Double-Bill,' *Plays and Players* (March 1971), p.76.
3. Interview with the author, Edinburgh, 18 October 1995.
4. *The Albright Fellow* (unpublished typescript), p.78.
5. Programme note to *Dear Janet Rosenberg, Dear Mr Kooning* (Meridian Theatre Company/Fifth Estate, Traverse Theatre, Edinburgh, July 1995).
6. Programme note to *The Albright Fellow* (Fifth Estate, Bedlam Theatre, Edinburgh, September 1995).
7. Interview.
8. Tom Gallacher, quoted in K. A. Berney (ed.), *Contemporary Dramatists* (London: St James Press, 1993), 5th edn, p.217.
9. *'Revival!' and 'Schellenbrack'* (Glasgow: Molendinar, 1978), p.44.

10. *Mr Joyce is Leaving Paris* (London: Calder & Boyars, 1972), p.32.
11. *Who Are You Anyway?* (Part One of *1 2 3*; unpublished typescript, Traverse Theatre Collection, National Library of Scotland, Edinburgh), p.41.
12. Tom McGrath, 'Notes for Toronto, September 1980' (unpublished typescript, Traverse Theatre Collection), p.2.
13. Tom McGrath, quoted in a synopsis of *The Android Circuit* (unpublished typescript, Traverse Theatre Collection).
14. Steve Grant, review of Traverse production at the ICA, London, *Time Out*, 15–21 September 1978, p.68.
15. 'Poetry and Drama', in *Selected Prose of T. S. Eliot*, ed. Frank Kermode (London: Faber, 1975), pp.145–6.
16. 'The Use of Poetry and the Use of Criticism', in *Selected Prose*, p.91n.
17. R. L. Brett, 'Ambiguity and Mr Eliot', *English* 8 (1951), p.284.
18. Interview with the author, Edinburgh, 7 November 1995.
19. *Losing Venice*, in Alasdair Cameron (ed.), *Scot-Free: New Scottish Plays* (London: Nick Hern, 1990), p.80.
20. See synopsis of *The Android Circuit* ('Brochure copy'; unpublished typescript, Traverse Theatre Collection).
21. Marion O'Connor, in Berney, p.217.
22. Interview with the author, Edinburgh, 31 October 1995.
23. John Clifford, 'New Playwriting in Scotland', *Chapman 43–4: On Scottish Theatre* (Spring 1986), p.97.
24. Noël Coward, quoted in Sheridan Morley, *A Talent to Amuse* (London: Pavilion, 2nd edn 1985), p.249.
25. Unnumbered draft of *Lucy's Play*, (unpublished typescript, Traverse Theatre Collection), Act One, pp.44–5.
26. Draft Three of *Lucy's Play*, Act Two, p.52.
27. Letter to John Hamilton Reynolds, 3 May 1818, in *Letters of John Keats to his Family and Friends*, ed. Sidney Colvin (London: Macmillan, 1928), p.105.

Ten

The New Wave

Peter Zenzinger

Scottish playwrights of today have a great advantage over the older generation: they can draw on a considerable number of Scottish works for the stage, whereas even twenty years ago Scottish drama presented itself as 'a series of almost totally isolated bursts of creative energy' with 'no immediately accessible link', as Hector MacMillan observed in 1977.[1] With the remarkable increase in Scottish plays illustrated in the preceding chapters, such links have become more and more apparent: never before has there been such a wide range of models, never before such a variety of themes and styles as at the present moment. Moreover, while the new works are informed by an artistic vision that is distinctly Scottish, they have largely moved beyond the self-conscious Scottishness of the earlier dramatic tradition, which often hampered its artistic realisation and limited its appeal outside Scotland.

One of the main characteristics of the new writing for the Scottish stage is its emphasis on strictly contemporary issues: this is true even of plays set in the past. Among its central themes are change and re-orientation, the loss of old beliefs, traditions and myths, and the search for new standards and values. Contemporary Scottish playwrights attempt to redefine Scotland's identity in the context of global changes. A case in point is David Greig (*Stalingrad*, 1992; *Europe*, 1993; *One Way Street*, 1995), who holds a mirror up to Scotland in his dramatic treatment of the upheavals in central and eastern Europe, impressing on his audience the intricate links that exist between nationalism and cultural identity and their controversial consequences, both political and personal. Similarly, the short play *New Frontiers* by 7:84 (1993) views the German experience from a Scottish point of view, and vice versa. Chris Hannan sets his tragedy *The Baby* (1990) in Rome at the end of Sulla's dictatorship, but it points clearly enough at Thatcherism through its nightmare images of policies emphasising law and order while allowing mass unemployment. Rona Munro turns to Northern Ireland in *Bold Girls* (1990) to describe the plight of women in a male-dominated world: like Sue Glover's *Bondagers* (1991), set on a Border farm in the nineteenth century, it is an appeal for a female solidarity and decisiveness that can challenge the convictions and codes of behaviour women have been brought up with. The redefinition of gender roles and of the role of the family is, of course, a central concern of the modern Western world; so are unemployment, public and domestic violence, drug abuse, the revolution in sexual ethics and Aids, environmental pollution, and the social change brought about by North Sea oil and new technologies, all of which have found artistic expression in recent Scottish plays.

The playwrights' formal and stylistic range is no less varied than their choice of themes. Slice-of-life realism and post-Brechtian theatre of estrangement, expressionist and absurdist tendencies, borrowings from the thriller and classical tragedy can be found side by side and, frequently enough, intertwined: the fund of traditions Scottish playwrights draw on is complemented by elements of the music-hall, the soap-opera and the pantomime, agit-prop, the happening and community theatre, the theatre of Artaud and Robert Wilson, and many more. This buoyant eclecticism is a general characteristic of late post-modern writing,[2] and it shows Scottish drama keeping pace with international developments and becoming less self-centred and stereotyped. At least in part, the Scottish theatre has turned into 'a forbidden garden of sensual, aesthetic, intellectual and moral riot'.[3]

Many plays by new Scottish writers are naturally fringe-oriented, and designed for shoestring-budget productions on the open stage. At the other end of the scale there is the million-pound pageant *The Big Picnic* by Bill Bryden (1994), for which a shipyard was turned into a First World War battlefield, or NVA's high-tech show *Sabotage* (1993), which took the audience on a journey through the human body and from birth to death, including a traumatic squeeze through the birth canal and an equally disturbing stay inside a pulsating human heart.[4] Even if the latter examples are exceptional, there is an increasing awareness of the non-verbal 'languages' of the theatre in Scottish literary or text-based plays. At the beginning of *Julie Allardyce* (1993), for example, sophisticated sound and lighting allows Duncan McLean to transform the theatre auditorium into the inside of a helicopter landing on an oil rig. The sharp lines and spots of bright colour McLean suggests for his play's set show the influence of Ukrainian Suprematist painting (especially Kasimir Malevich),[5] whereas Sharman Macdonald's *The Winter Guest* (1995), another play with a strong visual impact, has been likened to a Turner painting.[6] One of the lasting impressions of Rona Munro's *The Maiden Stone* (1995) is the stark contrast between red and white, particularly when, after Harriet has given birth to a baby, a bucket full of blood is thrown out over the snow.[7] The success of Sue Glover's *Bondagers* is no doubt partly due to the stylised costumes and ballet-like movements of the female workers hoeing in the fields, a device that finds its equivalent on a verbal level: although based on the rural Scots of the Borders, the cadences of the dialogue sometimes recall the verse drama of T. S. Eliot or Christopher Fry.[8]

The range of registers and local varieties of Scots and Scots-English that playwrights now make use of, as a matter of course, is amazing. Its richness can be illustrated by comparing the precise but stylised Glaswegian speech in plays by Iain Heggie (*A Wholly Healthy Glasgow*, 1987, and *Politics in the Park*, 1993, are superb examples) with the jazzy urban speech of Simon Donald's *The Life of Stuff* (1992); or the foul-mouthed Leith gutter language and drug-slang of Irvine Welsh's *Trainspotting* (adapted for the stage by Harry Gibson, 1995) with the genteel Edinburgh middle-class accent in Rona Munro's *Your Turn to Clean the Stairs* (1992), or the same author's Doric teenage jargon in *Saturday at the Commodore* (1989) – not to mention the richness of linguistic expression in plays by poets such as Liz Lochhead and Edwin Morgan.

Another of the major distinctive characteristics of recent Scottish drama is an uncommonly frequent use of song. Going far beyond Brechtian practice – and not always in keeping with it – this may rather be seen as an extension of the ceilidh formula popularised by John McGrath in *The Cheviot, the Stag and the Black, Black Oil* (1973). Again, what is striking is the great variety in the use of this device, which ranges from the traditional ballad and folk-song in plays such as *The Maiden Stone, Bondagers* or *Julie Allardyce* to ecclesiastical chanting in Sue Glover's *Sacred Hearts* and pieces from the music-hall, musical and rock traditions in *The Life of Stuff* or in the plays of John Binnie.

The following examples of recurring motifs and techniques in recent Scottish drama are necessarily only a selection, though one which is intended to be representative in its diversity. Some of the characteristic Scottish patterns of thought and social behaviour have taken the form of myths, similar to the myths of the American dream or the West in United States drama and literature. Among the most pervasive Scottish myths is that of the 'hardman', reflecting a view of the Scottish male largely indebted to Scotland's Calvinist heritage and its widespread industrialisation. The Scottish novel from R. L. Stevenson to Alasdair Gray abounds in images of the strong, inflexible male and often celebrates physical strength as a way of proving one's moral integrity: the same topos recurs in Scottish plays of the 'urban Kailyard' tradition. Arguably this renders the discussion of the gender roles more urgent in Scotland than elsewhere. In *Mary Queen of Scots Got Her Head Chopped Off* (1987), for example, Liz Lochhead underlines the problems of women in power – especially their difficulties in overcoming indoctrinated ideas of female submissiveness – using the dramatic device of having the roles of queen and serving maid played in turns by the same actress. As the following survey will show, many plays still centre around this kind of debate.

Tom McGrath made *The Hard Man* (1977) the title of a controversial play on the life of Jimmy Boyle, one of Scotland's most notorious criminals. The same author's *Buchanan* (1993), on the career of the famous Scottish boxing champion, also displays the traditional male attitude. Ken Buchanan stands for the honest Scottish lad of modest origin who has learned to channel his 'aggro' and has eventually made it to the very top. His only 'weakness' is that he is too good and naïve to use the same unfair tricks as his opponents in international competitions. After Buchanan's decisive defeat the new world champion scoffs at him: 'The Scotsman fights clean and expects the world to fight clean back. Them's old-fashioned attitudes. [. . .] Doing without dirt is a luxury.'9 Tom McGrath used documentary material for this play, but he also clearly confirms old stereotypes, including the jovial demeanour of the macho man. In the play's opening scene, for example, Buchanan introduces himself to the audience with a sexist joke in the style of a variety-stage compère: 'I was walking down there the other morn and I see six women coming towards me, their bellies like yon . . . Hey, I said, I hope they are not mine . . .'10

The glorification of the pugnacious, womanising Scot with a heart of gold is part of the working-class tradition, but has now come increasingly under attack. In 1974 Bill Bryden had already qualified the 'hardman' stereotype in *Benny Lynch*, a play about another famous Scottish boxing champion, one who enjoyed the fame of a folk hero for some time before dying in alcoholism and squalor. Significantly, Bryden's iconoclasm includes a scene showing the boxer's shabby behaviour towards a woman who is pregnant by him. The 'hardman' generally reduces woman to a commodity or at best grants her the role of a pliable companion; but the popular myth glosses over the cruelty, both mental and physical, which often enough goes with this attitude. Understandably, it is women writers who tend to object to this myth most vehemently. In her short play *The Letter Box* (1989)11 Ann Marie Di Mambro shows the plight of a woman who has been brutally treated and thrown out of her house by her husband and tries to explain her situation to her young daughter through the front-door letter box. This gripping dramatic monologue steers clear of sentimentality and also avoids overt condemnation: the woman's main concern is for her daughter's comfort and welfare and the cohesion of the family. Di Mambro's indignation is all the more powerful for being expressed indirectly: it also includes the indifference of society, in this case of the victim's neighbours, towards such acts of violence.

Rona Munro's *Bold Girls* (1990) is about different reactions to women suffering as a result of male savagery. Set against the background of the Belfast Troubles, the play views politically motivated violence as an extension of domestic violence, with women as the ultimate victims. Firmly rooted social conventions seem to make it impossible for women to change their situation, though the final scene does evoke solidarity among women as their only hope for a better future. Though this risks sounding a trite conclusion, borrowed from the storehouse of international feminist tenets, Munro handles the characters and the plot skilfully enough to give it a convincing ring. The theme of female solidarity reappears in *The Maiden Stone* (1995), which Munro sets in her native north-east Scotland in the early nineteenth century. The two formidable main characters are a pregnant, peremptory English actress who is trekking the desolate hills on foot with her small troupe, and a local wet-nurse, an archetypal mother-figure deeply rooted in folk traditions and guided by the practical wisdom of the people. In spite of their widely different cultural backgrounds, the two women become natural partners in moments of crisis because they share the same elementary womanly experiences linked with sexuality and childbirth. The play rejects the traditional demonisation of carnal desire in woman – given expression in the legend of the maiden stone (a vulgarisation of the Greek Daphne and Apollo legend) – and instead celebrates female sexuality as a powerful force. The plot of *The Maiden Stone* may not always be plausible, but the play has a wonderful theatrical intensity and poetic quality. Its rich north-eastern Doric is informed by the tradition of oral literature and serves as an apt frame for the inclusion of elements of fantasy and fable.

'There's naethin the deil's mair feart o' than a woman',[12] says Bidie, the wet-nurse, in Munro's play. But what about the Church? Sue Glover in *Sacred Hearts* (1994) evokes the ambiguous traditional Christian view of woman as either a madonna or a prostitute, or both, and suggests that churchmen, state officials and the man in the street are equally afraid of female sexuality – in which submissiveness and a menacing tendency to overthrow man's supremacy are sinisterly combined. Sue Glover's award-winning play *Bondagers* (1991) has been interpreted primarily as a protest against the exploitation of the female labour force by the mid-nineteenth-century agricultural system in the Lowlands, but in this context it also stresses the importance for women of analysing their situation and recognising their power. Propagated by popular tradition from the fairy tale and folk-song to the modern soap-opera, the cliché which promises an escape from male-induced miseries by an auspicious marriage is attacked as a cynical kind of wishful thinking. The traditional Scottish song 'woo'd and married and a'' runs through the play like a leitmotif, but the bride soon finds she is 'no so well off' in her new situation. One of the bondagers, Liza, functions as a spokeswoman for the author and challenges conventional aims of womanhood – getting married and bearing children – which, she claims, stabilise the system of male dominance and exploitation, if only by furnishing new labour for the master. The plot, however, ends in defeat, as it must for reasons of historical plausibility, but Liza's individual bravery plainly functions as a beacon to late-twentieth-century audiences.

The clash between the traditional view of what constitutes fulfilment in a woman's life and the modern woman's wish for self-determination is a pertinent theme in Sharman Macdonald's plays about the mother/daughter relationship. Her works of the 1980s, *When I Was a Girl I Used to Scream and Shout* (1984) and *When We Were Women* (1988), in particular, discuss the motives that govern the decision for or against marriage, childbearing or abortion. Occasional lapses into didacticism are not too obtrusive, thanks to the animated scenes of a girl's sexual awakening in the earlier play and the melodramatic plot of the latter.

But the new image of woman is not exclusively drawn by female writers. In *Julie Allardyce* (1993), Duncan McLean offers a multi-faceted portrait of a heroine who does a man's job on an offshore oil rig. The play raises questions about the nature of love and marriage, and how possibilities for a woman to become financially independent affect her private life. Julie is a high-tech-robot operator and holds one of the most responsible and best-paid jobs of her crew. But she is not a relentless careerist, and refuses to accept the brutal, inhuman standards of the male world of modern business, where profit even ranks higher than human lives. Eventually she returns to the family farm, worked by her brother. This neo-pastoral retreat is largely an illusion, for McLean has shown the fundamental changes the country areas of Scotland have undergone in the wake of the oil boom[13] and Britain's entry into the European Community, thus divesting rural Scotland of its romantic aura.

A discussion of the new gender roles and sexual politics, particularly in the age of Aids, would be incomplete without reference to lesbianism and male homosexuality. Particularly in small Scottish rural communities these are still largely taboo subjects. Rona Munro has dealt with lesbianism so discreetly in her short play *Saturday at the Commodore* that according to one reviewer 'the majority of the audience missed the point'.[14] Sharman Macdonald is somewhat more outspoken in *When I Was a Girl I Used to Scream and Shout*, which was rejected by the Traverse Theatre and performed by the Bush Theatre in London. Within Scotland it is the gay writer John Binnie who has given lesbianism the most overt treatment to date in *Accustomed to Her Face* (1993), which won a Fringe First Award.[15]

American dramatists have repeatedly written about Aids, often in connection with male homosexuality, and Tony Kushner's *Angels in America* has already gained the status of a modern classic. By comparison, attempts by Scottish playwrights to come to terms with these matters still occasionally resemble pieces of self-conscious theatrical journalism. In Ian Brown's *Wasted Reality* (1992) Jock, a secondary school headmaster, explains:

> Where I come from, where I come from geographically, but also socially, morally, emotionally, homosexuality was and is a sin. It's something that doesn't happen except in the plains of Sodom, not literally, but it's weakness, a perversion, something to laugh at, to pillory, to object to, to deny.[16]

Jock's gay son has died of Aids, and the play describes the difficulty the middle-class family has in accepting Michael's homosexuality and the death caused by the modern 'scourge'. Brown makes his characters role-bearers of contrasting stereotyped attitudes, but is obviously on the side of understanding and forgiveness. In Ann Marie di Mambro's short play *Brothers of Thunder* (1994) the moral debate is between a liberal Catholic priest and a homosexual student. Di Mambro gives this complex matter an admirably subtle and balanced consideration in which religious doctrine, tolerant rationality and personal vulnerability merge and glib solutions are avoided. Di Mambro's play was presented at the Traverse as part of a double bill, together with Joan MacLeod's *The Hope Slide*, which drowns the topic of Aids in religious fanaticism.

The major concern of John Binnie is to give voice to people marginalised in what he terms 'a very macho culture', and especially to pull down the barriers that isolate homosexuals in our society. Binnie has written close to twenty plays, primarily for his own troupe, Clyde Unity Theatre, but has now gained international recognition. After *Mom, Dad, There's Something I've Got to Tell You* (1986) he achieved his first major success in 1987 with *Killing Me Softly*, a play about the intense friendship between a gay man and a 'straight' woman. When the man discovers that he is HIV positive, his own brother turns against him and refuses to share a room with 'a bloody leper'. But Lil, his friend, stands by him and promises him that they will 'fight the world together'.[17] Her example eventually wins him back the affection of his family, and Lil is also held up to the audience as a model to be followed. *Killing Me Softly* toured in 1990 as part of an HIV-awareness programme, and a workshop and discussion were held after each performance to enhance the play's educational effect. This formula has become a hallmark of Binnie's plays. Having grown up in a small-town working-class community, and being gay, Binnie 'had never seen anyone on the stage with whom he could directly identify'.[18] Like the Glasgow Unity Theatre of the 1940s and 7:84 Scottish People's Theatre, Clyde Unity Theatre tries to reach an audience that would not normally go to the theatre, and seeks for modes of expression that suit the popular taste. Simple plots and clearly stated problems, uncommonly frequent insertions of popular music, and workshops and post-performance discussions are part of Binnie's strategy.

A *Little Older* (1992) and *Backgreen Belter* (1994) also link the gay/straight friendship motif with the plea for tolerance and mutual understanding. In *A Little Older*, which won the 1992 Independent Theatre Award, a young woman has fractured her skull in a car accident and lost her memory. She is at first unable to move and speak, but her devoted gay friend, who has known her since primary school, helps her remember and eventually leads her out of her stupor. In *Backgreen Belter* (1994) the issue of discrimination is widened to include foreigners as well as homosexuals. A German student spending the summer in a small town in Scotland is taunted with questions of the type, 'Whit did yir da' dae in the war?' But he is eventually accepted and loved by the local girls, among whom is Belter, a teenage rock star from the Glasgow backyards (or backgreens), whose music sets the tone for the first half of the play. A gay friend of theirs dies a violent death when he is discovered holding hands with another boy and chased through the streets by a gang of young roughs. At the funeral the young German steps forward and sings 'Flower of Scotland' as a token of his friendship and an expression of intercultural communication.

In his more recent plays, *Writings on a Frosted Windowpane* (1994), which was written, set and performed in America, and *Love Among the Juveniles* (1995), Binnie has included inter-racial couples in his cast and become less defensive in his attitude. The American play centres around a gay Jewish man, a black woman and their friend, while *Juveniles* puts a gay couple alongside a Scottish girl and her black African boyfriend and features stylised scenes of their love-making. Binnie's plays about individuals at odds with society include adaptations of two Glasgow novels by Margaret Thomson Davis (*Rag Woman, Rich*

Woman, 1991, and *Breadmakers*, 1995), and *Bone* (1995), which was developed in collaboration with the dance artist Rosina Bonsu and is an important step (after some tap-dance sequences in *Juveniles*) towards integrating movement and dance into the production style of Clyde Unity Theatre.

Faith in the stamina of the individual rather than contentment with the social and political situation leads to the relatively optimistic note on which most of the above plays end. One of the long-term effects of Thatcherism reflected in Scottish drama is the loss of a sense of solidarity. The fact that feminist drama urges women to show more solidarity corroborates rather than contradicts this thesis; and a play such as Tony Roper's *The Steamie* (1987) is, according to Alasdair Cameron, 'a warm and affectionate tribute to a community spirit in Glasgow which some remembered and many half-remembered or even imagined had existed',[19] but which is blatantly absent now. Even family bonds seem no longer to guarantee trust and mutual assistance. Chris Hannan illustrates this attitude in *Elizabeth Gordon Quinn* (1990):[20] though the play is set in a Glasgow tenement house in 1915, its psychology is informed by contemporary developments. The protagonist is an imperious woman who 'refuses to learn to be poor'. Her airs and graces, her stubborn individuality, lead her family to the brink of ruin, even if the grotesque consistency with which she maintains them give her a certain tragi-comical grandeur. Elizabeth's daughter Maura believes in the solidarity of the working classes and successfully organises a rent strike that saves them from being evicted from their flat, but when her brother comes home to seek a hideout after deserting from the army she is the first to undermine this kind of solidarity and informs the police.

The myth of the solidarity of the working classes receives a shattering blow in *The Cut* (1993) by Mike Cullen, an ex-miner turned playwright. Cullen's tightly plotted play about a power struggle among workers in a colliery depicts, in the words of Paul Taylor, 'a moral hell where people, forced to live like animals, come to think like them.'[21] Cullen sees in his play an allegory of 'the demise of socialism',[22] for the old socialist us/them opposition proves a fiction in the light of the ruthless selfishness of the workers, which mirrors the worst behaviour of their bosses. The brutality governing modern labour had already been illustrated by Duncan McLean's expressionist play *Julie Allardyce*. *The Cut* is an attempt at reviving the form of classical tragedy and relies on naturalistic conventions. These and other examples show that contemporary Scottish drama shares with its English counterpart a tendency – emphasised by recent scholarship[23] – to reactivate former genres, motifs and theatrical conventions, drawing its variety partly from this source.

Cullen's more recent play *The Collection* (1995)[24] is similarly disillusioning in its evocation of the selfish and brutal methods used in professional life, though it widens the focus to include the aspect of sexual harassment. Even more overtly than David Mamet in *Oleanna,* Cullen acknowledges that there may well be some justification for the charge that all men are potential rapists and that the most benevolent of male actions may be tinted by base instincts. There is more than a passing reference to the Scottish Jekyll/Hyde syndrome in *The Collection,* as there is in Rona Munro's black comedy *Your Turn to Clean the Stairs* (1992). The distinction between the serious and the comic has often been blurred in Scottish drama, and when David Kane describes the theme of his hilarious farce *Dumbstruck* (1994) as 'vice . . . rewarded and virtue ignored',[25] he is commenting indirectly on one of the diseases of modern society. With regard to the selfishness and depravity of its characters, the new Scottish city comedy – especially Chris Hannan's *The Evil Doers* (1991) – has been likened to the comedies of Ben Jonson and Thomas Middleton.[26]

One of the best Scottish plays of the 'new wave' is Simon Donald's *The Life of Stuff* (1992), which offers a frighteningly nihilistic, brutal view of contemporary city life. Significantly, it also presents its grim material as comedy, using all kinds of humour from slapstick, farce and the grotesquely absurd to parody, caricature and verbal irony. All the characters in this play are social drop-outs who try to overcome their boredom and sense of insignificance by taking refuge in a dream world of drugs, sex, and alcohol. But the 'stuff' their dreams are made of leads them even deeper into misery: health abuse, mutilation, murder and other kinds of drug-related crime are central issues. The industrial belt of Scotland has been suffering heavy unemployment for many years and in its wake has been facing serious drug problems and a high crime-rate. Donald's dramatic treatment of this subject – the play is set in a disco and its characters use a demotic urban Scots – allows his audience, and especially the younger Scots in it, to identify with the problem as one of their own, though the play's appeal is not limited to one particular area or social group, as was shown by its greatly acclaimed Berlin performance in German translation. *The Life of Stuff* also offers a further example of debunking of the hardman myth. The drug dealer Dobie wishes to rise to the top of his circle, surrounding himself with potential killers and 'dolls', but merely hides fear and an inferiority complex behind a mask of bravado.

Trainspotting (1994) moves through the highs and lows of the lives of heroin addicts, dwelling both on their reckless hedonism and their inevitable wasting away in mind and body. The play is even more sparklingly funny, and more depressing, than *The Life of Stuff*. Moments of elation alternate with others of relentless pain and squalor, and the corrosive wit of the dispossessed accompanies their bleak progression towards Aids and other drug-related illnesses. *Trainspotting* evokes sordid life in the neglected districts of the Leith docks, offering a view of Edinburgh disturbingly different from the capital's official tourist-oriented image.

Among Scottish dramatists who write for the English stage rather than the Scottish is Sharman Macdonald. Her escape from a male-dominated Scottish culture shows in the almost complete absence of adult men in her plays. A woman's bossy mother, whose callousness hides emotional crippling, generally replaces the 'hardman' of the traditional pattern, and if men appear as suitors, as in *When We Were Women* (1988) and *Shades* (1992), they are cowards who leave the women more miserable than before. *The Winter Guest* (1995), one of Sharman Macdonald's best achievements to date, sums up several of her major concerns. It is an almost plotless piece and in some ways has 'more in common with a Nordic tone-poem or a pre-Impressionist painting than with drama as it is usually defined', as Benedict Nightingale has put it.[27] The play's wasteland scenery – an ice-covered beach and deserted promenade dominated by a large grey sky in a bleak west-of-Scotland seaside town – sets the tone for four overlapping strands of action, revolving around the themes of loneliness, past happiness, present possibilities and the dread of an unknown future. The winter guest of the title is, of course, death, whose presence can be felt throughout the play and who strikes invisibly at the end. Macdonald does not, however, allow the elegiac mood to drift off into sentimentality but discovers elements of comedy in even the most serious circumstances. In the opening scene, for instance, two old women clad in black are waiting for a bus to take them to a funeral. During their incessant bickering they reveal that they are neither relatives nor friends of the deceased, but that they have made hearse-chasing their pastime, scanning the newspaper obituaries each day for exciting burials. Since none of their neighbours cares about them any more, they have made friends with the dead.

> *Chloe*: (*She nods at the paper*) Anyone we know?
> *Lily*: No. No I don't think so. Not yet.[28]

That death can be the basis for a life of greater awareness and intensity is also shown in the strand of action that centres on a widow and her mother, trying to come to terms with each other and eventually discovering a mutual yearning for love and understanding behind all their nagging and seeming coldness. In the two remaining strands, the theme of death is subtly balanced against that of awakening love and sexuality and the disquieting surmise of what this may entail. *Borders of Paradise*, Macdonald's second 1995 play, centres on adolescent angst. Disintegrating families, violence, racism, the uncertainties of the job market, environmental pollution and other curses of contemporary life render the transition towards adulthood particularly hazardous. *Paradise* is set in England, but Scottish youth faces the same problems, aggravated by the greater poverty of the country, as the final scenes of Binnie's *Backgreen Belter* illustrate.

Yet even if there is no reason for exaltation, neither Macdonald nor Binnie, nor, in fact, the majority of the new Scottish dramatists, see the future as a lost cause. In *Borders of Paradise* the central metaphor is surfing, with the risks and also the joy it represents, while Binnie turns to 'hi-energy' music to express the state of mind of Scottish youth in the 1990s. Both metaphors also sum up aptly the nature of Scottish drama on the threshold of maturity. There is an encouraging, pervasive sense of challenge and high energy, and a commitment to the crucial problems Scottish society faces at the approach of the new millennium, even if the overall aesthetic quality of the plays is still somewhat uneven. On the other hand, the number of dramatists who do succeed at this level is steadily increasing. Scottish drama will have to be taken more seriously by international directors and audiences.

NOTES

1. Quoted by Alan Bold, *Modern Scottish Literature* (London: Longman, 1983), p.278.
2. Cf. Herbert Grabes, 'The Subtle Art of Variation: The New Aesthetic', to be published in Herbert Christ (ed.), *Fremde Texte verstehen: Festschrift für Lothar Bredella* (1996).
3. Michael Coveney, *The Citz: 21 Years of the Glasgow Citizens Theatre* (London: Nick Hern Books, 1991), p.4.
4. See Mark Fisher's detailed description of *Sabotage* in *Theatre Scotland* 5 (1993), pp.24–34 and the same critic's comment in *Chapman* 73 (1993), pp.106–7.
5. Author's afterword to *Julie Allardyce* in *Made in Scotland: An Anthology of New Scottish Plays*, selected and introduced by Ian Brown and Mark Fisher (London: Methuen, 1995), p.237.
6. Benedict Nightingale, 'Paired off for a night of big chills', in *The Times*, 16 March 1995, p.30.
7. II.iv (London: Nick Hern Books, 1995), p.62.
8. See also my discussion of *Bondagers* in 'Looking for a Centre: Contemporary Scottish Drama and Theatre' in Bernhard Reitz (ed.), *Centres and Margins, Contemporary Drama in English*, 2 (Trier: Wissenschaftlicher Verlag), pp.67–81; 73–5.
9. *Buchanan*, Round Fifteen, quoted from the draft version published in *Theatre Scotland* 5 (1993), p.55.
10. Round One, p.41.
11. In *Scot-Free: New Scottish Plays*, selected and introduced by Alasdair Cameron (London: Nick Hern Books, 1990), pp.99–104.

12. *The Maiden Stone* (London: Nick Hern Books, 1995), p.36.

13. Other dramatic works that refer to Scotland's North Sea oil include John McGrath's *The Cheviot, the Stag and the Black, Black Oil* (1973), where the issue is presented as part of a pattern of capitalist exploitation of Scotland, and Tom Gallacher's *Sea Change* (1976), where an oil-drilling platform serves as the set for a re-working of Shakespeare's *Tempest*.

14. See the introduction to *Scot-Free*, p.xvii. The play is on pp.193–200.

15. See my discussion of this play in 'Looking for a Centre', pp.78–9, and the shrewd analysis by Joyce McMillan in 'Just not cricket', *Scotland on Sunday*, 27 February 1994.

16. I.iii, quoted from the author's typescript.

17. Quotations are from the author's typescript (scenes 19 and 23).

18. Anna-Maria Goossens, 'His plays evolve – with message', *Daily Hampshire Gazette* (Northampton, Mass.), 3 May 1994.

19. Introduction to *Scot-Free*, p.xv.

20. *Elizabeth Gordon Quinn* in *Scot-Free*, pp.105–46; p.140.

21. 'Coal Comfort', in *The Independent*, 22 January 1994, p.52. The playscript is included in *Made in Scotland*, pp.1–54.

22. Author's postcript, *Made in Scotland*, p.55.

23. Peter Paul Schnierer, *Rekonventionalisierung im englischen Drama 1980–1990* (Tübingen: Niemeyer, 1994).

24. *Theatre Scotland* 13 (1995), pp.31–44.

25. *Theatre Scotland* 9 (1994), p.32. The playscript is in the same issue, pp.33–46.

26. In a *Times* review of Chris Hannan's *The Evil Doers*, quoted in the backcover text of *The Evil Doers and The Baby* (London: Nick Hern Books, 1991).

27. In his review of the London production of the play, *The Times*, 16 March 1995, p.30.

28. *Plays 1* (London: Faber & Faber, 1995), p.177.

Eleven

Loose Canons:
Identifying a Women's Tradition in Playwriting

Audrey Bain

A recent critical study of British and Irish women playwrights has recognised the lack of attention devoted to the contribution of women to theatre in the standard British works.[1] Michelene Wandor and Marilyn Frye[2] have characterised the traditional, patriarchally sanctioned position of women in theatre as, respectively, understudy and stagehand, observations echoed by groups working towards the creation of women's history in Scotland:

> The experience of women in Scotland, very different from that of men, has been a well-kept secret. This experience must be described and analysed until through time it becomes part of the dominant myth and ensures that our children do not have to reform the women's movement year after wearisome year.[3]

Yet recent developments in the study of women authors in Scotland are giving momentum to the interest in women's writing for the theatre, as Carol Anderson has commented:

> There is a strong case for arguing that there is a women's tradition in our literature, not entirely separate from writing by men, but with its own qualities, and unduly neglected. This tradition should be highlighted and considered in its own right, as well as integrated into the more general view of our traditions.[4]

Indeed 1970 is a good point to begin investigating the emergence of a women's tradition in playwriting. Three writers of consequence – Ena Lamont Stewart, A. J. Stewart and Joan Ure – came to prominence during this time, and were involved in the formation of the Scottish

Society of Playwrights in 1973, though all of them had been writing for the stage for some considerable time. Ena Lamont Stewart had experienced great success with *Starched Aprons* (1945) and *Men Should Weep* (1947), produced by Glasgow Unity Theatre, but there were no professional productions of further plays from Stewart after the late 1950s. Following international acclaim with *The Man from Thermopylae* (1959) and a clutch of other successful stage and radio plays and television adaptations, A. J. Stewart was similarly deprived of an outlet for her work throughout the 1960s. Joan Ure, after a personal struggle to realise her ambition to write for the stage, had been one of the 'house dramatists' of the amateur Art Theatre Group of Glasgow (later Glasgow University Arts Theatre Club) during the 1960s. All three of these considerable talents achieved a greater measure of recognition in the 1970s and 1980s when their plays were published and revived in professional productions, reminding new audiences that women playwrights remained active.

During the 1970s Scottish Arts Council bursaries for playwrights, artistic directors receptive to new indigenous writing and the heady scent of devolution in the air, amongst other factors, resulted in an outpouring of talent and a crop of great plays which came to symbolise a 'Golden Age' of Scottish theatre. Though there was a great range of work taking place, it is for the major popular successes of the period such as *The Sash* (1973) and *The Slab Boys* (1978) which the 1970s are most remembered. Whilst being classics in their own right, the easily assimilable aspects of working-class life portrayed in these plays contributed to a certain notion of 'the Scottish play', one which many critics maintain has dogged new Scottish writing ever since. Joyce McMillan has speculated that in addition to the economic pressures dissuading artistic directors from commissioning new work in the 1980s, a certain orthodoxy in taste created by the great male-dominated plays of the 1970s was preventing women playwrights from receiving commissions at the major theatres.[5] Whilst it may be true that Scottish women were hampered by such attitudes, the 1980s did see the tentatively developing women's tradition in drama gaining greater confidence.

The appearance in the early 1980s of the talented Sue Glover led to talk of a school of women playwrights: Donald MacKenzie's prediction that the emergence of women playwrights would be one of the most exciting developments in Scottish theatre in the 1980s was less far-fetched than it might have seemed.[6] Certainly, the decade produced women playwrights of great distinction, including Liz Lochhead, Rona Munro, Catherine Lucy Czerkawska, Marcella Evaristi, Anne Downie and Sharman MacDonald. The late 1980s and 1990s have seen these writers mature and consolidate their reputations (though Evaristi and

Czerkawska have increasingly moved into radio rather than stage drama), and new talents such as Ann Marie Di Mambro and Lara Jane Bunting emerge.

Joyce McMillan's concern at the restrictions placed on women playwrights by a notional male 'canon' has a degree of validity. Though some felt relegated to the fringes at various points in their careers, many turned this situation to good effect by creating their own theatre companies, excelling in areas which once seemed marginal to traditional or 'legitimate' theatre but have now broadened our conception of what theatre can do. Formal experimentation has distinguished the contribution of women to Scottish theatre. Revue has been used to magnificent effect by Liz Lochhead, Marcella Evaristi, Rona Munro and Fiona Knowles (The MsFits), and Morag Fullerton. Lochhead and Jackie Kay are among those playwrights whose work as poets has led them to explore the relationship between verse and drama in a number of creative ways, such as in dramatised readings of their collections and specially devised work. Others, such as Aileen Ritchie of Glasgow's Clyde Unity Theatre Company, attempt to seize control of the creative process, avoiding playing roles demeaning to women, and the 'meat-rack of auditions'.[7] The recent formation by Gerda Stevenson of the all-woman company Stellar Quines is a promising new development in this area.

Scottish women playwrights have resisted and challenged the 'canon' by the retelling of history from a female point of view, both through an examination of the lives of historical figures and a revision of traditionally male domains such as the workplace drama. Ena Lamont Stewart's *Business in Edinburgh* (which received a dramatised reading at Glasgow Citizens in 1970, and an amateur production in 1980) documents the experiences of Sarah Hazlitt, coerced into divorcing her husband (the writer William Hazlitt) in order that he may marry a younger woman. Stewart's sensitive handling of Sarah's passage from the relatively secure position of wife of 'a man of genius' to the social pariah of a 'discarded' woman makes compelling drama. Particularly impressive is the writer's analysis of the experiential diversity of women of different classes. Stewart has Sarah speak up for all the silent women of history when she declares: 'the wives of great men are of no account: we seldom read of *them*. Well the world has never taken much account of women. Someday it may have to.'[8]

Later work in this category includes Liz Lochhead's *Blood and Ice* (1982), centring on the experiences of Mary Shelley, and Lara Jane Bunting's *Love But Her* (1993) which disentangles the life of Jean Armour from the Burns myth. Sue Glover's *The Straw Chair* (1988) and *Bondagers* (1991) are outstanding examples of the merit of these subjects for women playwrights. Adaptations too, such as those by Anne Downie of the work of Jessie Kesson (*The White Bird Passes*, 1986) and the autobiography of Betsy Whyte (*Yellow on the Broom*, 1989) are a valuable addition to the body of work dealing with women's lives.

The centrality of the unspoken histories of women to female playwrights in Scotland has led to the use of various discourses to uncover and articulate areas of women's experience occluded by patriarchal society. Dreaming, neurosis, and the creation of a work of art provide keys to the formation of meaning in Liz Lochhead's *Blood and Ice* (1982). Folkloric elements are also used extensively by a number of Scottish women dramatists to deconstruct both historically determined views of women, and the 'eternal feminine': this is a feature of such plays as Sue Glover's *The Seal Wife (1980)* and *Bondagers* (1990), Rona Munro's *The Maiden Stone* (1995), *Fugue* (1983) and *Piper's Cave* (1985). Taking the idea of competing discourses even further, Munro splits the character of Kay in *Fugue* and even has a character, Helen, who represents the landscape in *Piper's Cave*. The use of two actresses to portray Kay illustrates the forces battling for control of Kay's own psyche as she is menaced by an unknown female entity.

Like Munro and Lochhead, Ena Lamont Stewart, though radically different in technique, examines the category of 'woman' as a societal role, challenging the prevalent orthodoxy which views the domestic sphere as a depoliticised space. Employing the genre of domestic drama, derided as lightweight by its association with couthy 'kitchen comedy' in the pre-war era, Ena Lamont Stewart's *Men Should Weep* demonstrates the significance of the home both as the site of women's concealed, unpaid labour, and as the point of intersection between public and private discourses. Written in the 1940s and revised in the 1970s, the play explores the unresolved tensions at the heart of the Scottish working-class family. Giles Havergal's exciting new production of *Men Should Weep* for 7:84 Theatre Company in 1982 resuscitated the radical core of this classic social realist text by developing it in an epic manner, and Stewart at last received some long-overdue recognition. The fashionable view of many critics that plays written in the realistic mode are ultimately limited by collusion with the dominant ideology was thus confronted by the fact that a play rich in ideas and telling pertinent truths can grow beyond its original formal restrictions.

Stewart's pioneering work has enabled other women playwrights to interrogate the competing claims of public and private discourses in the domestic arena: Ann Marie Di Mambro's *The Letter Box* (1989) is a sensitive evocation of a mother's conflicting loyalties to herself, her daughter, and to a public ideology of self-sufficiency and propriety in the face of domestic violence. By distancing the play from the actual physical abuse of Martha by her husband, and instead concentrating on its results, Di Mambro silences the aggressor and allows his victim to take centre stage, a technique which avoids both sensationalism and melodrama. The mother's attempt to cope with the situation is presented as ambivalent rather than heroic (the martyrdom of women who 'keep up appearances' is often applauded in domestic melodrama), and there is a tragic irony in her urging of her daughter not to speak out, a demand itself supported by psychologically violent threats that she will be taken from her parents by the social services. Di Mambro's insistence that we view domestic violence as a social and not merely private problem is seen in the behaviour of the uncomprehending lovers who think the battered woman is simply drunk: the man leads his girlfriend 'protectively' away.

The work of Lara Jane Bunting provides an illustration of how the work of female playwrights in Scotland is simultaneously part of an emergent women's tradition, and of the development of Scottish drama as a whole. Writing in a period of great change for the industrial West of Scotland, when mines and factories were being closed and the towns, villages and people who depended on them were being forced to question their identities, Bunting confronts a reality devoid of the certainties of the traditional workplace drama. When the miner father in *My Piece of Foreign Sky* (1992) is stripped of his occupational role he suffers a profound spiritual crisis, no longer sure of who he is. His wife in turn loses the small freedom which she had enjoyed when he was at work, the absence of which is a threat to their marriage. Bunting deals sensitively, too, with the political dimensions of desire and imagination and their constriction by circumstance. *My Piece of Foreign Sky* asserts the spiritual importance of a sense of belonging. Yet whilst grief is expressed at the devaluing of community by capital, Bunting's work does not shirk from an engagement with the dangers of the small-town mentality, criticised in her first full-length play, *Vodka and Daisies* (1988).

The work of many Scottish women playwrights is marked by an interest in social responsibility, in particular how women can best manage the competing demands of individual desire and obligation to others in their roles as wives, mothers and daughters. Julie Davidson has written that the traditional position of Scottish women has been to 'hold the head of impoverished manhood at the cost of holding their own outside the home.'[9] In the recent past, the absence of any real social opportunities for women to exercise their talents often meant martyrdom on the altar of marriage, so that the family was seen as woman's greatest achievement. Playwrights from Ena Lamont Stewart to Marcella Evaristi have criticised maternal sacrifice as oppressive and fruitless. Maggie's self-abnegation in Stewart's *Men Should Weep* is exchanged for the ruthless pragmatism necessary to preserve her family, with the result that it is she, rather than her husband, who must be recognised as head of the household. The put-upon middle-class mother in Stewart's poignant *After Tomorrow* (*c.* 1956) discovers that her strength has been a factor in the emotional immaturity of her family. By accommodating their weaknesses she has shielded them from a knowledge of their own self-absorption. Marcella Evaristi's *Commedia* (1982/3) adds the traditional expectations of the Scots-Italian mother to the story of a woman's struggle for self-assertion. The rights of the widowed mother to live a life of her own, and to be a sexual being despite the disapproval of her family, are expressed in a play which is distinguished by a rich vein of humour.

The plays of Joan Ure deal imaginatively with women's rights and wrongs. A bold 'revision' of arguably *the* canonical text, *Something in it for Ophelia* (1979) presents the 'heroine', Hannah, distressed by a performance of *Hamlet* at the Assembly Hall:

> when the lights went up and I looked around it was as if all the men were Hamlet. They were clapping and clapping too. I got very frightened then. I had to remind myself of a few things. My own father's name . . . my brother's name . . . I kept saying all the names of boys and men I knew, so that I wouldn't be turning my head and seeing everyone clapping and clapping because they were seeing themselves as Hamlet.[10]

In a manner that anticipates Hélène Cixous' famous remark that going to the theatre was like witnessing her own funeral,[11] Hannah associates Ophelia's madness and death with an article she has read in *The Scotsman* reporting high suicide rates in young women, something which the men appear to applaud. After forcing the unwitting Martin to admit that as a man he may be responsible for the suicides of young women, she leaves him bereft by declaring that she was merely rehearsing an argument with him with which she intends to impress her colleagues from the bank. Ure's deft use of irony allows the articulation of male and female perspectives. As Ophelia is exploited by Hamlet and her father, the sensitive Martin is victimised by the materialistic Hannah. He is oppressed by the image of the masculine hero – 'You look at me as if I am riding a white and gold horse, and lo I am riding a white and gold horse!' – and by his mother's 'bloodsucking' love.[12] Ure's work has a refreshingly humanist outlook. Her inimitable lightness of touch and her creation of redoubtable heroines, who, like Fiona in the marvellously titled *Take Your Old Rib Back, Then* (1979), relentlessly research the human predicament with no heed to the casualties along the way, deserve much greater attention than they have yet received.

Rona Munro's *Piper's Cave* (1985) explores the conflicting demands of social responsibility and self-preservation. The heroine, Jo, has built up her physique after suffering a violent assault by a stranger, but after confronting her own violent feelings towards another potential attacker, she offers him help on her terms. The man's inability to receive Jo's help leaves her with no choice but to save herself. A mature and satisfying play, *Piper's Cave* demonstrates Munro's determination to find a means of preserving a traditionally feminine quality (one which is socially productive) without compromising a woman's rights as an individual (in this instance threatened by male sexual aggression). Jo's uncertainty about her body image and sexual orientation epitomises the conflicts and dilemmas facing contemporary women, and suggest the possibility of reframing gender to the benefit of society as a whole.

Women playwrights show a strong belief in the political power of theatre. Rona Munro's declaration – if we all have anything to say to each other that's one place to be saying it . . . and changing things'[13] – echoes the hopes of feminist scholars for the developing women's tradition, as Lynda Hart writes:

> As a form, the drama is more public and social than the other literary arts. The woman playwright's voice reaches a community of spectators in a public place that has historically been regarded as a highly subversive, politicized environment. The theatre is the space most removed from the confines of domesticity, thus the woman who ventures to be heard in this space takes a greater risk than the woman poet or novelist, but it may also offer her greater potential for effecting social change.[14]

It is to be hoped that women will continue taking the risks involved in writing for the stage, validating the early efforts of playwrights such as Ena Lamont Stewart and Joan Ure, and creating a space of their own in the spotlight.

The work of women dramatists can be considered an emergent tradition in Scottish playwriting, but it is one which enters into a dialogue with Scottish drama as a whole, informing and gaining strength from it. The notion of a 'canon' in Scotland is, as we have seen, a problematic one, since a continuous tradition of indigenous playwriting is still a relatively recent phenomenon. Now that women playwrights are gaining a foothold, the very non-specificity of the 'canon' may be a positive factor, allowing them recognition in mainstream theatre rather than defining their work negatively in relation to a more dominant tradition. At present, though certain concepts of the Scottish play derived from the 1970s renaissance may persist, the only firm criterion for canonicity in Scotland appears to be success. However set one's idea of 'a Scottish play' may become, the public is fickle, easily dazzled by talent and originality. Thus it was that Sue Glover's *Bondagers* sneaked up on the 'trendy city centre axis of Tramway and Traverse', 'eschew[ed] the orthodoxies of Glaswegian and over-ripe Lallans' and astounded us with its brilliance.[15] A play by a woman, about women and starring women is now part of the 'canon' – loosely speaking!

NOTES

1. Trevor R. Griffiths and Margaret Llewellyn-Jones (eds), *British and Irish Women Dramatists Since 1958: A Critical Handbook* (Buckingham and Philadelphia: Open University Press, 1993).
2. Michelene Wandor, *Carry On Understudies: Theatre and Sexual Politics* (London: Routledge and Kegan Paul, 1986); Marilyn Frye, *The Politics of Reality: Essays in Feminist Theory* (Freedom, California: Crossing Press, 1983).
3. Leslie Hills, 'Why Engender?', *Chapman* 76 (Spring 1994), p.49.
4. Carol Anderson, 'Listening to the Women Talk' in Gavin Wallace and Randall Stevenson (eds), *The Scottish Novel Since the Seventies* (Edinburgh: Edinburgh University Press, 1993), p.170.
5. Joyce McMillan, 'Women Playwrights in Scottish Theatre', *Chapman* 43–4 (Spring 1986), pp.72–73.
6. *Scottish Theatre News*, May 1980, p.4.
7. Aileen Ritchie used the expression 'meat-rack of auditions' in a talk given to Continuing Education students at the University of Glasgow in February 1992.
8. Ena Lamont Stewart, *Business in Edinburgh*, unpublished playscript in the Mitchell Library, Glasgow, SD 822 914 STE 3/BUS II 68–9.
9. Julie Davidson, 'Time of political reckoning for the modern Ma Broon', *The Scotsman*, 19 February 1979.
10. Joan Ure, *Something in it for Ophelia*, in *Five Short Plays* (Glasgow, Scottish Society of Playwrights, 1979), p.42.
11. See, for example, 'Soleil Protégé', Interview with Hélène Cixous by John McGroarty at the Traverse Theatre, May 1993, edited and reproduced in *Theatre Scotland*, 2, 7 (Autumn 1993), p.25.
12. *Something in it for Ophelia*, p.47.
13. Rona Munro, 'Community Drama', *Chapman* 43–4, (Spring 1986), p.83.
14. Lynda Hart, 'Introduction: Performing Feminism', in Hart (ed.), *Making a Spectacle: Feminist Essays on Contemporary Women's Theatre* (Ann Arbor: University of Michigan Press, 1989), p.2.
15. Catherine Lockerbie, 'Land Lover', *Theatre Scotland*, 6, (Summer 1993) p.30.

Part III

POLITICS AND PRACTICES

Twelve

From Cheviots to Silver Darlings

John McGrath interviewed by Olga Taxidou

OT: What position in the broader context of your work does the whole 7:84 venture occupy, and how did your interests develop towards it?

JMcG: The 7:84 venture is very central to the work I've done. I began with a commitment to theatre and with a deep involvement in popular forms of theatre and entertainment. Then I spent the first ten years after I left university trying to come to terms with how to reach a popular audience through television and through writing big movies, but my commitment was still to theatre – to the deeper areas of human life and culture theatre is able to operate in, but which film and television, because they're more cosmopolitan, don't seem really to be able to deal with in quite the same depth. They usually have a more surface appeal, not often dealing with the central issues of societies in such an intimate way.

I don't like theatre very much – I mean going to the theatre. I usually find it very irritating. I'm not over-impressed by the standards of the West End, or the nationalised or heavily subsidised theatres in England. The kind of theatre I wanted to do was one that would have a direct connection with its audience, and for ten years various attempts were made. I was involved in Centre 42 before Arnold Wesker got involved and screwed it up – it wasn't his idea, incidentally. The original idea was to find a building, either in Liverpool or Manchester, in a working-class area, in which we could make the kind of theatre that Joan Littlewood was making in the East End, and with the same kind of popular appeal. But we hoped to *get* a popular audience in, as opposed to what Joan was doing at that time, which was popular theatre without a popular audience. Subsequently, it did come, but at that time it was very frustrating for her and the company. We thought we'd stand more chance in the North where people do go to the theatre, and where they do get involved. So in 1963 or so I was involved in that, with a very interesting bunch of people.

OT: And it was part of a general movement as well?

JMcG: It was the start of a general movement, away from mainstream theatre. That was 1963: since 1961 or 1962 I'd been doing touring theatre with Mike Horowitz's 'New Departures Roadshow', a wonderful outfit. Then in 1968 I went to Paris to take part in the *événements* – to throw *pavés* at the CRS – and became more aware of the possibilities of popular action, mass action in Western Europe. So partly – not entirely – from that, I began to think that there must be a way to get through to this popular audience, and to carry a kind of involvement with that audience through a longer relationship. Then I went back to Liverpool, to the Everyman Theatre, and began to write plays for the new director, Alan Dosser. The first of these were bunches of short plays of local interest: where everything took off was when I decided to do a kind of rock concert which told a story. It was called *Soft or a Girl*, which was an ironical phrase my father used: 'Are you soft or a girl?', meaning are you silly or are you . . .

OT: Silly.

JMcG: We used that critically. The scenes in between the rock songs grew longer and the characters grew stronger and more interesting, but it was still basically a rock concert. There was a band up above the action and they sang songs which commented on the story or took it forward, and so on. It wasn't a posh sort of theatre. You could go in and get a pint as opposed to a bottle of fizzy beer: it was a very approachable, homely sort of place. There was a good feel about it: it didn't feel threatening in any way. After *Soft or a Girl* we got this huge audience and we kept on doing very exciting work there. I did thirteen shows of one kind or another in those three years from 1969 to the end of 1972, including *Fish in the Sea*, which I think is probably the best of them.

Alan Dosser and I shared great respect and love for Joan Littlewood, and we were all fascinated by Brecht – by the theories, but more by the practice; more by seeing Eckehardt Schall doing *Arturo Ui* than by reading the *Messingkauf Dialogues*, which are, I mean . . .

OT: Demonstrating the intellect.

JMcG: Which is not to say that I despised theory, or Brecht's theory. Brecht's theories were very, very interesting, but when you're trying to create you need a certain arrogance, and I felt I knew better what was going to work for me in the theatre from watching a good performance of Brecht than from reading the theories. In terms of theory, I was much more excited by Piscator than by Brecht. What Piscator was saying and his accounts of productions were very exciting because they were breaking down theatre conventions. Brecht was trying to build a new set of conventions of his own and I was much more interested in the openness of Piscator and the way he used new media to present stories of the issues. Brecht was an old Stalinist.

OT: No.

JMcG: Yes he was. Even though he had a lot more intelligence than old Stalinists tend to have, my basic quarrel with Brecht was that he became mystical about the power of science and the truth of science, and in the light of relativity and a lot of other scientific developments, I found this a senseless, almost nineteenth-century idea. One plus one equals two, therefore Stalin rules Russia – very dubious. I also found a lot of Brecht's personal politics a little bit dicey. But it was healthy dialogue, and he had an enormous influence on the way were thinking in Liverpool.

I wanted to carry on working in Liverpool, but it was becoming more and more difficult and I wanted to reach what you might call a more national audience. It seemed to me very important that there is such a thing as a working class, and that it has organisations, structures of solidarity, and allegiances with bits of other classes, and it seemed not only politically but theatrically very interesting to try to do work that would give some kind of voice to the whole of that class, or that movement as it existed in the early seventies. That's where 7:84 sprang from; not, originally, as 7:84 (England) but just 7:84 Theatre Company. Our first show, *Trees in the Wind*, I wrote in 1971 and directed for the Edinburgh Fringe, then we toured it to Cumbernauld, Aberdeen, Stirling and other venues in Scotland, including a couple in Glasgow. What we found, hardly surprisingly, was that Scottish popular audiences have a totally different set of traditions of popular entertainment – they have a different language, not only theatrical and verbal, but political and social. They have different customs and traditions. Of course we were aware of this, but not as aware as we should have been in terms of the contact in the theatre. For example, we did the John Arden/Margaretta D'Arcy play *The Ballygombeen Bequest*, set in the West of Ireland: this was tremendously successful, but it was not making the right kind of contact with Scottish audiences. We were speaking a different language – on all kinds of levels – and I thought that it was a bit imperialist, in the sense that here we were, parachuting in from London and trying to say to Scottish audiences 'be involved in this, this is part of you' and actually what they were saying to us was 'it's all very good and we like it and it's entertaining, but it's *not* part of us'.

Richard Eyre helped provide a new direction. The Upper Clyde Shipbuilders (UCS) yard had been occupied in 1971, and Richard

Eyre, who was working at the Royal Lyceum, suggested I might write about Glasgow being cleared in the same way that the Highlands had been cleared. I didn't write that, but it was the beginning of the idea that became *The Cheviot, the Stag and the Black, Black Oil*. I had been involved in the Highlands and Glasgow for a long time, since I met Elizabeth MacLennan in 1958, and I'd also spent a huge part of the sixties working in Sutherland and finding out what had gone on up there, so I knew the Highland audience very well. We had several Scots in the London-based company, and in 1973 we split the company in two: one touring England and Wales, one touring Scotland. The other people we got together in Scotland were all connected intimately to the Highlands and the Western Isles. So we did feel we knew and were close to the audiences, and that we could speak a language which was much denser, more allusive, and able to carry a lot more without being sentimental. We tried to voice a whole undertone of feeling and memory, of continuing awareness of historical events, and to put this in a form of entertainment that we thought people would be very familiar with. Happily, as it turned out, they were!

OT: Scotland is sometimes supposed to lack a theatrical tradition, because of its religion, or other historical accidents. But that is only if you refer to a specic type of bourgeois theatre. There are performative cultural forms that rely on notions of shared history, identity and collectivity. What were the forms in the Scottish tradition that you found particularly open or fruitful for your theatre here?

JMcG: There are several Scottish traditions. When it came to working with Highland audiences and making Highland shows, the music was obviously important, especially as it was being repopularised in the folk revival. Hamish Henderson and several others had also made available again a lot of songs which had just been sung in little corners, showing a whole tradition of music from the past was still alive; one strand in a wider, surviving tradition. This kind of music helped evoke an incredibly strong emotional reaction in the audience: they may or may not have known the melody, or the words – though of course many did – but they certainly knew what the feeling was and what it was about. Round about that time, there was also the beginning of the instrumental development of Scottish folk, Highland and Lowland, which went on into bands like *The Whistlebinkies* and *Silly Wizzard* who took basic folk-songs and turned them into modern music which was nevertheless still very sensitive to the feelings of the original.

The idea that people in Scotland simply stayed at home every night and said their prayers is ludicrous. In the Highlands people entertained themselves and each other with all kinds of music and stories – with their communal spirit, whisky included; with talking about what was going on. There were informal ceilidh evenings, and when we began to do the *Cheviot* there still were more formal concert parties going round from village to village.

The ceilidh was a form of popular entertainment. It didn't exist as theatre in any sense: it wasn't a narrative form. So I suppose what we did was to take the ceilidh form and use its potential to tell a story. We also did it to break down the whole naturalist thing. It could be used to involve and invoke larger ideas than the naturalist convention seems to be able to take on board, and to speak directly to the audience. But of course it was only one strand of the many that went to make up and keep alive the popular tradition.

I was interested in the people in the audience, where they were, where they worked, where they lived; in giving them a good entertaining experience first, an experience which broadened their vision of where they were, who they were, where they came from and where they were going; and an experience which raised questions about *why*? Perhaps this was what made us seem, to the Arts Council and others, threatening and political and terrible – because we dared to ask why this situation had come about, how things had come about historically and where they were going to. I wanted to raise the level of entertainment. Maybe it sounds arrogant, but it was done with quite a lot of modesty. The whole point of the way we structured the shows – the height of the stage that we took with us, the relationship between the actors and the audience – was that we began where the audience began and that the people who were involved were people who were very familiar with where the audience was coming from. We all were: we had acquired certain skills, and were using these skills to say – or help celebrate, or whatever – things that were there in the audience and in us. We weren't leading the audience by the nose to revolution, which is the image that I think some of the people who haven't seen the plays seem to have of us.

OT: There was a kind of left cultural project in the seventies that worked from the top down, a kind of avant-garde, in the literal sense of leading something. I can't see how you can altogether avoid that, especially if you're making theatre . . .

JMcG: I never believed in the Trotskyist 'General Staff' Theory of Revolution, nor were we 'avant-garde'.

OT: If you don't want to use the term 'avant-garde', you could use one of Antonio Gramsci's, like 'organic intellectual', with more of a sense of give and take.

JMcG: That's more like it. Gramsci was very important in a very early stage of our work. The first Gramsci translations were by Hamish

Henderson – of the letters from prison – though they weren't published at the time. But there were articles appearing slowly in the late sixties and early seventies, the first in Bob Tait's magazine *Scottish International.* I'd never been at all attracted, or committed, to any kind of Stalinist or Trotskyist orthodoxy. Because I'd been born in a religious family, and brought up in a fairly strict religion, when it came to these authoritarian rituals and disciplines, I refused. When the Trots appeared with similar, slightly more hysterical ideas of being powerful leaders of these poor, benighted people, again I felt 'No'. I'd done church. I was not now going to be an altar-boy for Lenin. But when Gramsci came along, I suddenly recognised a voice that was speaking a language I understood, and there was a certain amount of shared experience and concern. Only he was rather better at exploring it and saying it.

OT: Gramsci speaks very clearly about the relationship between central and peripheral cultures, and about the possibilities inherent in a national popular tradition, and he's one of the first left theorists to talk about a national culture critically. For historical and political reasons, there's almost a tradition of Gramscian studies in Scotland, more than in the rest of Britain. In a recent article, for example, and at a time in Europe when horrible things are riding on a nationalist tide, Tom Nairn made a case for what has been called 'Civic Nationalism' – a civic construction of nationhood, as opposed to an ethnic nationalism.

JMcG: I think it is tragically necessary to make that distinction. Nationalism should be a very fruitful movement, a fruitful communal emotion: it should be good that people take pride in the values of their nation and their culture, whatever that is. It should be something that gives people confidence, and takes *away* the kind of fears and phobias that lead to that terrible ethnic-cleansing rubbish that's been going on and is a sort of dreadful identification of nationalism with a form of fascism. It's very sad that you even have to make that distinction. Tom Nairn is quite right.

My feeling about it is that nationalism in the context of Europe is becoming increasingly important, particularly in terms of small nations, for a number of reasons. One is that the larger, more powerful nations are clearly going to dominate absolutely: Europe will take on the identity of Germany and France just as surely as European currency will take on the identity of the French and German currency. This multinational identity, however it is constructed, will tend to create another language, a meta-language on top of local languages and cultures; a culture above, or maybe alongside, local ones. Just as entertainment values from the United States have tended to erode British entertainment culture, so this meta-culture will tend to erode the sense of identity and the specifics of local and national cultures.

I think it would be a mistake to allow that to happen. You've got two models: you've got the United States model where there is the 'great melting-pot' theory – that when you become American you become American and nothing else. And then the second model: a version of the Canadian model, where you let everybody have their own identities: they're Canadian and Greek, they're Canadian and Chinese, they're Canadian and Jewish, whatever. I think that leads to a much more interesting society, and I would hope that in European terms there will always be two languages and two cultures. There will be a common culture which is European culture, European language, European currency, whatever, and existing alongside that will be national and local cultures.

OT: It's going to be English. It's still going to be the language of one nation.

JMcG: Okay, and existing alongside that will be national and local cultures.

OT: Isn't it slightly utopian to see national and local cultures just existing alongside hegemonic ones? A culture becomes dominant in the first place because it oppresses another: the model of happy co-existence and creative interaction is a very interesting one, but history has shown us so far that that simply doesn't happen.

JMcG: Well, it may be utopian. Or you could describe it as a political programme, which is a different way of looking at it: a political programme which has been embraced by large numbers of people involved in European politics. Members of the European parliament – representative of actual people, who elected them to go there – are very conscious of the need for cultural diversity and plurality not just to be encouraged, but actively worked for, to be financed. And that *is* going on.

OT: I understand that, but there's also another way of reading that relationship between dominant and peripheral cultures: through the idea of hybridity, seeing two cultures not as distinct, separate and 'pure', but each in a hybrid relation to the other. There is really no such thing as a pure English person, or a pure Scot, if you like, and it's the areas of overlap that are interesting culturally.

JMcG: I think there's a danger of emphasising the interest of the overlap and ignoring the basic existence of what's there in the first place. Given the demographic changes going on all over the world, and particularly all over Europe, local and national cultures are not going to be embalmed or purified. I'm talking about them being able to develop in their own ways – in the light of demographic, historical and other changes taking place in their area – without being *forced* to develop as the United States cinema has forced the Czech cinema to develop, i.e. to become a tributary of Hollywood.

Local cultures have got to change, and always will change, but for reasons people can't explain very often. One factor will be the huge movement of people around the world. The Highlands are no longer the Highlands of twenty-five years ago. When we started touring they were very, very different. But traditions are alive and have got to stay alive. What I'm saying is that unless there is a political programme to help them to stay alive, and to change in their own way, then either they will be obliterated completely, or forced to change in the direction of the dominant culture, or some other culture, probably the United States's.

This is where you come back to the question of nationalism which you asked me in the first place. The one way to help or allow those cultures to develop is to break up the larger monolithic structures like the United Kingdom, if you like, into federal structures: but in the case of Scotland – which is and always has been a nation – there's no reason for that federation to be dominated by, or even related to the United Kingdom, or England. Scotland should be able to relate to England as part of a federated Europe, but still have the means to control certain areas of its own life and development: that is the kind of nationalism that I'm interested in.

OT: Or nationhood, let's say.

JMcG: Or nationhood, but the idea that there would be some sort of ethnic barrier set up around Scotland is totally ridiculous. I'm English for Christ's sake, or Irish.

OT: Yeah, you'll get kicked out.

JMcG: Well, I'd get kicked out back to England. Then because they don't allow political asylum there anymore, I'd get sent back to Ireland, where my granny came from.

OT: And I'd have to go back to Greece, then Asia Minor . . .

JMcG: You would.

OT: Anyway, what you're talking about is a more dynamic, dialectical construction of nationhood, not a monolithic thing that excludes a group of people.

JMcG: No. Nor ethnicity, which is an appalling concept, an absolutely disgusting concept.

OT: Do you still see a place for your construct of nationhood within alternative theatre?

JMcG: Well, theatre is one way culture gets around. It's also a way of making audiences and cultures cohere, of making people feel part of something. When we played the Highland shows in Glasgow, we got a huge audience of Highlanders: there was a reaffirmation of some sense of identity.

OT: You could play them in Canada too, couldn't you?

JMcG: We did. We played several of the shows in Cape Breton, and in Toronto two or three times. We performed *There is a Happy Land* in Cape Breton for a conference on alternative and community theatre, and they found to their amazement they couldn't get in, because word had gone round that this was Scots Gaelic and the theatre was full because the locals had all come early. We had to do another show, then we were dragged across the island to do more bits of it, ending up in a place called Iona, on Barra Strait – a beautiful place on the edge of Bras d'Or Lake – where we did the whole thing again for an audience half of whom were joining in the Gaelic songs, even though their families had left Sutherland because of the Clearances; some even before then.

OT: Left-wing thinking suggests that for something to be truly cosmopolitan it has to be local. You can't really start the other way round, because then your work belongs nowhere.

JMcG: I believe that in film, as well as theatre, very much. Because you hope to show a film all over the world, and because people have different expectations, there's an element of film-making that demands an almost mythological structure, and that there has to be somebody for the audience to identify with. You have to have a basic structure and narrative devices so that people all over the world can see what's going on, so that the movie is approachable by a lot of people from different cultures. But those people love the movie more if the way you tell it – the specifics of the characters and their lives – is very, very accurate, and local, and works locally. I know from writing movies that if you try to write one archetypally, with pure Joseph-Campbell myth-making, then it doesn't connect on any sort of particularly good level with an audience, but it does if you do something specific. My favourite example is Milos Forman and Ivan Passer's movies in Czechoslovakia in 1967/8: *Peter and Paula* and *Blonde in Love*, which are very simple stories. Bill Forsyth is another example in his early films: it's the kind of film-making where anybody can see what the story's about because it's generally approachable, but it's terrifically locked into its own place, and specific. That works, I believe, even in movies. In the theatre, still more so.

OT: A debate has been going on over the last few years about the need for a Scottish National Theatre. Is there a need for one? If so, of what kind, and how would it work?

JMcG: One of the more interesting things the Scottish Arts Council came up with was the idea that we don't need a Scottish National Theatre because all the companies already in place, and touring all over Scotland, *are* the Scottish National Theatre. It was probably an excuse for not funding another institution or taking money away from those in existence to give to another institution: there is an absolutely practical question, at a time when budgets are being reduced, about how a Scottish National Theatre is going to be funded. Is it going to take funding away from the Royal Lyceum, the Citizens', Wildcat or the smaller companies? Is it going to stop other new companies from getting grants to do new work? Is it going to be a kind of glorification of the established Scots theatre pundits, whoever they may think they are?

When you talk about a national theatre, the image that immediately comes to mind is of that great concrete bunker on the South Bank of the Thames, or of some enormous Comédie Française – which is there only to have stones thrown at it and is a completely useless object. Both of them are useless objects. They're there for national glorification, closely connected to the kind of Rattko Mladic school of nationalism. If there's going to be a healthy theatre in Scotland, there should be bases that add up, in all the constituent parts of Scotland, making sense not in terms of local government particularly, but in terms of a cultural programme. The money that would otherwise be going to a new concrete bunker would go to those living institutions, living forms of expression of what's going on in particular areas, contributing to a two-way flow between all the constituent parts and a National Theatre. Individual parts would be responsible for garnering theatrical experience from their own communities; putting it on, helping it, celebrating it and showing it to other people. They would also have a responsibility for bringing in shows from other parts of Scotland, but also from the rest of the world, mixing the local and international – so that there is a theatrical culture which is actually alive and informed and knows what theatre can be.

The country's repertory theatres are obviously under-funded and need to drag in their audiences. So they're certainly not culturally internationalist. The Citizens' Theatre on the other hand has been a prime example of a kind of internationalism that should be alive and well and thriving in all corners of Scotland if there's to be a proper National Theatre. It shouldn't be based in Edinburgh, Glasgow, Stirling or wherever: it should have five, six or seven constituent parts. That's my programme for a National Theatre of Scotland.

You've got to allow for initiative in theatre. The arts establishment has got to learn again what the good old liberal tradition taught in the sixties and early seventies: that you have got to respond to initiatives from creative people and not sit there legislating and handing out prognoses. They must stop doing what they're doing at the moment, which is satisfying bureaucratic egos by prescribing what will happen theatrically. If you prescribe what will happen theatrically it just won't happen because it's got to come from people who are actually going to do it.

OT: In the seventies, in Scottish theatre in particular, there was a clear sense of direction and purpose, and a reliance on a liberal system of funding. Now that system isn't there, would your five, six or seven regional companies – despite their distinctive differences – still be able to create that clear sense of purpose and clear direction?

JMcG: I don't think theatre alone can generate a sense of purpose. The sense of purpose during the seventies was generated by a terrific and generalised sense of purpose about Scotland which led to the referendum in 1979. When the referendum was defeated, or rather out-manoeuvred, there was a terrible sense in Scotland of vacuum, which I experienced very personally. I wrote *Joe's Drum* as a direct response to that vacuum, trying to find a character who would say 'Wake up!' and 'Do something!' Movement and purpose in the theatre has got to be associated with a sense of renewal of the whole scene, of the whole nation: I hope that if there is a successful move towards a Scottish Assembly – if that begins to make sense and have some political direction – then Scottish theatre will recover that terrific sense of purpose.

OT: In a devolved Scotland?

JMcG: Devolved sounds passive. It sounds as if it has *been* devolved. What theatre should do is to refuse the passive mode and make self-government into an active assertion of what it means to be alive in Scotland at this time. It should have a much more meaningful say in what's going on in Scotland. The other thing that began in 1979, of course, apart from the results of losing the devolution vote, was the growth of a sense that Scotland was completely impotent, that it would continue to be castrated by the London Tories.

OT: Some critics have seen in recent Scottish theatre another kind of crisis: a reliance on adaptations rather than original plays. Given that a large part of your work is occupied by adaptation – whether from novels to theatre, or from theatre to the cinema – how do you see the creative processes involved?

JMcG: I don't think there's a crisis. Adaptation is simply a process of creating something new. It is never – or very, very rarely – a process of simply transferring something from one medium to another. You've got to start with the idea that you're going to do something brand new, and that the raw material is going to be provided by somebody else. (I leave aside the question of what I mean by 'raw material'.) In order to do it, you've got to be really enthusiastic about it, but you've also got to bring your own feelings to it, feelings not only for the material itself, but for the form, the shape it's going to take in its new existence. There is a sense in which any writer faced with creating a new work which deals with a whole thematic will find it helpful to refer to other works which have already explored it. Sometimes the relationship is very direct. In *The Silver Darlings* I responded very, very strongly to the narrative, and to the area, the geography, the story, and to the meaning of that story. I wanted to see it as a piece of theatre because I thought people would find that view of the novel interesting and useful, so it was adapted as a piece of theatre in one particular way.

I've now rewritten it as a screenplay, which is a completely different thing – a kind of raid on the novel. If you start with the idea that you're going to make a faithful film transcription of the novel, you find yourself in all kinds of trouble. When you want to say something, and you know someone else has already said it very well, it's almost perverse to go on trying to write it again. In *The Silver Darlings*, for example, it would be stupid to recreate a story about what happened to the people that were cleared to the coast, to live on a cliff edge; or a story about a boy growing up and his relationship with his mother; or to explore what I think is the most crucial relationship in terms of violence, that between mother and son. Neil Gunn's novel, *The Silver Darlings*, does all this very well. I needed to explore how a boy can grow to a kind of wholeness, a maturity, and so be able to see his mother as another person, trying to escape from the psychic conflict within that relationship. However deviously and distantly, these are issues which seem to me to be at the root of an awful lot of the violence and aggression that goes round the world. Okay, I could have started all over again on all that, but there was this book which I'd responded to very strongly.

OT: Political theatre – Brecht's for example – often doesn't rely on new stories but on different ways of telling old ones, just as in Greek Tragedy it's the comment on the myth that's going to matter.

JMcG: That's right: it's your job to make the story relate to the audience that's sitting there watching, to make it work for them, and that's a political activity, I guess. But on the subject of newness, one of the big problems with Scottish theatre is that when a play has been done, even in a small hall in Edinburgh, it is considered undoable by any other theatre in the land. At least for the last thirty years, plays have been commissioned by theatres, done, and because they're identified with that theatre none of the others will consider them. There are obvious exceptions: the *Slab Boys* trilogy and *The Steamie* broke through because they were sentimental, Glasgow-populist, naturalistic and easy to do, and so several theatres did them. But *The Cheviot* wasn't done again in a professional theatre from 1973 to 1993. There is a huge pile, hundreds of very good plays, which are never done again. It's quite extraordinary.

OT: Not only in *The Silver Darlings* but throughout your career your work has always been a creative interaction between theatre, cinema and television, though you could also say that you have distinct careers in each of these areas. How do you see the relationship between theatre and television, which is sometimes seen as a kind of National Theatre itself?

JMcG: I've always, as you say, tried to keep these parts of my creative life separate. The theatre to me is one whole area, one whole world. Television is a different world altogether, a different geography, and cinema is another world still. Having said that, they obviously overlap in places. Doing *Border Warfare* and *John Brown's Body* in the Tramway was made possible financially by my being able to offer them to Channel Four, each in the form of three sixty-minute programmes. Channel Four got them cheaply because they were all set up, ready to shoot, and they were shot very quickly. Because I was writing and directing both versions, there were ways of making it all work. That kind of overlap is largely for financial reasons.

OT: It's not only financial, though, is it? In *A Good Night Out*, you say that one way that you could deal with two hundred years of history in terms of narrative is by means of editing techniques and concepts of montage you used in television. Your latest film, *Long Roads*, is an epic film: I mean 'epic' as in 'epic theatre'. It has these conventions there, in place.

JMcG: I've never been over-analytic about that. I don't think I can be. I think the play that is most interesting from that point of view is *The Wicked Old Man*, produced three years ago in the West Yorkshire Playhouse. We were able to use this space to make statements which positively evoked cinematic images, though we never made the mistake of trying to make a movie, just a show on the stage.

I learned about trying to make movies in the theatre very early on. In the late sixties, I wrote a screenplay based on a book about Winstanley, the leader of the Diggers. Then somebody 'did' Cromwell, so they all said 'Oh well, we've done the English Revolution – why do we need a film about the Diggers?' So there was this nice, literate screenplay with a strong story-line, and I showed it to Sean Kenny the designer, offering to make a theatre version of it, but he said that it would do as I had written it. I thought at the time 'will it work?' It didn't work, because it was a movie and it's just a different thing. So there are overlaps I don't believe in, and some that I do.

OT: Going back to that sense of purpose in the seventies, the kind of 'grand narratives' of class conflict, national identity, ideological questioning which shaped left-wing theatre at that time – at the time of *The Cheviot* – are nowadays said to be in crisis. What is the role of political theatre – and of the whole concept of political engagement – in this new context, if any?

JMcG: This I presume invokes the postmodern abuse of 'grand narratives'?

OT: I did avoid using the term postmodern.

JMcG: Yeah. Well, the postmodern distaste for 'grand narratives' is really a way of denying the existence of easily identifiable historical facts and truths, and a lot of this attack on 'grand narratives' is trying to say that everything exists only on a micro level; that the only real level is the personal, and that the person's ability to live a solipsistic or exclusive life is all that matters. It's a wonderful way of avoiding political involvement of any sort, and allowing a kind of terrible fatalism about the power of government to take over people's lives. I thinks it's dangerous. I think postmodernism on the whole creates a pre-fascist mentality that's growing here and in the United States. It's like the kind of existentialism which Nazi Germany thrived on in the early thirties: the idea that if something had happened then it had happened, and there was nothing else – it was going to happen, it was fully determined, and there it was, it happened! There's a sense in which this idea of 'the end of grand narratives' is telling everybody to give up any idea of intervening in the larger issues of society, and life, and to subscribe instead to Thatcher's theory that 'There's no such thing as society'. It's trying to disempower people, to encourage them to cultivate their gardens and to keep their noses out of things which other people know more about than they do. It goes along with the cult of the expert, and of course if you analyse the whole thing it is actually about the power of multinational corporations to rule the world. That's what it's about.

OT: So it's business as usual as far as you're concerned?

JMcG: No, I don't think that at all.

OT: For the political theatre?

JMcG: In relation to political theatre it can't be business as usual. The whole scenario has changed because of this highly financed and very organised onslaught on personal and political responsibility, and on the idea that a person is part of a society. This has had a profound effect on the generations growing up in the eighties. Maybe in the nineties as well – I'm not sure. Political theatre has to redefine its role as a much more questioning one, and can no longer assume that an audience will respond in the way that it used to respond. It can't assume class solidarity: it can't assume that any of the larger emotions are going to be present in the audience.

OT: So it has to reinvent itself?

JMcG: No, political theatre has got to do what we've always done, in a basic sense, which is to start where the audience is. The audience is now in a very different place from where it was in 1972. You start where the audience is now, and you work from there: you work from there to finding out what is driving that audience, and then you put that in the context of what you know and have learned about society, history and life. That's all. I think political theatre now, particularly in Scotland, and particularly if Scotland has a new lease of life, is probably experiencing its most interesting and exciting challenge. We've learned an awful lot from the onslaughts that have undermined the work that was done in the past, and we've also learned a lot about our own assumptions, ones that were maybe a bit glib. The theatre has a fantastic possibility now to meet that challenge, and I think a lot of great work could come out of it.

Thirteen

Epic Theatre in Scotland

Olga Taxidou

I. BRECHT AND AFTER

Epic theatre has come a long way since Brecht's somewhat schematic formulations in the 1930s.[1] Either in dialogue or in debate with these programmatic formulations, later generations of theatre theorists and practitioners have re-invented or adjusted the term 'epic theatre' to suit both their historical contexts and their means of production. This chapter sets out to explore the applications – or even deconstructions – of the term within the context of contemporary Scottish theatre. In line, however, with Brecht's theoretical and political aspirations, epic theatre is read in this study as that form of theatrical production which is self-reflexive in its conventions, historical in its themes, engaging and critical towards its audience, and interventionist in its relationship with hegemonic cultures.

With the benefit of hindsight, and with more information available to us about theatre history and performance theory, Brecht's epic theatre acquires both a specific theoretical context – that of the project of Modernity – and a historical dimension. In particular, it is possible to consider epic theatre continuing a long line of popular performance traditions in Europe. This fact, however, seems often to have been obscured by Brechtian epic theatre's political immediacy and by its upfront attack on contemporary schools of bourgeois naturalism: both aspects were crucial in trying to establish a language for political drama as an answer to the attempts of fascism to appropriate theatre – and in particular to hijack 'folk art' – for its own ends. Like much of the work of Walter Benjamin (an inspiring commentator on Brecht and epic theatre), Brecht's somewhat 'crude thinking' – as he himself termed it – has to be read in the light, or shadow, of this threat of fascism. Working in this context, Brecht was looking for ways of breaking with tradition, and not of establishing links with it. The potential of popular theatrical modes like the *commedia dell'arte* or medieval theatre therefore remained almost totally ignored in his work: in general, there is a pervasive nervousness when dealing with notions of tradition, whether popular or literary. It is only later, and under the influence of left theorists such as Antonio Gramsci, that tradition and traditional forms come to be viewed as possible sites of critique.

On the other hand, theatre practitioners like Dario Fo[2] in Italy and John McGrath[3] in Scotland look towards popular performance modes as part of a long tradition of irreverence and critique, and as a set of conventions that can help rejuvenate the term 'epic theatre'. Gramscian notions of the dynamic potential of popular tradition, of the role of organic intellectuals,[4] and, most importantly, of the tensions between peripheral and central cultures, inform for each author a type of theatre that at once relies on popular culture and, at the same time, rewrites it as part of a political project. What the *commedia dell'arte* represents for Dario Fo, the medieval theatre (in the most recent productions) and working-class traditions such as music-hall and pantomime represent for McGrath. In both cases what makes the work significantly different from Brecht and his epic theatre is a strong sense of place.

The politics of locale, space and geography seem to be particularly relevant to any theatrical project that claims to be political, especially if, as in the case of Scotland, it is functioning within a culture that exists within a centre-periphery dynamic. More specifically, theatre is three-dimensional and engages in spatial politics more than other art forms. Where an event is taking place, how it conceptualises its relationships with the audience, how it relates to the rest of the city are all factors that help construct the politics of performance. Brecht's epic theatre, admittedly in many cases for reasons beyond his control, remained within the confines of bourgeois theatrical institutions. The post-war popular theatre movement, however, placed great importance on the venue of an event. Whether in factories of Italy or in the town halls of the Scottish Highlands, the locale of popular theatre was just as important as its themes and conventions. Any reading of epic theatre in Scotland over recent years would have to take account of such spatial relationships.

This study proposes to examine carefully significant examples of epic theatre in Scotland in the late 1980s and early 1990s. The productions discussed all propose different versions of epic theatre. *Border Warfare* (1989) and *John Brown's Body* (1990) by John McGrath present notions of epic theatre significantly different from those found in Bill Bryden's

The Ship (1990) and *The Big Picnic* (1994). Another theatrical project which made an impact in Scotland was Peter Brook's *Mahabharata* (1988). Although this has been described as an 'Indian Epic' its use of the term is decidedly non-political and pre-Brechtian. Brook's production will enter this analysis as it helps highlight the tensions between local and hegemonic cultures by proposing a kind of aesthetics that shuns matters of locality and history, supposedly in favour of the global and universal.

II. SPACE AND THEATRICAL CONVENTIONS

Dealing with the difficult historical relationship between England and Scotland, *Border Warfare* was the second performance to be held at the Tramway. The first was Peter Brook's production of the *Mahabharata*. No two productions could be more different in the way they relate to the specific locality of the event and to its audience, in the way they appropriate and re-write traditional and popular theatrical forms, and in the overall cultural ideology they promote. It is interesting to compare briefly these diverse versions of epic theatre as cultural projects and to see how they both, in a sense, re-create the space of the Tramway and in doing so propose very different relationships with local cultures.

The Tramway was Glasgow's old transport museum, which Peter Brook saved from demolition when he chose it as a venue for his *Mahabharata*. A year earlier John McGrath had made a similar attempt to take over the Tramway in order to house 7:84. His endeavours proved fruitless. Where McGrath failed, Peter Brook succeeded and with the *Mahabharata*, the Tramway hosted instead a production which had already achieved critical acclaim on the international festival circuit. It is tempting to speculate how the whole development of the Tramway might have taken a completely different course had it been taken over by John McGrath. As it is, the first two productions held there made two drastically different statements, using the same space, but applying almost opposing notions of the 'traditional' and the 'popular'.

The *Mahabharata* arrived in Glasgow carrying with it all the veneer and the glamour of an international production. It had been successful in Paris and in other parts of Europe and had already been heralded as the 'theatrical event of the eighties'. The *Mahabharata*, however, has more recently evoked a new wave of criticism, mainly within the context of postcolonial theory, which problematises some of its basic thematic and aesthetic assumptions. Through the myth of the Mahabharata, and utilising a combination of theatrical conventions vaguely labelled as 'eastern', Brook sets out to narrate nothing less than the 'poetical history of mankind'. Brook's quest has always been for 'essential' truths and, in this case, what he constructed as Indian 'traditional tales and techniques' offered the perfect theatrical language for these eternal truths to be told. This enterprise – which apparently assumes it can pick and choose theatrical conventions from anywhere in the world, regardless of their history and context, and then proceed to essentialise them – has rightly been read as a form of orientalism and 'othering'. Invariably the cultures borrowed from are ones which have had a colonial relationship with the West, or are economically dependent on it. Brook's notion of what is traditional about the tale of the Mahabharata is in fact a construct; one that first creates the idea of the traditional in the other culture, then proceeds to essentialise it as universal and eternal. In the process it also constructs a type of epic theatre that is 'transcendental' and mythopoeic rather than historical. In other words, Brook's use of epic theatre is pre-Brechtian, a form of the term which remains conservative and coercive, unaffected by Brecht's radical, modernist revisions. Rustom Bharucha's critique of the *Mahabharata* within the context of postcolonialism provides some very useful insights:

> Peter Brook's *Mahabharata* exemplifies one of the most blatant (and accomplished) appropriations of Indian culture in recent years. Very different in tone from the Raj revivals, it nonetheless suggests the bad old days of the British Raj, not in its direct allusions to colonial history – the *Mahabharata*, after all, deals with our 'ancient' past, our 'authentic' record of traditional Hindu culture. For Brook's Vyasa, it is nothing less than 'the poetical history of mankind'. Within such a grandiose span of time, where does the Raj fit? Not thematically or chronologically, I would argue, but through the very enterprise of the work itself: its appropriation and re-ordering of non-western material within an orientalist framework of thought and action, which has been specifically designed for the international market.[5]

When Brook toured with his production one thing he almost always did was to find a 'new' theatrical space. This was usually not a conventional theatre venue, and more often than not it was in an area that was not renowned for its cultural activity. So in Greece he found an abandoned quarry in a working-class area on the outskirts of Athens. In India he had changes made to an existing theatre so it could look 'traditional', and, when the result was 'too traditional', he had it renovated again. This way of using space – which Bharucha calls 'the aesthetics of waste' – is typical of Brook. There is nothing inherently wrong with utilising non-conventional theatre spaces and staging productions in working-class areas. The history of political theatre is also a history of how to use spaces other than the proscenium arch. There is a significant difference, however. Having chosen the space, Brook proceeds to empty it of all sense of history or locality. It becomes one of his 'empty spaces', suitable for hosting universal and essential truths. The production of the *Mahabharata* in the Tramway could have taken place anywhere in the world. The fact that it was in Glasgow was coincidental.

Border Warfare and *John Brown's Body* engage with the space of the Tramway in very different ways. The fact that it was an old transport museum (and previously, repair depot) and the references to the industrialisation of the city that this implied are factors that informed both productions. In fact *Border Warfare*, which traces the history of Scotland and England, and *John Brown's Body*, a play about the making of Scotland's industrial classes, couldn't have found a better venue. All the contradictions created by the establishment of the Tramway as a performance/cultural centre and the heralding of Glasgow as a cultural capital of Europe for 1990 were present in the making of these two productions. Whereas the *Mahabharata* could have taken place anywhere in the world, the Wildcat/McGrath productions could have taken place only in the Tramway. This, however, does not mean that they remain 'provincial' or of limited 'local interest'. The politics of the debate between peripheral and central cultures is something that McGrath has always taken into account. He writes:

> I do not accept the following assumptions: 1. that art is universal, capable of meaning the same to all people; 2. that the more 'universal' it is, the better it is; 3. that the 'audience' for theatre is an idealised white, middle-class, etc., person and that all theatre should be dominated by the tastes and values of such a person; 4. that, therefore, an audience without such an idealised person's values is an inferior audience; and 5. that so-called 'traditional values' of English literature are now anything other than an indirect cultural expression of the dominance over the whole of Britain of the ruling class of the south-east of England.[6]

The Tramway productions seem to be taking this debate further. The Tramway is similar to many cultural centres all over Europe at the moment, where old industrial spaces are gradually emptied of their local identities and turned into 'cosmopolitan', 'neutral' spaces, suitable for comparable cultural events. Together with the rise of International Festivals, these spaces present 'new' and ahistorical ways of relating to locality. The Wildcat/McGrath productions keep these issues in view in their themes and in the conventions that they choose to use. These two large-scale shows dealing with the political and cultural history of Scotland in a sense re-historicise the Tramway itself, and offer a critical use of its space.

McGrath's and Bharucha's statements about aspects of cultural colonialism are strikingly similar. Indeed, the two may be illuminatingly compared in terms of the complex networks of meanings and exchanges that result from a colonial history, and the similar tensions and contradictions that arise between local and hegemonic cultures. Postcolonial criticism over recent years has offered very helpful insights in reading these exchanges. Continuing the work of Gramsci and of Franz Fanon, postcolonial theory has explored new ways of reading the relationship between marginal and dominant cultures. Rather than setting up a simple and non-dialectical opposition between right/wrong, powerless/powerful, it explores the 'in-between' spaces, the spaces of conflict, of emergence between two or more cultures. These 'spaces', which are often described in performance terms, are seen as helping create the possibility of critique. The revised role of tradition in this context is very important. As Homi Bhabha writes:

> Terms of cultural engagement, whether antagonistic or affiliative, are produced performatively . . . The 'right' to signify from the periphery of authorised power and privilege does not depend on the persistence of tradition; it is resourced by the power of tradition to be reinscribed through the conditions of contingency and contradictoriness that attend upon the lives of those who are 'in the minority'. The recognition that tradition bestows is a partial form of identification. In restaging the past it introduces other, incommensurable cultural temporalities into the invention of tradition. This process estranges any immediate access to an originary identity or a 'received' tradition. The borderline engagements of cultural difference may as often be consensual as conflictual; they may confound our definitions of tradition and modernity; realign the customary boundaries between the private and the public, high and low; and challenge normative expectations of development and progress.[7]

Border Warfare occupies such an in-between space. In charting the history of England and Scotland, it also re-invents the notions of tradition, the past and the present. It inhabits one of those consensual/conflictual spaces that triggers a critical and dialectical relationship with tradition and the 'new', history and the present. The opening sequence is characteristic of this. Denying the audience the comforting solace of a 'happy monolingual

and monocultural past', it presents a conflation of past and present in the
form of a corpse, which is wheeled on in a pram:

CORPSE
I was a Pict and slain by a Scot,
An Anglian peasant by an English army,
A Gael by a Gollach,
A Presbyterian tortured by Mary's men,
A Tim shot through the head by an Orangeman,
A Piscy by Cromwell,
A Highlander by Cumberland,
I was a heretic burnt by Knox,
A Comyn stabbed by Bruce,
A Crofter's child with cholera on the boat to Nova Scotia,
I was the flower of Scotland
Broken at the stem,
I was a soldier on the Somme, I was drowned in the Minch,
A young wife with TB in the slums of Paisley:
I was a miner when the roof went,
A witch at the stake,
A still-born child,
A baby with Aids:
Let me now lie in peace.
Put me in earth with decency and thoughtfulness.[8]

This evocative image seems to dwell between a number of locations,
cultures and meanings: life/death, past/present, hope/despair. The
accuracy and the concreteness of historical place names and events
scattered throughout the sequence fails to offer the comfort of familiar
and historically charted territory. In a sense, this misleading familiarity
together with historical shifts – which occur throughout the text –
only serve to further problematise any received notion of cultural or
historical identity. This corpse appears as a kind of historical ghost, as
an emblematic inhabitant of a hybrid in-between space. Indeed, much
of the rest of the performance explores the historical circumstances and
the contradictions that have helped create this creature, and possible
ways of resuscitating it.

  Just as *Border Warfare* examines the borderlines between Scotland
and England, *John Brown's Body* sets out to examine more opaque and
complex relationships. In many ways the two pieces are in dialogue with
each other. Both see history and politics, the local and the international
as interwoven entities. It is a monumental work that traces the 'History of
Scotland's Industrial Classes', as the subtitle suggests. Industrial is indeed

the key term as in its three sections – The Wealth of Nations, Discipline and Flourish, The End of History – the play delineates the development of monopoly capitalism and its evolution into the free-market economy of the multinationals.

This is essentially a play about work. But it does not proceed uncritically to celebrate work or to present an undifferentiated mass of working people. The whole concept of work is presented as a site of various discourses, sometimes merging, sometimes conflicting. So, in this way, work is different for a woman, different for a man, different for a soldier, different for an unemployed person, different for a manual worker, different for an intellectual. The idea of 'freedom' receives the same treatment. The Enlightenment promise of more freedom, coupled with the idea of progress, runs throughout the three sections of the play and forms one of its structural principles. How work, freedom and the pursuit of happiness all interrelate as concepts, and why they help create so much unhappiness and oppression, are some of the questions the play constantly puts before us. In many cases it provides us with an answer, but there are also instances where it stubbornly refuses to do so. For *John Brown's Body* inhabits one of the great dialectics set up by the Enlightenment idea of freedom: the freedom that creates exploitation and oppression also helps create the idea of hope and the belief in change. Aligned with the critique of history established by Michel Foucault, and its referring freely to *fin-de-siècle* nihilist and neo-conservative rhetoric, *John Brown's Body* follows the great ideals of the Enlightenment and the age of reason, and proceeds to question whether they are still valid today. To trace such a journey through the concept of work is exciting and innovative in both ideological and aesthetic terms. It is not, however, new.

The Russian/Soviet Constructivists of the 1920s and 1930s also found in the concept of labour not only a theme for their theatrical projects, but also a form that helped them shape them.[9] They were also one of Brecht's main sources of influence. For the Constructivists, plays were not only going to be about work, but the way labour was structured and organised was also to provide them with a new theatrical language. In this context it does not seem so strange that Meyerhold, despite his fervent radicalism and his commitment to dialectical analysis of theatrical conventions and processes (in ways that foreshadowed Brecht), managed to find inspiration in the capitalist industrial practices introduced by Taylorism. Such practices of fragmenting the labour process led directly to Fordism as a mode of production: in terms of labour relations it only helped to establish further the classic Marxist concept of alienation. Like Lenin before him, Meyerhold nevertheless saw in Taylorism a

capitalist process that he thought could be adapted, appropriated within
a radical project. Through his complex system of bio-mechanics, bodily
movements are broken down, fragmented and repeated, in imitation of
Taylorist work processes.

In their uncritical glorification of labour, the constructivists believed
they had an ally in technology. Indeed, Taylorism together with
technology presented the great hope for the workers of the future.
Their utopian, almost romantically naïve faith in technology was in
line with much modernist thinking that saw technology as emancipatory,
as the force that would finally free people from labour, bridge the gap
between manual and intellectual worker and lead the working class to
happiness. The theatrical designs and directions of Meyerhold, and other
Soviet Constructivists such as Popova and Tairov, all bear witness to this
belief. *John Brown's Body* engages with this tradition in very challenging
ways, both formally and thematically. It neither glorifies nor ignores it,
but chooses to set up a dialogue with it. In an age where labour has
not only lost faith in Fordism and technology as emancipatory forces,
but has 'progressed' to more and more inhuman and alienating modes
of production like post-Fordism[10] and information technologies, the
utopias of constructivism can hardly be accepted uncritically.

The pseudo-constructivist set designed by Pamela Howard comments
on the grandness and the aspirations of that tradition, but maintains a
weariness and a critical distance from it. It is at once a homage and a
critique. It is not bold and shiny with the promise of a better future.
It is more reminiscent of a fun-fair than a factory. In fact it looks tired
and run down, like a constructivism that has lost its conviction. And the
repetitive movements made by the actors throughout the play are exactly
that: tired and repetitive. There is no bold Meyerholdian thrust. *John
Brown's Body* seems to be saying that this kind of labour dehumanises,
it does not liberate.

This dialogue that the play sets up with the whole constructivist
tradition is not always successful and at times the sheer scale
of the design seems to take over. Where *Border Warfare* utilises
medieval performance traditions such as pageant and processional
stages, *John Brown's Body* relies wholly on a performance tradition
that is decidedly avant-garde rather than popular. The dynamism,
the immediacy and historical relevance of the popular tradition seems
to be taken over by the self-consciousness of a modernist one. *Border
Warfare* belongs to the post-war European theatrical tradition that
looks back to the medieval stage not only for inspiration, but also
for political relevancy. In this sense it is like Arianne Mnouchkine's
1789 and Luca Ronconi's *Orlando Furioso*. *John Brown's Body*,

however, does not seem to be as comfortable with its performance conventions.

This kind of unease is taken further in another production that also deals with the industrialisation of Scotland, Bill Bryden's *The Ship*. Also produced in 1990 and staged in a non-conventional theatrical space – the Harland & Wolff Shed – it dealt with the rise and fall of Glasgow's ship-building industry. This is seen as having helped create the identity of the city. The sometimes awkward and uncritical use of contructivism and the problems entailed in transferring an avant-garde technique, or language, that was more or less specific to a particular modernist sensibility seem to become even clearer in this production. We should not forget that constructivism, despite its utopian aspirations, was basically an abstract 'aesthetic' rendition of Taylorism. Within the project of Modernity and with all the aspirations placed on the liberating effects of technology this seemed to be a plausible, even radical, position. Within the context of post-Fordism, the seemingly unreconstructed glamorisation of labour presented in *The Ship* appears ahistorical and uncritical. This was a production where the audience first observed the building and then the launching of a whole ship in almost true dimensions. The labour process seemed to be merely aestheticised rather than understood in any historical or political way.

III. AN HISTORICAL IMAGINATION

This tendency to utilise epic modes of theatrical production while, in a sense, dehistoricising the subject matter tackled is also undertaken by Bryden in *The Big Picnic*. In his writing on Brecht, Walter Benjamin states that epic theatre requires a historical imagination, a way of politicising aesthetics.[11] And this is a crucial aspect of epic theatre which differentiates it from other modes of theatrical production. In *The Big Picnic*, however, this imagination almost seems to go against history. Despite the subject – a group of Glasgow men and their involvement in the First World War – the perspective of the production never properly includes a sense of history. Like many a war movie it tends to read the war as a set of personal journeys of development from innocence to experience: it is personal and psychological in its outlook, appearing more like a study in masculinity than an analysis of the war and its effect on people's lives. This last issue could have been developed further: there are readings of war that draw parallels between the personal and the political around the axis of masculinity such as Frank McGuinness's *Observe the Sons of Ulster Marching Towards the Somme*. Bryden's play, however, is more reminiscent of plays such as Irvine Shaw's *Bury the Dead* in its expressionist tones and its fascination with personal character. Such qualities might work well in a quasi-naturalist or even quasi-expressionist piece, but not as a form of epic theatre. And indeed Bryden's imagination seems to be more visual than historical:

> The first idea of the whole thing was an image of the maypole or the market cross which, in every village and town, became a war memorial. There's not a famous war memorial in Govan but I thought it would be good if that was the target of the play – that the play finished with us creating that memory.[12]

Brecht's view of war as 'a continuation of business by other means, making the human virtues fatal even to those who exercise them' [13] seems a far cry from the slightly sentimentalised and even 'patriotic' view proposed here. Brecht's version of epic theatre also seems irrelevant in this context. This production would have been more at home behind a proscenium arch rather than in the vast space of the Harland & Wolff Shed.

Epic theatre has a long and glorious history. Either in its Brechtian ramifications or in its later more popular renditions it distinguishes a type of theatre that is purposefully non-naturalist and interventionist. The whole rubric of conventions and styles available to this kind of theatre becomes particularly relevant at times when notions of historicity and political engagement are mocked. The richness, the adaptability – as these examples show – and the potential of the epic tradition become even more pertinent for smaller cultures that are resisting appropriation and homogenisation. Throughout the 1980s and early 1990s, during years of European Cultural capitals, International Festivals, and strong government policies that promote the commodification of culture, the epic tradition in Scotland provided the basis for some of the most exciting theatre in Britain.

NOTES

1. See John Willet (ed. and trans.), *Brecht on Theatre*, 1957 (London: Methuen, 1993). For a recent study on the impact of Brechtian notions of theatre on twentieth-century performance, see Peter Thomson & Glendyr Sacks, *The Cambridge Companion to Brecht* (Cambridge: Cambridge University Press, 1994).
2. See Dario Fo, trans. Joe Farrell, *Tricks of the Trade* (London: Methuen, 1991).
3. See John McGrath, *A Good Night Out* (London: Methuen, 1981).
4. In Gramscian terms, intellectuals are those people who give a social group 'homogeneity and awareness of its own function'. Organic intellectuals, as opposed to traditional intellectuals, are those who emerge from out of the group itself, rather than impose themselves from outside it; usually from above. An example of an organic intellectual is a worker who becomes a political activist, while an example of a traditional intellectual would be the figure of the priest, that is, those figures who represent and help reproduce the cultural hegemony of a specific class. For a more detailed analysis see Antonio Gramsci, trans.

William Boelhower, *Selections from Cultural Writings* (London: Lawrence and Wishart, 1985).

5. Rustom Bharucha, *Theatre and the World* (London: Routledge, 1993), p.68.
6. See *A Good Night Out*, pp.3–4.
7. Homi Bhabha, *The Location of Culture* (London: Routledge, 1994), p.2.
8. John McGrath, *Border Warfare*, unpublished typescript (1989), p.4.
9. See Lars Kleberg, *Theatre as Action* (London: Macmillan, 1993).
10. See Werner Bonefeld & John Holloway (eds), *Post-Fordism and Social Form* (London: Pluto, 1991).
11. Walter Benjamin, trans. Anna Bostock, *Understanding Brecht* (London: Verso, 1992).
12. Bill Bryden interview, 'War Memorial', in *Theatre Scotland*, 3, 10, (1994), p.28.
13. See *Brecht on Theatre*, pp.219–20.

Fourteen

Scottish Drama and the Popular Tradition

Femi Folorunso

> Ella: I thought Scotsmen were supposed to be strong and silent.
> Dennis: Aye, well, that's the A side of the cliché. On the other
> side's me, a Scottish joke invented by Harry Lauder and the
> English, all stuck up with tufts of Tartan, wi'a wee bent stick
> and a clacking tongue, standing forever in front of the footlights
> by the banks of Loch Lomond, singing 'Oh, you'll tak the high
> road and I'll tak the low road . . .' Mind you, Ella, you've got a
> grand wee foghorn of a voice yersell . . .
>
> Stanley Eveling, *Mister*[1]

When Stanley Eveling decided to write a play incorporating the myth of
the hard man, arguably the most extensively quarried among those myths
that continue to animate Scottish writing, it seemed perfectly natural
that he had to recall, as the above lines suggest, the role and impact
of the music hall in fastening that myth to popular imagination.[2]

It is not only Eveling who has been attracted to the music hall in this
way. In nearly every modern Scottish play, recognisable bits and pieces
of music-hall aesthetics can be found. Where they are not explicit – for
example in techniques of performance – they are implicit in dramatic
consciousness. From the irreverent jokes and scabrous humour in Liz
Lochhead's *Mary Queen of Scots Got Her Head Chopped Off*, to the
witticism and songs in almost every play John McGrath wrote for 7:84
Scotland – even Peter Arnott's sombre revaluation of national themes,
symbols and characters – the impact of the music hall is everywhere
discernible.

Eveling's recalling of music hall, moreover, is more than an intertextual
experiment. From Dennis's speech, it is clear that the playwright is
criticising 'the structure of attitude and reference' (to borrow Edward

Said's words[3]) which has been built around the Scottish personality, much of it ingeniously disseminated through popular artistic forms. As it happens, probably no other cultural form has exerted as much imaginative influence on the popular mind in Scotland as the music hall and its confederates. So it is not surprising that there is no other cultural phenomenon – the Kailyard school of writings apart – that is being more rigorously reassessed in contemporary discussion. Regrettably, much of the resulting reassessment (which constraints of space will not allow us to examine here[4]) has been unfavourable. But whatever the prejudice against the music hall, a number of facts about it are worth noting. Firstly, there is David Hutchison's important observation that a native (Scottish) tradition of theatrical entertainment developed around this colourful form.[5] Secondly, it needs to be pointed out that from its introduction until the late 1940s, it was the most popular and richest form of entertainment in Scotland: it is also important to note that it has declined more slowly in Scotland than anywhere else in the United Kingdom. Thirdly and more importantly, the music hall occupied the middle space in a direct line from seventeenth-century popular entertainment to contemporary drama in Scotland.

It is against the norm, whether in literary criticism or cultural debate, to suggest that there *is* a tradition of drama in Scotland. Yet, if one looks critically at Scottish drama as a whole and not the works of lauded playwrights or theatre companies, its continuity and commitment cannot be doubted. The drama has consistently sought to be at the social centre, continuing to do so throughout the twentieth century – the works of the coal-miner playwright, Joe Corrie in the late 1920s, or more recently, John McGrath's, inevitably generating controversy because of the immediacy of their politics.[6] Remaining close to the issues of daily life, Scottish drama aims to capture and reconstruct experience and reality from and for the popular consciousness.

As well as McGrath's work, there have been many examples of this since the 1920s. Whether through social realism, workers' theatre movements, working-class drama, plays dealing with historical subjects/themes, or even the innocuous drama of entertainment of amateur drama groups, what is encountered is a drama which keeps close to the popular spirit. The techniques of popular performance, its conventions and goals are freely adopted, adapted and utilised. The dominant attitude in this drama is to speak about the nation, to reinforce the sense of values of community, either directly through plays that draw on national symbols or motifs, or indirectly through plays that question them and chart new courses altogether. Consequently, what we have is an art which deliberately dramatises, addresses or legitimates national feelings. Thus, when its aesthetic structure, language and the author's and the audience's attitude to the drama are scrutinised, what emerges is a tradition of popular drama, a drama driven as much by a desire to please as by socio-national complexities. The historical emergence of this drama and its growth are to be seen both in terms of its roots in the traditional performing arts of the Scottish people and its more direct, immediate antecedent in the agents of the transformation of these performing arts.

Contrary to what always seems to be the first impression, popular drama is neither inferior nor subordinate to what is often assumed to be the aesthetic drama. Indeed, critical examination of the inner movements and the crucial points of theatre history will reveal that the division between the two is often tenuous and unnecessary. As David Mayer points out, 'those plays which have received the respectful attention of critics are those which reveal the material of popular culture worked and controlled by an artist'.[7] There is truth in the basic premise, which is that popular materials have a greater vitality and flexibility, which cannot be ignored or passed over even by supposedly 'serious' dramatists. This of course makes light of the complex relationship between the popular and the aesthetic drama and may give the impression that popular drama simply serves as raw material for aesthetic drama. Bearing in mind that all drama, popular drama included, is united by certain shared characteristics such as mimesis, presence of participants, a recognisable structure and an audience, we will need to set out the differences between popular and non-popular aesthetics more clearly, even if only in the form of a rough guide.

In critical terms, popular drama is antithetical to the aesthetic drama in two important areas. Firstly, the dramatic experience it tries to generate in its audience is not private, but rather communal and consensual. At the heart of this is the subordination of aesthetic considerations to 'the exigencies of public rite, whether political, religious, or social'.[8] It is often the case, therefore, that popular drama more readily responds, formally and thematically, to pressures external to drama. Secondly, the audience of popular drama is on the whole not a select one, for the drama is always playing to a large and general audience – an entire nation, rather than a select group or class.

A census of plays written in Scotland between 1900 and 1980 would perhaps reveal that about 85 per cent are based on Scottish history, mythologies or issues within the Scottish social environment.[9] Of the remaining 15 per cent 10 would probably be those plays aiming at 'high art' while the last 5 per cent will occupy the grey area between the two. We can ignore for the moment what attitude or position a particular play or playwright takes to a particular myth, or what interpretation is given to a particular aspect of history. What is important is the selection itself, the decision to write about Scottish history and issues, although of course the idea of dramatists using history and myths as source material is not new. In popular drama, however, the idea has a depth which goes beyond a mere search for heroic models. Popular dramatists have an intuitive attitude towards history and myth as sources of creative power. As repositories of values and the ethos which informs a particular society's definition of itself, myth and history embody their own meanings and attributes. Since they are usually well known and easily recognised by everybody within that society, they can be a powerful means of communication between the creative artist and his audience; a means of establishing the kind of collectivity Michael Bristol identifies when he remarks that 'by favouring a certain style of representation and a particular etiquette of reception, the institutional setting of a performance informs and focuses the meaning of a dramatic text and facilitates the dissemination of that meaning through the collective activity of the audience'.[10]

Randall Stevenson, in surveying Scottish drama from the 1950s to the late 1980s, not only acknowledges the high number of plays dealing with history, but goes on to defend such plays with his comment that 'contemporary political feelings made recreations on stage of certain parts of our history significant gestures in themselves.'[11] This comment is in effect suggesting that there can be a direct political response to events which goes further than the material of the plays themselves. What needs to be carefully examined, then, is the nature of such events and what the response to them is intended to achieve. If, on one hand, the producers and the audience of this drama are united in the interpretations given to these external events, and if on the other, the agreed interpretations reveal the nature, fears and sentiments of their own society, then we need no further proof that here is a popular drama.

Writing about her experience as an actress and co-founder in what was the original 7:84 Scotland Theatre Company, Elizabeth MacLennan draws attention to how the self-defining cultural practice in the country was a dominant factor in shaping the orientation and direction of the company. She remarks that:

We had become increasingly aware of the cultural and political differences between the situation in the south-east and the north of England and Wales, and between their preoccupations and those of people in Scotland. Scotland is distinguished by its socialist, egalitarian tradition, its Labour history, its cultural cohesion and energetic participation in argument and contemporary issues. Within its separate educational, legal and religious systems is a strong but not chauvinist sense of cultural identity. Culture and politics are not dirty words. We felt our plays there should reflect and celebrate these differences in language, music, political identification and carry on the arguments. This would need a different but related company.[12]

Other Scottish playwrights have made similar comments. Peter Arnott and Liz Lochhead, for example, indicate that their works often respond to the kind of interplay of culture and history MacLennan identifies.[13] This culture-as-social-practice MacLennan discusses obviously defines the experience of audiences as much as artists.

The difference between Scotland and other parts of the UK is neither as superficial – not just a matter of stepping over a border – nor as tenuous as it might seem from discussions of Scotland's participation in the Enlightenment, for example, or recognitions of its full collaboration in the building of the British empire. The practice of difference has recognisably deeper historical roots, going back, as scholars and commentators always acknowledge, to the union of the Scottish and English crowns, and later parliaments, in the seventeenth and eighteenth centuries. Consequently, the cultural practice of difference is ultimately an articulation of what has always been, from the point of view of the Scots, a disturbing historical accident. In a recent article, Martin Kettle describes as follows this aspect of 'difference':

The persistence of this seemingly ineradicable difference after so many centuries is a powerful fact. However much England and Scotland are united under common rule, by a common currency, by a common language and the rest, they remain clearly different from one another. They have experienced so much together, yet they remain quite distinct.[14]

Conflicting affiliations to 'Scottishness' and 'Britishness' continue to inform political and cultural debate, and are a source of urgent concern among the Scottish intelligentsia.[15] Consciously or unconsciously, it has become part of ideological commitment on nearly every subject, and through artistic forms and cultural expressions it is being kept alive and continuously rekindled among the populace. David Daiches obviously has this in mind where he remarks that Scottish literature has often seen itself as the most credible symbol of the opposition to the Scotland-England relationship.[16]

In the words of the sociologist David McCrone, Scotland was the second nation to undergo 'the comprehensive process of industrialisation',[17] but has suffered an equally comprehensive post-industrial decline. Although the discovery of oil and gas off its coasts in the 1970s ignited a new optimism about economic renewal and prosperity, none of it seems to have been realised. Though such developments clearly have more to do with the crisis of capitalism on a global scale, they have of course added to the specific complexities of Scottish 'difference'. It is in a bid to come to terms with these complexities that 'difference' has taken the form of a more assertive but non-xenophobic nationalism in recent years.

As Raymond Williams once pointed out, one of the difficulties of criticism is that while there is a general acceptance that some relation must exist between social and material environments on the one hand, and on the other the nature of artistic creativity and the changes taking place within it, this is always very difficult to demonstrate in detail. Williams argues further that it is because of this difficulty that 'people (usually) find good reasons for joining in the general retreat which would promote or relegate art to an autonomous area'.[18] I believe that Scottish drama does demonstrate the truth of the relationship between art and socio-political developments, although also the retreat that usually arises from the difficulty of demonstrating this relationship in detail. Since the 1920s, when the drama became a marked addition to Scottish writing, its tone and orientation have been towards public affairs – whether in the plays of Red Clydeside, or of the workers' theatre movement, whose best achievement is probably Joe Corrie's work, particularly *In Time o' Strife* (1928),[19] or in the post-Glasgow Repertory explosion of drama on Scottish themes, from Anthony Rowley's *A Weaver's Shuttle* (1910) to J. A. Ferguson's *Campbell of Kilmohr* (1914). According to one critic, James Bridie's interest in drama was stimulated by plays put on at the Glasgow Repertory,[20] and indeed his first play, *The Switchback*, was offered to (and rejected by) the company in the second phase of its existence.[21] The same orientation towards public affairs also appears in the urban realism or historical interests of drama from the 1940s to the 1960s, in plays such as James Barke's *Major Operation* (1941), Robert McLeish's *The Gorbals Story* (1946), Ena Lamont Stewart's *Men Should Weep* (1947), Robert McLellan's

Flouers o' Edinburgh (1948) and Stewart Conn's *I Didn't Always Live Here* (1967). Much the same interests remain in the contemporary drama, which has made serious questioning of accepted truths the norm in plays such as Peter Arnott's *Thomas Muir's Voyage to Australia* (1986) or Liz Lochhead's *Mary Queen of Scots Got her Head Chopped Off.* What we have in all these plays is a drama which, collectively, most often sees itself directly responding to the physical and psychological conditions of the nation. Collectivity of response has occasionally even led playwrights to focus on the same theme or character, as when Bill Bryden and Peter Arnott each modelled a play on the life of Benny Lynch, the 1935 Scottish world flyweight boxing champion. Consequently, the forms, modes and meanings of this drama can be appreciated as structured reflections of society in all its complexity, from the pattern of social relations to the principles – ideological, intellectual, political – which guide it. This is the sense in which Scottish drama represents both the expressive and instrumental elements of Scottish culture and nationalism – as a crucial, and inherently populist response to 'difference'.

I began by drawing attention to the role and impact of the music hall, and conclude by re-emphasising its importance as a repository of what may be described as the Scottish tradition. Although music hall came to Scotland in the early nineteenth century purely as a commercial enterprise, it immediately encountered a number of other factors. The most significant of these was the slow recovery by the nation from the assault on secular and especially dramatic entertainments made by the Scottish reformed church from the mid-sixteenth century onwards. Although various critics offer substantial discussion of this assault, its severity and very long-lasting effects are still largely under-investigated. We now know, for instance, that a pattern of utilitarian drama was established in Scotland before the Reformation.[22] This pattern achieved its highest standards in Sir David Lyndsay's *Ane Satyre of the Thrie Estaitis.* A close scrutiny of the language and techniques of this play suggests very much the kind of imposition, discussed earlier, of literary order on popular elements in order to make some urgent, serious political statements. While there are still many gaps to be filled in the subsequent history of Scottish drama, I believe that what is already known can be used as basis for some productive speculations. One such is that from the sixteenth century – especially after the time of *Ane Satyre* – many of the growing or already advanced forms of entertainment in Scotland were submerged or forced into undesired, incongruous mergers by the brutality of the Reformers. Another is that by looking closely at the Scottish pantomime, we can see it perpetuating elements of the weird, wonderful and supernatural which may initially have been inspired by Celtic folklore, or descended partly from seventeenth-century circus and mountebank shows. If we examine closely the patterns of development apparent in the various popular forms, we would become less inclined to support the whimsical argument that Scotland lacks a tradition of drama. Instead, this tradition can be seen as continuously inflected in forms of popular entertainment. Despite the Reformation's assault on Scottish drama, it remained strong, if in one way silenced, or, in Eveling's terms, with only its 'B' side, its popular forms, still clearly playing.

Further evidence for the strength of popular tradition may be drawn, for example, from George Emmerson's well-researched *Social History of Scottish Dance*, in which he draws attention to the dramatic features of all well-known Scottish dances, pointing out that these have often been ignored in analyses of them. He concludes that there are other traditional performances which include such dramatic elements, though these are unrecognised because so little attention has been paid to them.[23] Surveying the various forms of popular entertainment in Scotland, it is difficult to disagree with Emmerson. From the Highland games to the ceilidh, or the Burns supper, the dramatic impulse has a very strong presence. One unavoidable speculation concerning the dynamism of the Scottish music hall is that once it secured a footing, it became the agent for coalescing and transforming the diffused elements of Scottish popular arts, which it then used to expand its own scope. As entertainment, it was convivial and full of revelry. As theatre, its core was the spontaneous recreation of popular experience and reality.

Materials from the music hall and its confederates have not only been appropriated in contemporary Scottish drama: the appropriation has itself become the technical means of continuing the popular base of the drama. Like much of music hall, contemporary drama has continued to draw from living arts and discourses – the embodiments of current feelings and sentiments of the people in the form of songs and newly borrowed popular witticisms, for example. In so far as we cannot speak of a progressive evolution from music hall to real drama, since every form of artistic entertainment ultimately derives its values from the circumstances which foster it, the continued occurrence of music-hall motifs, routines and awareness in contemporary drama ought to be seen as a key aspect of the powerful popular impulse that dominates Scottish entertainment.

NOTES

1. *A Decade's Drama: Six Scottish Plays* (Lancaster: Woodhouse Books, 1980), p.55.
2. The myth of the hard man is a derived popular myth, which goes back to the Calvinist ideas that influenced the Scottish Reformation. See Trevor Royle, *The Macmillan Companion to Scottish Literature* (London & Basingstoke: Macmillan, 1983), p.56, and also his entry on John Knox, pp.166–7.
3. Edward Said, *Culture and Imperialism* (London: Chatto & Windus, 1993), p.73.
4. The Scottish sociologist David McCrone has provided a summary of these views in an essay appropriately titled 'Representing Scotland: Culture and Nationalism' in McCrone, et al (eds), *The Making of Scotland* (Edinburgh: Edinburgh University Press, 1989), pp.161–74.
5. Cf. David Hutchison's 'Scottish Drama 1900–1950' in Cairns Craig (ed.), *The History of Scottish Literature*, Vol.4 (Aberdeen: Aberdeen University Press, 1989), p.164.
6. See Linda Mackenney's 'A National or Popular Theatre' in *Chapman* 43–4, on the kind of controversies that surrounded Joe Corrie's works. The controversies generated by the works and attitudes of John McGrath and the 7:84 Scotland Company are yet to be documented in a full and comprehensive manner. However, there are bits and pieces of explanation and references to it by Elizabeth MacLennan throughout her book, *The Moon Belongs to Everyone* (London: Methuen, 1990).
7. David Mayer, 'Towards a Definition of Popular Drama', David Mayer & Kenneth Richards (eds), *Western Popular Theatre* (London: Methuen, 1977), p.267.
8. Ibid., p.265.
9. See also Alan Bold, *Modern Scottish Literature* (Essex: Longman, 1983), p.275.
10. Michael D. Bristol, *Carnival and Theatre* (New York & London: Methuen, 1985), p.3.
11. Randall Stevenson, 'Recent Scottish Theatre: Dramatic Developments?' in *Scotland: Literature, Culture, Politics* (Heidelberg: Universitatsverlag, 1989), p.196.
12. Elizabeth MacLennan, *The Moon Belongs to Everyone* (London: Methuen, 1990), p.43.
13. Cf. Greg Giesekam, 'Connecting with the Audience: Writing for a Scottish Stage. Interview with Peter Arnott', *New Theatre Quarterly*, 6, (Nov.1990), pp.318–34; Ilona S. Koren–Deutsch, 'Feminist Nationalism in Scotland: *Mary Queen of Scots Got Her Head Chopped Off*', *Modern Drama*, 32, 3 (Sept. 1992), pp.424–32.
14. Martin Kettle, *The Guardian*, 23 September 1995, p.23.
15. The references here are too numerous and cut across disciplines. Representative examples can, however, be found in the critical work of Robert Crawford, David McCrone, Christopher Harvie etc. But it is in the activities of the Saltire Society that the aspiration has its most eloquent expression. Any of the society's numerous publications will do for reading.
16. David Daiches, *The Paradox of Scottish Culture* (Oxford: Oxford University Press, 1964).
17. McCrone, op. cit. p.7.
18. Raymond Williams, *The Long Revolution* (Harmondsworth: Penguin Books, 1961), pp.271–2.
19. This date and others cited refer to the first performance of each play.
20. David Hutchison, op. cit., p.172.

21. Alan Bold, op. cit., p.287.
22. Cf. Robb Lawson, *The Story of the Scots Stage* (Paisley: Alexander Gardner, 1917) and James Dibdin, *Annals of the Edinburgh Stage* (Edinburgh: 1871). Although these books are very useful, especially as general introduction, they both lack detailed analysis. The best work I have come across in that direction in Sarah Carpenter's 'Drama and Politics: Scotland in the 1530s', Meg Twycross et al (eds), *Medieval English Theatre*, 10, 2 (1988).
23. George S. Emmerson, *A Social History of Scottish Dance* (Montreal and London: McGill-Queen's University Press, 1972).

Fifteen

Talking in Tongues:
Scottish Translations 1970–1995[1]

Bill Findlay

Goethe, Schiller, Büchner, Hofmannsthal, Kraus, Brecht, Ahlsen, Dorst, Dürrenmatt, Kastner, Schnitzler, Hochhuth, Fassbinder, Ibsen, Tolstoy, Chekhov, Lermontov, Gogol, Racine, Molière, Beaumarchais, Balzac, de Musset, Genet, Arrabal, Cocteau, Sartre, Goldoni, Pirandello . . . plays by these and other European dramatists feature among a remarkable body of some seventy translations by the outstanding translator working in Scottish theatre over the past quarter-century: Robert David MacDonald, co-director, translator, playwright and actor at Glasgow Citizens' Theatre since 1972. A significant number of those translations were done for the Citizens' and, as Cordelia Oliver has said, 'his presence in the company has had the effect of opening up the whole spectrum of European drama to Glasgow audiences in a way that is certainly rare in Britain'.[2] Rare in Britain, too, is the long relationship that MacDonald has enjoyed as resident translator with one company over a quarter of a century; a relationship that has more in common with the Continental European (and especially German) practice of having resident dramaturges attached to theatres.

MacDonald's skills as a multi-lingual translator have made a defining contribution to the Citizens' reputation as a theatre that, in Michael Coveney's words, 'has provided the most exciting European-based repertoire in the British theatre over the past twenty years'.[3] Because of MacDonald's special empathy with German drama, German plays have made a distinctive contribution to that 'European-based repertoire', as can be seen in the impressive number and range of German plays performed, from the classic to the recondite, commencing with Brecht's *Happy End* in 1972 through to Schiller's *Don Carlos* at the 1995 Edinburgh Festival. Notable 'firsts' have been the English-language première of Karl Kraus's epic play, *The Last Days of Mankind* (1983, Edinburgh Festival); the world première of Rolf Hochhuth's *Judith* (1984); and a rarely staged work by Goethe, *Torquato Tasso* (1982; revived at 1994 Edinburgh Festival). In recognition of his German translations, MacDonald was awarded the prestigious Goethe Medal in 1984, the citation of which stated: 'Robert David MacDonald has given new perspectives to the transfer of German culture into the English-speaking world and built bridges of understanding between our two peoples'.[4]

His sustained practice of the translator's art, and the quantity of plays he has translated, distinguish Robert David MacDonald from other Scottish translators over the period. Also, his undeviating use of Standard English (in a writing style that he has humorously described as 'gutter mandarin'[5]) sets him apart from a significant linguistic trend in Scottish translations over the last quarter-century. A few other translators, of course, have taken Standard English as their translation medium. For example, the playwright C. P. Taylor did so in the 1970s in his adaptations of work by Brecht, Sternheim and Ibsen.[6] So, too, did another dramatist, Tom Gallacher, in what he has described as 'appropriate period English' translations of Rostand's *Cyrano de Bergerac* (1977, Pitlochry), Strindberg's *The Father* (1980, Dundee), and Ibsen's *An Enemy of the People* (1979, Royal Lyceum), *A Doll's House* (1980, Little Lyceum; 1982, Perth Theatre), and *The Wild Duck* (1987, Perth Theatre).[7] But, as will emerge from the following discussion of the Traverse's promotion of play translations, employment of a non-Standard medium has characterised the majority of translators' work over the period under review, and from 1980 especially.

The only other Scottish theatre to enjoy an international reputation rivalling that of the Citizens' is Edinburgh's Traverse Theatre; and, like the Citizens', that reputation rests in large part on translations (as reflected in the Traverse receiving in 1994/95 the International Theatre Institute's Award for its promotion and development of international new work). Whereas Citizens' translations have concentrated almost exclusively on the historic repertoire (Rolf Hochhuth's work being an exception), the Traverse has specialised for the most part in premiering contemporary plays (with some exceptions, as I will discuss). And whereas the Citizens' has become identified with one particular translator (though it has occasionally used others), the Traverse has always drawn on a wide variety.

The importance of translations as one of the Traverse's *raisons d'être* was signified from the outset, for the first ever production in 1963 was the UK première of Fernando Arrabal's *Orison* in a double bill with Jean Paul Sartre's *Huis Clos*. But, perhaps surprisingly, the Traverse's present exclusive focus on contemporary playwrights is a development that commenced only in the 1980s. Translations of contemporary foreign plays have featured in programming throughout the Traverse's existence (excepting the period 1976–83 when emphasis was placed on contemporary British writing), but the 1960s and 1970s saw classic work in translation staged, too. In the 1970s, for example, we find *Elektra* by Euripides, *Woyzeck* by Büchner, three plays by Brecht, three plays by Strindberg, and an adaptation of Ibsen's *Peer Gynt*. The number of classic plays thus rivalled that decade's total of nine contemporary plays in translation (by Handke, Fassbinder, Kroetz, etc.).

The period from 1980 to 1995 has seen a reorientation in the Traverse's promotion of foreign work. Adaptations of *Medea* (1983) and Gogol's *The Gamblers* (1987, in a co-production with the Tron) were the only classics staged. In contrast, the eleven years from 1984 to 1995 saw an impressive fourteen UK premières of contemporary foreign plays in translation; and the popular and critical success of many of those plays has made a key contribution to shaping present perceptions of the Traverse as a cutting-edge theatre with an exclusive focus on new work. Those fourteen plays are as follows (translators' names are given in parenthesis):[8]

> 1984 *Sandra/Manon* Michel Tremblay (John Van Burek)
> 1985 *Through the Leaves* Franz Xaver Kroetz (Anthony Vivis)
> 1985 *Aus der Fremde (Out of Estrangement)* Ernst Jandl (Michael Hamburger)
> 1986 *Burning Love* Fitzgerald Kusz (Anthony Vivis and Tinch Minter)
> 1986 *Kathie and the Hippopotamus* Mario Vargas Llosa (Kerry McKenny and Anthony Oliver-Smith)
> 1987 *Man to Man* Manfred Karge (Anthony Vivis)
> 1987 *The Prowler* Enzo Cormann (James Kelman)
> 1988 *A Man with Connections* Alexander Gelman (Stephen Mulrine)
> 1988 *The Conquest of the South Pole* Manfred Karge (Tinch Minter and Anthony Vivis)
> 1989 *Blending In* Michael Vinaver (Ron Butlin)
> 1990 *The Bench* Alexander Gelman (Stephen Mulrine)
> 1992 *The House Among the Stars* Michel Tremblay (Martin Bowman and Bill Findlay)
> 1992 *Moscow Stations* translated and adapted from a novel by Venedikt Yerofeev (Stephen Mulrine)
> 1995 *Stones and Ashes* Daniel Danis (Tom McGrath)

A notable feature of the above list is that, of the fourteen translations, half were by Scots. In the early 1980s English and Canadian translators predominate, but that changes in the mid-1980s. With the exception of *The Conquest of the South Pole* in 1988 (though it was acted in Scottish voices), all of the translations since *The Prowler* in 1987 have been done by Scots (Kelman, Mulrine, Butlin, Bowman/Findlay, McGrath). Moreover, almost all of those translations have drawn on distinctive varieties of Scots speech (mostly but not solely an urban demotic Scots). An apparent exception is Stephen Mulrine's Russian translations, which seem to be in Standard English. But here, too, there is a Scottish inflection, for Mulrine has said: 'I'm conscious that my own speech rhythms, non-Standard English as they are, remain fundamentally unchanged when I'm ventriloquising as a translator.' For example, of Alexander Gelman's *A Man with Connections*, he has commented: 'I made the translation educated Glaswegian, basically my own speech, with a liberal sprinkling of Americanisms, which come with the territory.'[9]

This emergence of Scottish translators of contemporary foreign plays, drawing in the main on varieties of Scottish speech, coincided with a wider development in Scottish theatre in the 1980s that is detectable in the programmes of both building-based and touring companies, and that is bound up in large part with two writers with whom Scottish audiences seem to have felt a special affinity: the Italian dramatist Dario Fo and Quebecer Michel Tremblay.

Within a decade there were no fewer than seven Scottish productions of Fo's work. Morag Fullarton directed *Female Parts* for the Tron in 1982 and Theatre Workshop did *Accidental Death of an Anarchist* in 1983. In 1985 Fo was given a distinctive Scottish voice when Ian Brown (now at the Traverse) directed for TAG Theatre Company *Can't Pay? Won't Pay!* in a Glaswegianised adaptation by Robert Walker and Alex Norton. This linguistic lead was followed when, in 1986, Borderline Theatre Company began a highly successful association with Fo's work by staging *Trumpets and Raspberries* (revived in 1995), followed by a double bill of *The Virtuous Burglar* and *An Ordinary Day* (1988), *Mistero Buffo* (1990), and *Can't Pay? Won't Pay!* (1990), which were adapted to Scottish speech by, variously, Morag Fullarton, Joseph Farrell and Alex Norton. (It should be mentioned, too, that Borderline scored a popular success in 1993 with another foreign work done into Scots: Carl MacDougall's adaptation of Jaroslav Hasek's novel *The Guid Sodjer Schweik*.)

Since 1989 there have been five Scots translations of Michel Tremblay's work in a collaboration between a Montrealer, Martin Bowman, and a Scot, Bill Findlay. Glasgow's Tron Theatre staged *The Guid Sisters* in 1989 (revived 1990 and 1992), *The Real Wurld?* in

1991, and *Hosanna* in 1991; London-based LadderMan Productions, in association with the Tron, staged *Forever Yours, Marie-Lou* in 1994; and the Traverse staged *The House Among the Stars* in 1992 (with a second production by Perth Theatre in 1993). Worth mentioning, too, as an example of how translations can prove a vehicle for showcasing Scottish theatre abroad, is that the Tron took *The Guid Sisters* to the World Stage International Theatre Festival in Toronto in 1990, and to the Centaur Theatre in Montreal in 1992 for a four-week run as part of the official British contribution to the city's 350th anniversary celebrations; and the Tron also took *The Real Wurld?* to the Stony Brook International Theatre Festival, Long Island, New York, in 1991.[10]

Other notable Scottish translations of contemporary work in the period, in UK premières, were Stephen Mulrine's translation into 'Glasgow demotic'[11] of *Cinzano* by Ludmilla Petrushevskaya, produced at the Tron in 1989 as part of a season of Soviet Arts in Glasgow (Mulrine's other work, at the Traverse, has already been noted); and the Standard English adaptation by Tom McGrath, from the translation by Ella Wildridge, of Tankred Dorst's two plays, *Merlin* and *Merlin – the Search for the Grail*, staged at the Royal Lyceum in 1992 and 1993, respectively.

What can account for such extensive interest in translation for the Scottish stage, especially marked since the mid-1980s? One partial explanation might lie in a kind of delayed effect arising from the burgeoning of indigenous drama in the 1970s and playwrights' new harnessings of the particularities of Scottish speech at this time. A further reason perhaps lies in the even greater expansion of indigenous theatre activity that was witnessed in the 1980s, and a related rise in confidence in the distinctiveness and health of Scottish theatre culture – a confidence that was expressed partly in a wish to forge direct contact with contemporary happenings in foreign theatre. Given the linguistic distinctiveness of most of these translations, a further reason might appear in a more general trend discernible over the same period to assert with new-found confidence the validity of Scottish voices on our stages in performing non-Scottish plays, whether translations or English-language plays ranging in period and place from Shakespeare to Mamet. That this shift was accomplished without alienating audiences – indeed, quite the reverse – suggests that a similar change was taking place in audience attitudes, perhaps as a reflection of the wider cultural and political nationalism that was evident in Scotland in the 1980s.[12]

This language-related trend can also be seen, firstly, in the number of new Scots translations of classic plays that, with significant coincidence, were produced over the same period; and, secondly, in the popular success that most of those translations enjoyed, as confirmed by the number of revivals that occurred relatively soon after first productions. Since 1985, for example, five plays by Molière have been translated into Scots:[13] *A Wee Touch o' Class* by 'Rabaith', 'the both' being Denise Coffey and Rikki Fulton (1985, 1986 and 1988, Perth Theatre); *Tartuffe* by Liz Lochhead (1986 and 1987, Royal Lyceum; 1992, Dundee Rep; 1995, Nippy Sweeties); *Patter Merchants* by Liz Lochhead (1989, Winged Horse); *The Hypochondriak* by Hector MacMillan (1987, Royal Lyceum; 1993, Dundee Rep); *The Bourgeois Gentilhomme* by Hector MacMillan (1989, Royal Lyceum; 1995, Dundee Rep, retitled *Noblesse Obleege*[14]). There were also two Goldoni translations by Marjory Greig and Antonia Stott: *The Weemen Stratagem* (1987, Perth Theatre), and *La Serva Amorosa (Where Love Steps In)* (1992, Fifth Estate). And there were a number of single play translations by different dramatists: Donald Campbell did a version of Ibsen's *Ghosts* (1980, Scottish Theatre Company); Hector MacMillan translated and adapted *The Barber Figaro!* from *Le Barbier de Seville* by Beaumarchais (1991, Perth Theatre); Bill Dunlop adapted *Klytemnestra's Bairns* from *The Oresteia* by Aeschylus (1991 and 1994, Edinburgh Fringe); and Edwin Morgan translated Rostand's *Cyrano de Bergerac* (1992, Communicado). In that they give further support to the trend I am arguing for, I should also mention the two rival Scots translations of Shakespeare's *Macbeth* by R. L. C. Lorimer and David Purves, both published in 1992 but not yet staged.[15]

The significance of these Scots translations of classic plays can be gauged from the fact that those mentioned above exceed in number the sum total that previously existed. The first translations appeared in the 1940s when Glasgow Unity Theatre staged a Scots version of Maxim Gorki's *The Lower Depths* and Edinburgh's Gateway Theatre produced Robert Kemp's Molière translation *Let Wives Tak Tent*. The 1950s saw another Molière by Kemp, *The Laird o' Grippy*, and two plays by Aristophanes translated by Douglas Young, *The Puddocks* and *The Burdies*. (Two sixteenth-century Latin plays by George Buchanan, *Jephthah* and *The Baptist*, were translated by Robert Garioch and published in 1959 but the translations have never been staged.) And in the 1960s Victor Carin translated Molière's *The Hypochondriack*, Goldoni's *The Servant o' Twa Maisters*, and Heinrich von Kleist's *The Chippit Chantie*.

In surveying the period 1980–1995, then, we find more Scottish translations produced than at any previous period in Scottish theatre history. Moreover, we find that the majority of those translations drew on varieties of Scots: mostly an urban Scots in the case of contemporary plays, and various kinds of 'traditional', 'aggrandised' or 'experimental'

Scots in the case of classic plays. Whilst I believe that these developments are a sign of health in Scottish theatre culture, the repertoire of Scots translations is nevertheless still fairly limited. Extraordinarily, it would seem that no contemporary foreign play had been translated into Scots before the 1980s,[16] so we have made a late start in remedying that deficiency and in consequence have only a relatively modest number of contemporary plays in translation. Also, the Scots translations of classic plays that existed prior to the 1980s were limited in number and circumscribed in range; and although that number has been substantially added to in the past fifteen years, the fact that, for example, Molière translations predominate as they did in the earlier period – and now to an even greater extent – suggests that the range of authors translated needs to be broadened.

That said, the Scots translations that we now have serve to demonstrate the value of the linguistic options that translators in Scotland have available, being able to draw not just on Standard English and 'Scottish English' but on varieties of Scots, whether urban or rural, regional or 'standardised', historic or contemporary, literary or experimental. On the basis of 'horses for courses', and fashioning a translation medium best suited to any given work, I believe that Scottish translators are at an unusual advantage in the English-speaking world in having at their disposal such a rich and flexible linguistic resource.

The Chilean playwright Ariel Dorfman said something relevant to this when he was in Edinburgh in the summer of 1995 for the world première of his play *Reader* at the Traverse. Interviewed by the *Glasgow Herald*, he remarked: 'The dilemma the Scots have about language is a dilemma of many people around the world. It is a dilemma of the bilingual and it's a good dilemma to be in. Rather than seeing it to our detriment, it should be something which enriches our lives.'[17] Although there is welcome evidence that attitudes are changing, for long enough Scots was viewed negatively as a problem, and as posing a 'dilemma' for writers *vis-à-vis* writing in Standard English. I do not want to oversimplify the reasons for this, but a contributory factor was and is that, from an English perspective, the use of 'dialect' for serious literary purposes is regarded as odd and outwith the literary mainstream (witness the response of many London reviewers to James Kelman's work). Yet, as Ariel Dorfman reminds us, 'bilingualism' – whether between two distinct languages, between two related languages, or between Standard and non-Standard varieties of the same language – is an historic and contemporary linguistic reality in many countries. In short, what might strike some as idiosyncratic about Scotland in British terms is not necessarily so when viewed in an international context. The truth of this – and the continuing value and relevance of our Scots resource for translation purposes – can be seen from the language of some contemporary playwrights whose work has been staged in Scotland: Franz Xaver Kroetz writes in the dialect of the Bavarian under-class, Michel Tremblay in *joual* (the east-end Montreal dialect of Quebec-French), Dario Fo in a variety of North Italian dialects (sometimes enriched with dialectal archaisms), and Enzo Cormann in a localised French vernacular.

The availability of Scots, then, presents the translator with special opportunities in approaching both contemporary and classic plays. As regards the latter, for example, in discussing his translation of *Cyrano de Bergerac*, Edwin Morgan said: 'I decided that an urban Glaswegian Scots could offer the best basis, supplemented where necessary, to meet the range of tones and tongues in the original, by other kinds of Scots and English'.[18] That reference to 'the range of tones and tongues in the original' lends support to my belief that the long-standing predominance of Standard English translations in British (and, until relatively recently, Scottish) theatres – more often than not delivered in the class-associated accent of Received Pronunciation, with the 'mechanicals' sporting regional accents – has misrepresented both the 'non-Standard' or 'bilingual' nature of much Western drama and its rootedness in the texture of a particular national or regional culture (in the case of *Cyrano*, that of Gascony). That is, Standard English can sometimes have a homogenising effect as a translation medium and can disfigure the work being translated. Edwin Morgan's award-winning translation of *Cyrano de Bergerac* proved so arresting partly because in honouring the original text and its 'range of tones and tongues' his language thereby differed radically from previous English-language versions and offered a startlingly new way of seeing Rostand's play.

The kind of language options that Morgan could draw on for *Cyrano* also help to explain why Molière enjoys a popularity in Scotland unknown in England; that is, it would seem that a Scots translation releases qualities in Molière which Standard English does not. For it is noticeable that Molière has never quite enjoyed the popularity on the English stage that his status warrants. As one reviewer concluded in a review of a London production of *Le Malade imaginaire*, 'If truth be told, is he not in English the most uninteresting of world dramatists?'[19] In contrast, the popularity of Molière on the Scottish stage in the post-war period has made him almost a Scottish playwright-by-adoption, as evidenced by Noel Peacock's study, *Molière in Scotland 1945–1990*.[20] In large part, Molière's success in Scotland can be explained by how well he translates into a Scots idiom, and how alive his work thereby becomes for

Scottish audiences. Whilst Liz Lochhead's 'theatrical Scots'[21] translation of *Tartuffe* differs from the more traditional Scots of Molière translations by Kemp, Carin and MacMillan, her rationale for using Scots supports the view that there is a gain over using Standard English: 'There seemed to be a sensuous and sensual earthiness in Molière's masterpiece, a comedy both classical and black, and with an ending of quite explicit political satire which bland English translations totally lost'.[22]

However, in saying all of this, I do not want to seem to downplay the importance of Standard English as an effective and natural medium for Scottish translators, too. It is, after all, part of our linguistic inheritance and daily experience, and it gives us reciprocal access to English-language theatre cultures elsewhere.[23] Our foremost translator, Robert David MacDonald, writes in it; and essentially, so, too, does Stephen Mulrine, who has emerged in the last decade as an accomplished translator of Russian drama.[24] As their respective examples show, use of a Standard English medium is of real assistance in achieving international accessibility and in having one's translations staged by companies in other English-language countries. But, whilst acknowledging and applauding those individual achievements, in this essay I have focused in the main on Scots because, along with the unprecedented number of Scottish translators at work, the number of Scots translations, is, I believe, the other significant development in the period covered by this volume.

My own view is that English and Scots are not rival but complementary and overlapping translation mediums that can be used not just in isolation from one another in single-medium translations, but used either in contrast within the same work or in a commingled brew of a writer's own devising. Just as Scottish society reflects the linguistic diversity that flows from this English-Scots duality – with style-switching shifts in speech between English and Scots and commingled varieties of the two – Scottish translations, in their various mediums, do so, too. Whilst I am personally interested in harnessing that diversity for translation purposes, so far as translators who choose other options are concerned, I would resist prescriptiveness in defining what, linguistically, constitutes a 'Scottish' translation. Choice of translation medium is in the final analysis a personal matter; and, in any event, one cannot hope to create theatrically effective translations by following some kind of linguistic manifesto. What is important, I think, is to celebrate that the Scottish translator may, depending on such factors as upbringing, individual preference, or the demands of a given work, employ Standard English (for instance, Robert David MacDonald), or one of the varieties of Scots (for instance, Hector MacMillan), or counterpoint English and Scots in the same translation (for instance, Bowman and Findlay in Tremblay's

The House Among the Stars), or creatively forge an individualistic Scots-English medium (for instance, Morgan's *Cyrano* and Lochhead's *Tartuffe*). As Ariel Dorfman said, being 'bilingual' is 'a good dilemma to be in'.

NOTES

1. In this essay I use the word 'translations' in a loose manner to encompass not just direct translations from a source language but 'translations' of the kind that may be variously described in theatre credits as 'translated by', 'adapted by', or 'in a version by' and that have been fashioned from an intermediary English direct translation, whether literal or literary. Scottish practice is not unusual in this last regard, for the word 'translations' is commonly used in this elastic sense in theatre internationally.

2. Cordelia Oliver, *Glasgow Citizens' Theatre, Robert David MacDonald and German Drama* (Glasgow: Third Eye Centre, 1984), p.11.

3. Michael Coveney, *The Citz: 21 Years of the Glasgow Citizens Theatre* (London: Nick Hern Books, 1990), p.1.

4. *Glasgow Citizens' Theatre, Robert David MacDonald and German Drama*, p.5.

5. Quoted in *The Citz: 21 Years of the Glasgow Citizens Theatre*, p.137.

6. Translations/adaptations by C. P. Taylor for the Traverse are detailed in years 1973, 1974, and 1975 of 'A Chronology of Traverse Productions 1963–1988 Compiled by John Carnegie', in Joyce McMillan, *The Traverse Theatre Story* (London: Methuen, 1988), pp.137, 139, 143.

7. In a letter to me of 25 October 1995 Tom Gallacher kindly provided these production details, and described his translation medium thus: 'In all but one of the titles mentioned, the language I used was appropriate period English. With *The Father*, however, I used patrician Scottish of the period, since I'd moved the location to Scotland.' He also informed me that his adaptations of Ibsen's *A Doll's House* and *The Wild Duck* have been re-translated and used by various Scandinavian theatre companies. He discusses adapting Ibsen in an article, 'Play Surgery', in *Scottish Theatre News*, May 1982, pp.6–11.

8. All translations staged at the Traverse between 1963 and 1987 are listed in John Carnegie's chronology in *The Traverse Story*. [The chronology purports to cover '1963–1988' but its coverage actually ends in 1987.] My list of translations staged between 1988 and 1995, inclusive, was confirmed with the Traverse.

9. These quotations come from a letter to me of 24 November 1995 in which Stephen Mulrine kindly provided production details about his translations and answered my queries about how he would describe his translation medium.

10. For detailed discussion see Martin Bowman and Bill Findlay, 'Québécois into Scots: Translating Michel Tremblay', in *Scottish Language*, 13 (1994), pp.61–81.

11. Letter of 24 November 1995.

12. Of relevance here, too, is the increase in public interest in Scots language in the 1980s as evidenced by the publishing success enjoyed by works such as *The Patter*, *The Concise Scots Dictionary*, and *The New Testament in Scots*.

13. For details of all Molière productions in Scotland from 1945 to 1990 inclusive see Noel Peacock, *Molière in Scotland 1945–1990* (Glasgow: University of Glasgow French & German Publications, 1993).

14. In a letter to me of 13 November 1995 Hector MacMillan kindly confirmed these production details and explained that his preferred title of *Noblesse Obleege* had been changed by the Lyceum management to *The Bourgeois Gentilhomme* for the first, 1989, production. He also informed me that *The Hypochondriak*

has been translated from Scots into Finnish because of the difficulty in making Molière funny when translated directly from French. Hamish Glen directed the first production in Finland in 1994, and the translation has subsequently proved a popular and critical success at a number of theatres.

15. R. L. C. Lorimer, *Shakespeare's Macbeth Translated into Scots* (Edinburgh: Canongate, 1992); David Purves, *The Tragedie o Macbeth: A Rendering into Scots of Shakespeare's Play* (Edinburgh: Rob Roy Press, 1992).

16. Bowman and Findlay's *The Guid Sisters* was completed in 1979 but no theatre proved interested until the Tron staged it in 1989. *The Guid Sisters* was a conscious attempt to extend into translations what writers had been doing with a contemporary Scots idiom in original plays in the 1970s.

17. *Glasgow Herald*, 26 July 1995, p.16.

18. Edwin Morgan's 'Introduction' in the programme for Communicado's 1992 production.

19. *Plays and Players*, 411 (December 1987), p.21.

20. See note 13.

21. From the 'Introduction' to: Liz Lochhead, *Tartuffe: a Translation into Scots from the Original by Molière* (Edinburgh and Glasgow: Polygon and Third Eye Centre, 1985).

22. Ibid.

23. Since we are part of a larger English-speaking theatre community, English-language translations from outwith Scotland have and will continue to be staged by Scottish and visiting companies. Because of this, more translations of plays (by classic authors, in particular) have been staged in Scotland since the 1970s than I have been able to discuss because of my article's focus.

24. Stephen Mulrine prefers not to be typed as a 'Scottish' translator (letter to me of 24 October 1995). He has sometimes drawn on distinctive Scottish forms: in addition to Petrushevskaya's *Cinzano*, his adaptation of Leskov's *The Lady Macbeth of Mtensk* for BBC Radio 3 was in 'a thinly demotic Scots'; and the dog in his adaptation of Bulgakov's *Mongrel's Heart* for the Royal Lyceum (1994) 'was very deliberately in Glaswegian, since it was for Bill Paterson'. But most of his translations have been into a sufficiently standard English to allow them to be performed by companies in London, Australia and the USA (where, the Traverse production of *Moscow Stations*, starring Tom Courtenay, is currently running at Union Square Theatre in New York). Nevertheless, Mulrine's flexible command of different idioms supports my argument for the benefits that a translator can derive from being shaped by a culture marked by linguistic diversity.

TRANSLATIONS 1980–1995

Chekhov, Anton, *Three Sisters*, translated by Stephen Mulrine (London: Nick Hern Books, 1994).

Dorst, Tankred, and Ursula Ehler, *Merlin*, adapted by Tom McGrath from the translation by Ella Wildridge, in *Theatre Scotland*, Vol.1, Issue 1 (Spring/Summer 1992), pp.19–37.

Dunlop, Bill, *Klytemnestra's Bairns* (Edinburgh: Diehard, 1993).

Gelman, Alexander, *A Man with Connections*, translated by Stephen Mulrine (London: Nick Hern Books, 1989). [Also anthologized in *Stars in the Morning Sky: New Soviet Plays*, introduced by Michael Glenny (London: Nick Hern Books, 1989).]

Goethe [Johann Wolfgang von], *Faust: Parts 1 and 2*, translated by Robert David MacDonald (London: Oberon Books, 1988).

Goethe [Johann Wolfgang von], *Tasso (Torquato Tasso)*, translated by Robert David MacDonald (London: Oberon Books, 1994).

Goldoni, Carlo, *Mirandolina and The Housekeeper*, translated by Robert David MacDonald (London: Oberon Books, 1988).

Ibsen, Henrik, *Brand*, translated by Robert David MacDonald (London: Oberon Books, 1991).

Lenz, Jakob, *The Soldiers*, translated by Robert David MacDonald (London: Oberon Books, 1993).

Lochhead, Liz, *Tartuffe: a Translation into Scots from the Original by Molière* (Edinburgh and Glasgow: Polygon and Third Eye Centre, 1985).

Molière, *School for Wives*, translated by Robert David MacDonald (London: Oberon Books, 1986).

Petrushevskaya, Ludmilla, *Cinzano and Other Plays*, translated by Stephen Mulrine (London: Nick Hern Books, 1991). [Stephen Mulrine has informed me that the Glasgow demotic of the staged translation was 'toned down a fair bit' for this published version.]

Pirandello, Luigi, *Enrico Four*, translated by Robert David MacDonald (London: Oberon Books, 1990).

Rostand, Edmond, *Cyrano de Bergerac*, translated by Edwin Morgan (Manchester: Carcanet, 1992). [Also published in *Theatre Scotland*, Vol.1, Issue 3 (Autumn 1992), pp.29–58.]

Schiller, Friedrich, *Mary Stuart and Joan of Arc*, translated by Robert David MacDonald (London: Oberon Books, 1987).

Schiller, Friedrich, *The Robbers*, translated by Robert David MacDonald (London: Oberon Books, 1995).

Schiller, Friedrich, *Don Carlos*, translated by Robert David MacDonald (London: Oberon Books, 1995).

Tremblay, Michel, *The Guid Sisters and Other Plays* [the title play translated by Martin Bowman and Bill Findlay] (London: Nick Hern Books, 1991). [The Scots of the performed translation was 'anglicised' a fair amount by the publisher in a wish to make the text more accessible.]

Tremblay, Michel, *Forever Yours, Marie-Lou*, translated by Martin Bowman and Bill Findlay (London: LadderMan Playscripts, 1994).

Yerofeev/Mulrine, *Moscow Stations: a play by Stephen Mulrine translated and adapted from 'Moscow-Petushki' by Venedikt Yerofeev* (London: Oberon Books, 1993).

Sixteen

Directing for the Scottish Stage

Ian Brown

I arrived in Scotland on April Fool's day in 1984 to become Artistic Director of TAG (Theatre-About-Glasgow) Theatre Company. I immediately set about commissioning and auditioning in Scotland to bring to the company a Scottish slant on an international repertoire which would play to mainly young audiences in Strathclyde Region.

I decided to continue the TAG tradition, established by Ian Wooldridge, of doing adaptations of Shakespeare for Upper Secondary pupils. I programmed one adult tour a year and one play for younger pupils in Secondary Schools. My opening play was a production for primary schools of Volker Ludwig's *Eddie and Ellie*, originating from the Gripps Theatre for Young People in Berlin. I was particularly proud of the cut-down Shakespeare in schools. I remember being in an Easterhouse Secondary School and seeing the fourth and fifth years watching *As You Like It* and enjoying it! Producing Shakespeare for TAG also gave young Scottish actors their first chance to speak Shakespeare since they had left college.

During my time at TAG I began to work collaboratively with actors, movement directors, composers, designers and writers, trying to fuse all the elements together. This work culminated in *Great Expectations*, adapted from Dickens's novel by John Clifford. I co-directed this with Gregory Nash, the choreographer and dancer, and it was ground-breaking in the fact that the fusion between movement and acting was largely successful. This production won 'The Spirit of Mayfest' award in 1988 and subsequently toured India, Iraq, Sri Lanka, Bangladesh and Pakistan under the auspices of the British Council.

Of all the Scottish revenue-funded companies, TAG has perhaps the most difficult balance to strike. It is possible, on the one hand, to become too oriented toward the general public, or, on the other, to fulfil the company's specific commitment to young people but feel that such work is still often marginalised by both press and the public itself. But running TAG for four and a half years was a marvellous opportunity to sow seeds for the future. Fast, colourful and direct were probably the adjectives that could best describe my work with the company: *As You Like It* in an hour and a half, with Andrew Price and Tamara Kennedy wearing street clothes from 'Boy' as Rosalind and Orsino; C. P. Taylor's *Operation Elvis* with primary school children unable to believe that someone was actually singing and playing the guitar in front of them; *Can't Pay? Won't Pay!* bringing Alex Norton's Scottish version of Dario Fo to the Citizens' Theatre, and forging Andy Gray, Maureen Carr, Sandy Morton and Anne Downie into a fine ensemble company.

I also commissioned Scottish writers to write for young people, most successfully in the case of Ann Marie di Mambro's *Visible Differences*, a play about racism for lower secondary pupils. David Ian Neville cleverly adapted Joan Lingard's novels about Belfast for the same age-group, and all these plays were accompanied by a workshop – a first for TAG at that time – dealing with the difficult issues of sectarianism and racism. The challenges were plenty and the repertoire varied: I hope that my five years at TAG helped provide a training ground for new Scottish writers, designers, composers, choreographers and actors.

SCOTTISH ACTORS

One of the joys of working in Scotland is the actors it produces. Trained largely by the Royal Scottish Academy of Music and Drama in Glasgow, or – less often – Queen Margaret College in Edinburgh, these actors form the basis of an ever-changing but ever-present repertory company for Scottish theatres. Successful actors in this country move easily between theatre, television, radio, film and the odd commercial. Familiarity with each other and a shared background in their training helps produce a style of Scottish acting which at its best can be very exciting, energetic and dangerous, as well as emotional and sensitive, and often as adept in comedy as in tragedy. Most importantly, Day One of rehearsals often sees the beginning of a company spirit which helps enormously in overcoming the problems short rehearsal periods force on most companies.

It is a great pity that the flow of work between London and Scotland isn't freer. Too often up-and-coming actors make the move south and rarely make it back for theatre work. Good Scottish actors are rarely without work for long, and an agent operating between Scotland and London would be extremely beneficial to individual careers and the future of Scottish theatre in general.

SCOTTISH WRITING

For twelve years I have been in the business of commissioning Scottish writers to produce original work, to translate foreign drama into Scots, or to adapt existing material into a Scottish idiom. I believe playwrights have a special view on society, and that there is a rare value in their observation; their fictionalising of human behaviour; their attempts to make sense of the world and to make a statement about the human condition. To write a play and hold an audience for two hours in a theatre is no mean feat and not to be underestimated. That Scottish playwrights are generally unappreciated as artists is a sad symptom of the current cultural environment, and of the way theatre is marginalised in the Press.

Yet after a time of feeling gloomy about the future of new Scottish theatre writing, I believe that there are once again distinct signs of life, and it is essential that this momentum is kept up. Two 'young Turks', known locally as 'the two Davids', have made their presence known to Scottish audiences. David Greig and David Harrower display considerable talent, enthusiasm and fearlessness in tackling big issues and taking risks. Above all, they enjoy theatre and prove that it is a medium that young people can get excited about. Mike Cullen also has an understanding of the way theatre can excite people, and he enjoys the contribution that particular actors can bring to the development of a play, often writing specifically for those actors.

The previous generation of writers is going through a difficult period. Some of them have been tempted away by companies in London who seem unable to interpret the Scottishness of what they write. Others have found themselves writing solely for television or film. The older generation did not find the larger stages they should have reached after their initial success and may have become demoralised. Some have been discouraged by poor reviews, particularly for second plays, which critics sometimes slam for the same qualities they praised in a debut. The lessons are plain for anyone to see. If the new generation is not to suffer the same fate, and if there is to be the diversity of opportunity which the range of available talent deserves, more ways must be found of producing new Scottish plays on the stages of Scottish repertory theatres. The Scottish Arts Council perhaps has a role in cushioning any risk for a larger theatre in producing a new play.

Scottish writers do not form a cohesive band of similar and like-minded people. The diversity of styles is very refreshing, though it means that no single theatre can take full responsibility for the development of all writers in Scotland. Differing artistic tastes make it impossible for a writer to produce work that one particular director will always respond to, and it is impossible to direct a play unless the director is fully behind it. With the Tron in Glasgow having considerably reduced its output of new work because of lack of money, it worries me that an unreasonable burden now rests with the Traverse. One of the hopeful elements of the early 1990s was the work done by the independent companies such as Fifth Estate and Wiseguise, but it has been hard for them to continue their output without funding. For new writing to flourish in Scotland, proper development work has to be done on scripts, whatever the cost, and new money would help the bigger and smaller theatres produce the best plays possible.

Over the past two years at the Traverse, the dramaturg Ella Wildridge, Associate Director Philip Howard and I have embarked on a comprehensive programme of development work with writers. This means offering commissioned writers the chance to workshop their scripts with actors, as and when they feel it could be useful to the process of writing the play. Writers exploring ideas for possible plays are also offered workshops. This is a policy which has certainly begun to bear fruit. Regular writers' groups run at the Traverse, and David Greig works one day a week as a Script Associate. A women's play-writing group has now entered its second year of activity and showcases work by new women dramatists.

THE TRAVERSE SINCE 1988

I became Artistic Director of the Traverse in its twenty-fifth anniversary year, 1988. This was also the time when the Traverse shed its club status and became a public theatre, making full compliance with fire regulations more difficult, and making more obvious and frustrating the limitations of space in its Grassmarket home. I think it was on my first full day in the job that the General Manager, Anne Bonnar, mentioned that there was a good chance of a new theatre in the proposed office building in Castle Terrace. We soon decided that a move was an exciting prospect for the theatre, and that if we could be sure that the actual auditorium would be exactly what we wanted, then it was an opportunity not to be missed. It wasn't long before we found ourselves in front of Edinburgh District Council, in whose gift the theatre was, bidding against the Royal Lyceum, who were to lose the Little Lyceum as a result of the sale of the land known as 'the hole-in-the-ground'. Miraculously, as it now seems, the Traverse was awarded a 150-year lease and £3.4 million for the fitting out of the shell by the developers. One of the world's first studio theatres, whose alleged scandals and depravities had regularly shocked readers of *The Scotsman*, had finally achieved recognition by the city fathers. It was an amazing deal, and one not dreamed of by previous Traverse regimes, though these had been wishing for larger premises ever since the 1970s.

The Traverse had almost total say in what the new theatre in Cambridge Street would be like. The brief to the architect, Nicholas Groves-Raines, was to have a fully flexible 250-seat auditorium, with access all around it for audience and actors. There was to be flying space above the acting areas and, if possible, access to the stage from beneath. Due to volcanic rock and a stream which runs underneath the auditorium, this last requirement could not be met: all the others were. As a result, the Traverse has one of the best and most up-to-date theatre spaces in the country. Moving to it, however, was an act of faith for a small arts organisation, though one boldly believing it could cope with the uncertainties of an expansionist future. We managed the 'fit-out' ourselves, going only slightly over budget in doing so. This shortfall was met from reserves and money from the Sponsored Seat fund, so we began our new life with a clean slate, and firmly in the black. On our installation in the New Traverse, we proclaimed the theatre to be the first purpose-built space for new drama since Shakespeare's Globe – grandiose claim that this is, it remains worth celebrating.

We had pledged ourselves to doubling the audience in the first year, and we did. The opening play, Michele Celeste's *Columbus*, hit the kind of stormy waters the real Columbus had largely avoided: perhaps it was a sacrifice on the altar of first-night expectations. Simon Donald's *The Life of Stuff* fared better and was the hit of the 1992 Festival: the Traverse was back 'on track'. Brad Fraser's *Unidentified Human Remains and the Nature of Love* came next, followed by Michel Tremblay's *House Among the Stars*, translated by Martin Bowman and Bill Findlay, and Stephen Mulrine's adaptation of Yerofeev's *Moscow Stations*, starring Tom Courtenay. Tom McGrath returned to the Traverse to write *Buchanan*, the lively story of Edinburgh's champion light-heavyweight boxer, though it was a subject neither critics nor public seemed to have much taste for.

The new theatre also worked out a new way of running its affairs, with a new management structure and management team established in the autumn of 1992. The theatre recommitted itself, ahead of any other considerations, to the job of putting on seven new productions a year, commissioning four new plays annually, and, in general, to an artistic policy of producing new Scottish plays and British premières of international work. The Traverse is now the principal producer of contemporary work in Scotland, and has begun to assume a national role in the development of new writing at a time when other theatres have generally stopped producing new plays in any quantity. In 1996, the theatre is deficit-free, and – in addition to its seven annual productions – undertakes regular tours to the Highlands and Islands, also often transferring work to London. Fully programmed for most weeks in the year, Traverse One and Traverse Two present a wide range of theatre, dance and music companies. A full developmental programme for writers continues, and an educational policy is being shaped and expanded.

Keeping the Traverse open is a complex business. In an era where profit-share companies are generally more respected than companies which pay wages, it is unfashionable to draw attention to things such as sponsorship, good administration, marketing and being commercially minded where revivals, touring and transfers are concerned. Yet for an institution to survive and flourish I would put all these things high on the agenda. Since moving to Cambridge Street, the Traverse has had no significant increase in funding. It has afforded a larger operation by increasing its sponsorship, its earned income from the box-office and profits from the bar. So far, it has managed to stay in business without a deficit: the challenge for the future will be to maintain that position. The Traverse also has its part to play in training people in all areas of activity: to maximise its chance of success, increasingly, a theatre has to attract high-quality personnel in all areas, and they deserve proper remuneration.

I have believed very strongly in trying to maximise the shelf-life of productions: while new work must always be produced, it is a good thing to extend the existence of some plays. The Traverse has earned substantial amounts from bringing back productions after initial success. The theatre's reputation is enhanced by taking them further afield; by finding a wider audience. Revivals give people an opportunity to see challenging work which – second time around – comes with a 'proven quality' label. Writers, actors and directors also gain much from revivals, which give them the chance to have another go at something. It also contributes to the formation of a repertoire of work, which is a norm in other countries, though for some reason seems less valued in Scotland.

There are challenges ahead. If subsidy doesn't increase, then the solution to making ends meet will be simple: earn more or cut back on productions. The Traverse doesn't overpay its employees, and holding together skilled workers on small wages will get harder and harder. Audiences in Edinburgh are being stretched to the limit by the arrival of an extra two thousand seats for sale every night at the new Festival Theatre. There is little discussion of how important the two producing theatres – the Traverse and the Royal Lyceum – are to Edinburgh in particular and to Scottish theatre in general. Theatres should also be valued for training people in all sorts of areas, including writing, design, marketing, stage management, finance, administration, sponsorship and commercial operations. A small, regular increase in public funding would make a huge difference, but it seems likely that arguments for this are falling on deaf governmental ears. I don't know how much longer the present situation can continue without some serious casualties. What use will beautiful empty theatres be without companies working in them?

CRITICS

New theatre in 1996 seems to be unfashionable. Although Scottish broadsheet newspapers still devote a considerable amount of space to reviews, previews and background articles have been steadily dwindling. Most of the 'style magazines' don't mention theatre at all, and the rapid turnover of arts editors is symptomatic both of tricky balancing acts in newspaper offices and of a lack of clarity in the kind of coverage newspapers think their readers want. New policies for arts pages have been introduced in Scottish broadsheets, trying to be trendier and ending up less thorough and thoughtful. The standards of theatre criticism are also currently under debate. It is an extremely difficult area if one is to escape the charge of merely whingeing about bad reviews.

Reviewers seem to come and go and the feeling of responsibility and overview is missing. A critic who is a lover of theatre and has experience of many years' output from a theatre is more able to put things in perspective and trace themes, working methods and developments. Hit-and-run reviews prevent theatre-makers from receiving much-needed analysis and feedback. On-the-night reviewing seems to be back in fashion, which for some plays simply won't do. Snap judgements about important works do not do the reviewer, producer and reader many favours. The column article, where three or four disparate reviews are put together to form some kind of thesis, also seems to be irrelevant to needs, and often unfair. Scotland needs less sensationalism in its reviews, less axe-grinding, more love of theatre and a desire to support play-makers and encourage audiences to try something different. Angry reviewers don't write fair reviews. Critics who know and love their theatre and want the best from us earn respect even if they give us bad reviews.

New work from playwrights deserves careful handling. Sometimes I read reviews, particularly for second plays, and wonder if reviewers aren't simply being gratuitously nasty. Usually, they are the same ones who eulogised 'Scotland's New Voice' – sometimes far above the first play's merits – only to knock the next one doubly hard. This can stop playwrights in their tracks: what good does that do any of us? People get so defensive about this area that debate is difficult, but it would improve the situation if there could be a proper discussion between both sides, and if some kind of code of conduct could be agreed.

My time at the Traverse is coming to an end. It's been a tricky period for the theatre. As an organisation, it has changed beyond recognition, yet the work it produces is just as new and fragile as it was thirty-three years ago. Our support seems to lie with a wider, more amorphous audience, rather than the elites and cliques that supported the Traverse until the 1980s. Some people haven't forgiven us for opening the doors to everyone, but I for one think the situation is much healthier now.

I'm proud of *Ines de Castro* by John Clifford, *Hanging the President* by Michele Celeste, *Loose Ends* by Stuart Hepburn, *The Hour of the Lynx* by Enquist, *The Struggle of the Dogs and the Black* by Koltes, *Tally's Blood* by Ann Marie di Mambro, *A Light in the Village* by John Clifford, *The Pursuit of Accidents* by Peter Mackie Burns, *Welfare My Lovely* by Anthony Neilson, *Bondagers* by Sue Glover, *The Life of Stuff* by Simon Donald, *The House Among the Stars* by Tremblay (translated by Bowman and Findlay), *Moscow Stations* by Venedict Verofeev (translated by Stephen Mulrine), *The Bench* by Alexander Gelman, *Unidentified Human Remains and the True Nature of Love* and *Poor Super Man* by Brad Fraser, *Europe* by David Greig, *Buchanan* by Tom McGrath, *Knives in Hens* by David Harrower, *Stones and Ashes* by Daniel Danis (translated by Tom McGrath). I'm proud of the beautiful new Traverse, a theatre that has a highly motivated staff which can still manage to attract audiences to difficult work.

It's been the most fantastic job and I'm grateful for all the help and support I've had during my time at the Traverse. There *is* a 'Traverse spirit' and it comes from the sense of excitement that every first night brings when a new play is launched. There's nothing quite like that feeling, and in thirty-three years, whatever else has changed, that hasn't.

Seventeen

Economics, Culture and Playwriting

David Hutchison

Anyone contemplating the arts scene in Scotland in the mid-1990s could not avoid the conclusion that the last twenty years have been a remarkable period of expansion. In the musical world not only has Scottish Opera established itself in its permanent home, Glasgow's restored Theatre Royal to which it moved in 1975, but ensembles ranging from the medium-sized Scottish Chamber Orchestra to numerous quartets and trios have been set up, and now perform throughout the country. Created out of Western Theatre Ballet in 1969, Scottish Ballet has also put down strong roots, while in the theatre new buildings have been constructed for the repertory companies in Pitlochry and Dundee and for the Traverse in Edinburgh. Major refurbishments have also been undertaken at Perth, the Lyceum, and the Citizens'. New performing spaces have been created at the Tron and Tramway in Glasgow, at Inverness and in various arts centres. Most spectacularly, Edinburgh's Empire has been magnificently restored as the Festival Theatre. Alongside the development of performing spaces, there has been a growth in touring companies which utilise a wide range of venues for their presentations.

None of this could have been achieved without a substantial infusion of public funds. The principle of on-going public finance of the arts dates from the establishment in 1940 of the Council for the Encouragement of Music and the Arts, which led to the setting up of the Arts Council by the 1945–52 Labour government, and is a part of the post-war settlement which was strengthened under both Labour and Conservative administrations thereafter. It is one aspect of that settlement which has survived the Thatcher years tolerably intact. During that period there was an enthusiasm for increasing the amount of private sector patronage, and there was clearly a barely suppressed hope that state subvention might be cut substantially in the future, as business and commerce increased their contributions. As is noted in the 1994–95 report of the Arts Council of England, however[1] the proportion of income secured by the ACE's clients from sponsorship in that year represented 5 per cent of their total income, with the Council providing 41 per cent. In the same year, the Scottish Arts Council's major clients also derived 5 per cent of their income from sponsorship while 37 per cent came from the Council.[2]

What this means is that almost all professional arts activity in the UK is dependent on public subvention for its survival. It is also the case that the expansion of state funding has not kept pace with the demands placed upon it by the many arts organisations which have a reasonable claim for support. There was a time in the very early 1960s when the gentleman in charge of the Scottish Committee of the Arts Council, as it was then known, was happy at the end of the fiscal year to return a surplus to London – indeed the individual in question is held responsible for attempting to strangle Scottish Opera at birth[3] – but that day is long gone, and the problem the Scottish Arts Council has in the mid-1990s, when its budget is not increasing, is finding ways of expanding existing provision while also allowing some room for innovation. A further complication stems from the reorganisation of local government: subsequent to the 1975 reorganisation, arts funding was shared by the district and regional authorities, and a number of regions, such as Strathclyde and Lothian, have been particularly supportive of the national companies and of more local ventures. The move to unitary authorities in 1996 could well mean that the local authority contribution – running in 1994–95 at a total of £9.1 million in revenue grants to SAC-funded organisation – is diminished, for the district authorities on which many of the new unitary authorities are based have had rather a patchy record of support for the arts. The advent of capital funding for arts projects such as the provision of new buildings – from the proceeds of the National Lottery is proving to be of little help, since a likely outcome is that even more requests will be made for revenue support, the budget for which has not been increased.

Audiences for the arts are substantial: it is often claimed, for example that more people attend live theatre performances in the UK than go to professional football matches. But the arts compete with a range of other activities in a world in which, for those with reasonable incomes, leisure opportunities have expanded remarkably. This is particularly true of the domestic environment, where the post-war improvement in comfort and space has combined more recently with an ever-increasing range of video and hi-fi equipment to make 'home entertainment' an attractive option and a relatively cheap one, after the hardware has been purchased. So, although it is easy to argue that audiences for live arts performances could easily be doubled and trebled, if only the latent interest in music and drama which people profess in opinion surveys could be translated into actual attendance at concert halls and theatres, it is difficult to be confident that such advances are probable in the near future.

The arts, then, are having to operate in a situation where neither state revenue funding nor audiences are likely to increase. Given the propensity of inflation to be higher in the arts than in other sectors of the economy – a propensity that it is difficult to understand completely – there are clear consequences for the level at which arts organisations can expect to function, as Scottish Opera discovered in 1995 when a Scottish Arts Council-sponsored report suggested that its house orchestra be disbanded, and that music in the pit should be provided by other ensembles. Not so many years previously it would have been easy to resist such a proposal with confidence, but that is no longer the case. Despite the fact that public expenditure has continued to rise – to a significant extent as a direct result of the cost of maintaining a section of the population in unproductive idleness – the climate of the 1990s is one in which it is very difficult to argue for an increase in arts funding, for example, to avoid the disbanding of an orchestra. There is now an assumption, which has seeped into general discourse, that there are clear limits to public expenditure, beyond which our society has passed. Whether this is true is very much a matter for debate – the percentage of gross national product taken by taxation in the UK is lower than in most countries of the European Union – but there can be little doubt than in a contest between the second foreign holiday and increased public expenditure on the arts – or on other worthy causes – for many citizens the holiday would win. The theatre is affected by this climate of the times as much as other art forms.

Theatre needs actors, directors, designers, and a host of other professionals, but does it need living writers? The contrast with broadcasting in this respect is instructive. In radio and television the premium is on new material, with repeats being regarded by audiences as inherently undesirable, unless there are overwhelming reasons to justify them. This means that in drama there is a constant need for new scripts to meet the varied demands of series, serials and single plays. Although there are revivals and repeats and, particularly in radio, the use of scripts originally presented in the theatre, there is an enormous amount of material which has been specifically created for radio and television, will be performed once or twice, and never seen or heard again. There are disadvantages for the writer in this situation – it is difficult to become established as a dramatist of note without turning out rather too many plays – but the clear advantage is that there is a continuing market for the contemporary playwright who can meet the needs of the broadcast media. In theatre, on the other hand, it is perfectly possible for managements to mount season after season without including a single new play, and very easy to restrict the presence of living writers.

If playwrights whose talents take them into theatre wish to make a reasonable living in their own country, certain conditions have to be fulfilled. In the first place, there has to be an infrastructure of theatres which are willing to première new work, to revive and circulate it, and, with the help of publishers who specialise in drama texts, to enable it to move far beyond its place of origin. Within such a network there must be a number of theatres which specialise in developing and nurturing new dramatists. Thirdly, there has to be an audience which is interested in seeing new work, and is prepared to thole the indifferent, in the belief that something far superior will emerge sooner or later. Crucially, the funding arrangements must be designed to make all of this possible. It is also highly desirable that there are opportunities for plays and writers to cross over into the broadcast media, and film.

A cursory glance at the English theatre shows that the conditions for the development of new writing are fulfilled there. London dominates theatre, as it dominates other aspects of English life, but because of its size it is possible for there to be both relatively well-funded high-prestige ensembles like the National Theatre and the Royal Shakespeare Company at one end of the scale, and at the other, small, relatively impecunious and more transient operations, with a range of ventures in between. It would be foolish to suggest that all London theatres are interested in nurturing English playwriting, but even the overtly commercial West End draws heavily on the core work of the subsidised companies in the development of indigenous drama. While it falls to theatres like the Royal Court and the Bush – and beyond them a range of fringe companies – to concentrate on finding new plays, both the large subsidised companies also feel obliged to be active in this area, and to revive the work of living dramatists. Beyond London the record is patchier, but there are a reasonable number of provincial theatres which are only too happy to mount productions of plays which have succeeded in the capital, and some of these theatres also commission and present new work. As London is the theatrical capital of England, so it remains the centre of the media world also, although both Birmingham and Manchester have established significant presences in broadcasting. There is constant traffic between theatre and radio and television drama: a traffic in actors and directors, and also in writers. What all of this means is that it is perfectly possible for playwrights to make a good living in England and to do so without having to write themselves out. A dramatist like Alan Ayckbourn clearly thrives on endless production, but he has no economic motive, for the royalties from continuing revivals of half a dozen of his most successful plays must be more than adequate to secure him in comfort for the rest of his life. Writers as different as Tom Stoppard and Willy Russell have been able to combine more modest productivity with a steady income, which, even if they were to stop writing now, would continue for a long time to come.

The conditions which make this situation possible do not exist to anything like the same extent in Scotland. This is a small country with a weak theatrical tradition, no obvious centre to compare with London, a small population base, and consequently fewer theatres. If a Scottish dramatist wishes to emulate the financial success of his southern colleagues – or even to attain a more modest but tolerable income – it is not easy in his native land. The two most successful Scottish dramatists to date have been James Barrie and James Bridie: Barrie wrote exclusively for the London stage, and Bridie, despite starting his career in Scotland, and despite his commitment to the development of theatre in that country, saw to it that a large proportion of his plays were premiered south of the border. There was no alternative at the time when these writers embarked on their careers, if they were to make a living. Bridie died in 1951 fourteen years after Barrie, and since then the repertory theatre movement in Scotland has expanded considerably, but it still cannot offer more than a handful of dramatists a reasonable income. The market, to use current parlance, simply cannot support them. It might be argued that in this situation the sensible Scottish playwright should be thinking of the British market and not the Scottish one, as Bridie clearly did. Indeed it could be said that the success of the contemporary generation of Scottish fiction writers south of the border, and beyond, demonstrates that an overt Scottishness in subject matter, language or both, is not a barrier to acceptance elsewhere. This is a seductive argument, although for some distinguished Scottish dramatists language can remain a problem. John Byrne, who has made the transition from theatre to television, won much critical acclaim for the networked *Tutti Frutti*, but the acclaim was not matched by the size of the audience in England, and some metropolitan critics muttered darkly about the need for subtitles; our proletarian novelists, even although they seek to render urban Scots dialect, are careful not to deviate too far from standard English prose in their narrative passages.

There is another relevant factor: several of the Scottish novelists who have recently achieved prominence have been published initially by small

Scottish houses, which do not have the advantage of lucrative back lists; they have had to find new writers, otherwise they themselves would perish. There is no parallel in the Scottish drama: Scottish theatres do not need new, or even dead, Scottish writers in order to stay in business, for the world is full of dramatists from outside of Scotland, dead and alive, whose work is universally available for presentation, much of it written in English. No publisher, not even the largest on the planet, could handle the full range of dramatic material from around the world which every theatre nevertheless has always at its disposal.

A market for Scottish dramatic writers does exist in the broadcast media: BBC Scotland in the 1990s has been expanding its television output, most obviously in comedy, but also in series drama, such as *Hamish Macbeth*, and in single plays/films. The major ITV contractor, Scottish, continues to concentrate on series – *Taggart* and *Dr Finlay* – and the recently-saved soap opera, *High Road*. There has also been a growth in the – still very small – number of films made in Scotland targeted at the cinema rather than the broadcast market. BBC Radio also continues to offer some opportunities to Scottish dramatists, although that market appears to be static, if not declining, for complex internal reasons.

The commissioning fee which is paid for a new play by Scottish theatres in the mid-1990s is around £5,200, and with royalties of normally 10 per cent of the net box office on top of that, total income from a production in a reasonably sized venue could be around £8,000. The minimum fee for a series episode is £10,000 and for a television feature film £19,000, while a sixty-minute radio play attracts a minimum fee of £1,300, with the possibility of repeat fees in the event of further transmission.

On the basis of these figures, it would be reasonable to conclude that it is possible for very flexible and hard-working Scottish writers, who are able to move from medium to medium, to increase their incomes to a tolerable level, but in practice this only diminishes rather than altogether solving the underlying problem. In 1995 a Scottish Arts Council-commissioned report discovered that only 4 per cent of 483 artists – visual artists, actors and writers – who were interviewed by the researchers earned £30,000 per annum or more, and that the average income was £8,700; among the 51 writers – dramatists were not categorised separately – there was one individual who earned more than £30,000, and one who earned over £20,000 from their craft.[4] One suspects, too, that these individuals may have been novelists. John Clifford, a writer whose work has attracted much praise, has commented thus on the predicament of the Scottish dramatist as he has experienced it:

> being a professional writer, and exercising one's professional skills
> to the best of one's ability, should not entail – as it now does –
> a continual and demoralising insecurity and a dependence on the
> lunacies of the social security system[5]

If it is accepted that it is desirable that Scottish playwriting should be encouraged, and that the natural starting point of the Scottish dramatist should be the Scottish theatre – since in contrast to the situation when Barrie and Bridie were embarking on their careers, we now do have a theatrical infrastructure in the country – then the responsibility of the individual Scottish theatre is a substantial one, much more substantial, it can be argued, than that of the individual English theatre, which is a member of a much larger assembly. Any objective observer would have to conclude that this responsibility has never been discharged in a consistently diligent way across the Scottish theatre, and over the years, in a sustained fashion. It is perfectly possible to point to the programmes of, for example, the Gateway in Edinburgh in the late 1950s and early 1960s, the Citizens' in the 1950s and the Traverse in the late 1970s and early 1980s, as examples of a very strong engagement with native drama; indeed it could be argued that sometimes the commitment shown by these companies was so strong that it included staging indifferent work which should never have seen the light of day. However, as any trawl round the London fringe demonstrates, the price of encouraging talented writers to develop is giving the mediocre dramatist the chance to discover that he has no future in the theatre. That price is well worth paying if over time – and time is crucial – the mediocre writers are swept aside by the writers of real talent, and perhaps the odd one or two of genius. It is obviously impossible to reproduce the English theatrical and media milieux in Scotland. What can be done, however, is to recognise the fundamental structural difficulties facing the Scottish-based dramatist and then to design policies which are geared, at the very least, to counteracting the worst features of the current situation. A major responsibility remains with the individual theatres; it is up to them to shoulder the burden of ensuring the continuing development of Scottish drama.

As was pointed out at the beginning of this essay, however, the arts in Britain are sustained by public funds; and it is the Scottish Arts Council which ultimately must ensure – through the deployment of the admittedly limited resources at its disposal – that it is possible for talented Scottish dramatists to establish themselves in Scotland and beyond. It is not satisfactory to argue that the SAC is not in the business of telling companies what their artistic policies should be, for this is done all the time in subtle – and not so subtle – ways across the range of the Council's activities: in order to justify the use of public funds to support its activities the smallest music club in the land is obliged to submit details of proposed artists and programmes with grant applications. Yet for understandable reasons, the Council has fought shy of affirmative action of the kind that is necessary in drama. The time has nevertheless come when a more radical approach is called for. That approach could take the form of an insistence that *all* Scottish theatre companies in receipt of public funding are expected to have a minimum proportion of Scottish work – new and revived – in their programmes. If companies chose not not to follow this route, a cut could be made in their grants, and the money redirected to others which are prepared to make better use of it. Such a proposal might well be greeted with horror in some quarters, and characterised as a device for encouraging the parochial and third-rate. The most fitting response to that criticism is to ask whether the English Arts Council would be happy with a situation where English writing featured erratically, and usually in a minority position, in English theatres.

It is instructive to consider how another country, which lives in the cultural and economic shadow of a powerful neighbour, has dealt with a similar problem. Canada has developed a range of policies designed to hold at bay the cultural colonisation of the country by the USA. This has not been an easy task, particularly as far as the electronic media are concerned, but there have been some successes. In the theatre, where English cultural colonialism was as much a problem as the American variety, public subvention to the growing network of theatres from the federal Canada Council and provincial governments was providing 50 per cent of funding by the 1970s, and in 1971 a Council inspired-conference came up with the suggestion that with such a level of subsidy a similar proportion of presentations should be of Canadian plays. The effect of this suggestion was that theatres began to pay far more attention to indigenous work and, as a result, by 1986 a survey of 65 theatres could demonstrate that of 324 plays presented in one season, 30 per cent were new Canadian ones, and 29 per cent Canadian revivals.[6] The process continues at the present time, with the Council having as the first of its assessment criteria the contribution its clients make to the development of Canadian theatre and Canadian theatre artists. In the mid-1990s, as a consequence of the approach taken by the Council, and also no doubt the general cultural atmosphere, 72 per cent of presentations in Canadian theatres were of Canadian plays: in the French-speaking theatre the figure was 69 per cent, and in the English-speaking theatre 76 per cent.

By Scottish standards, these are astounding figures. If a similar scheme were to be tried in Scotland, there would be no guarantee of geniuses arising in the immediate future, but at least there might be an end to the kind of misery described by John Clifford, and over time there would be a very good chance of a repertoire of plays emerging which collectively would command rather more enthusiasm than the list of the top one hundred dramas compiled in 1993 by the promoters of the Scottish National Theatre project.[7]

NOTES

1. Arts Council of England, *Annual Report 1994–95* (London, 1995).
2. Scottish Arts Council, *Annual Report 1994–95* (Edinburgh, 1995). The difference in the figures is largely accounted for by the higher local authority contribution in Scotland, 17 per cent as opposed to 10 per cent. The figures may not be directly comparable, however, as they are not collected on exactly the same basis: the ACE ones refer to all clients, the SAC ones to major clients.
3. See Conrad Wilson, *Alex: the Authorised Biography of Sir Alexander Gibson* (Edinburgh: Mainstream, 1993).
4. *Socio-economic Study of Artists in Scotland* (Edinburgh: Scottish Arts Council, 1995).
5. John Clifford, 'New Playwriting in Scotland', *Chapman* 43–4 (Spring 1986), p.93.
6. See the entry on Theatre in the *Canadian Encyclopaedia*, second edition (Edmonton: Hurtig, 1988), in which David Gardner explains developments in discussion of the subject.
7. See *Theatre Scotland* 2, 8 (1994) for the full list and a discussion of its merits.

The Scottish Theatre since 1970: A Bibliography

Alison Lumsden

I) PLAY TEXTS

Adam, Agnes, *Birds of Prey: A One Act Scots Comedy* (Glasgow: Brown, Son and Ferguson, 1973)

——, *Coffee Morning: A One Act Scots Play* (Glasgow: Brown, Son and Ferguson, 1971)

——, *The Bachelors' Club: A Play About Robert Burns* (Glasgow: Brown, Son and Ferguson, 1973)

Barron, Charles, *The Buchan Trap: A Play in One Act* (Glasgow: Brown, Son and Ferguson, 1976)

——, *Groomsnicht: A Play in One Act* (Glasgow: Brown, Son and Ferguson, 1979)

——, 'The Mannie' in *Triad 26* (Macclesfield: New Playwrights' Network, 1980)

——, *As the Bat at Noon* (Glasgow: Brown, Son and Ferguson, 1981)

Brown, Ian, and Mark Fisher, eds, *Made in Scotland: An Anthology of New Scottish Plays* (London: Methuen Drama, 1995)

Bryden, Bill, *Willie Rough: A Play* (Edinburgh: Southside Ltd, 1972)

——, *Benny Lynch: Scenes from a Short Life: A Play* (Edinburgh: Southside Ltd, 1975)

——, *Old Movies: A Play* (London: Heinemann, National Theatre Play, 1977)

Byrne, John, *Still Life* (Edinburgh: Salamander Press, 1982)

——, *Cuttin' a Rug* (Edinburgh: Salamander Press, 1982)

——, *The Slab Boys* (Edinburgh: Salamander Press, 1982)

——, *Tutti Frutti* (London: BBC Books, 1987)

——, *Your Cheatin' Heart* (London: BBC Books, 1990)

——, *Colquhoun and MacBryde* (London: Faber and Faber, 1992)

——, 'Threads' in *A Decade's Drama: Six Scottish Plays* (Todmorden: Woodhouse Books, 1980)

——, 'Writer's Cramp' in *Scot-Free: New Scottish Plays*, edited by Alasdair Cameron (London: Nick Hern Books, 1990)

Cameron, Alasdair, ed., *Scot-Free: New Scottish Plays* (London: Nick Hern Books, 1990)

Campbell, Donald, *The Jesuit: A Play* (Edinburgh: Paul Harris, 1976)

——, *Somerville the Soldier: A Play* (Edinburgh: Paul Harris, 1978)

——, *The Widows of Clyth: A Play* (Edinburgh: Paul Harris, 1979)

Carruthers, George Sutherland, *Highland Fling: A Light Hearted Comedy in One Act* (Glasgow: Brown, Son and Ferguson, 1975)

——, *Toon Affairs: One-Act Scots Comedy* (Glasgow: Brown, Son and Ferguson, 1976)

Clifford, John, *Light in the Village* (London: Nick Hern Books, 1991)

——, 'Losing Venice' in *Scot-Free: New Scottish Plays*, edited by Alasdair Cameron (London: Nick Hern Books, 1990)

Cochrane, Alan, *The Deil's Awa!!!: A Play: A Roistering Tale of Smugglers in the East Neuk* (Glasgow: Brown, Son and Ferguson, 1978)

——, *The Campbells are Comin': A Play* (Glasgow: Brown, Son and Ferguson, 1978)

——, *Scots Wha Hae: A Stirring Tale of the Times of Robert Bruce* (Glasgow: Brown, Son and Ferguson, 1979)

Cullen, Mike, 'The Cut' in *Made in Scotland: An Anthology of New Scottish Plays*, edited by Ian Brown and Mark Fisher (London: Methuen Drama, 1995)

Conn, Stewart, *The Burning: A Play* (London: Calder and Boyars, 1973)

——, *The Aquarium, The Man in the Green Muffler* and *I Didn't Always Live Here* (London: John Calder, 1976)

——, *Thistlewood* (Todmorden: Woodhouse Books, 1979)

——, 'Play Donkey' in *A Decade's Drama: Six Scottish Plays* (Todmorden: Woodhouse Books, 1980)

Dallmeyer, Andrew, *The Boys in the Backroom* (Edinburgh: Salamander Press, 1982)

Di Mambro, Ann Marie, *Tally's Blood: Rehearsal Script* (Edinburgh: Traverse Theatre, 1990)

——, 'The Letter-Box' in *Scot-Free: New Scottish Plays*, edited by Alasdair Cameron (London: Nick Hern Books, 1990)

Donald, Simon, 'Prickly Heat' in *First Run: New Plays by New Writers*, edited by Kate Harwood (London: Nick Hern Books, 1989)

——, 'The Life of Stuff' in *Made in Scotland: An Anthology of New Scottish Plays*, edited by Ian Brown and Mark Fisher (London: Methuen Drama, 1995)

Dougall, Edwin, *Tatties and Herring: A Farce* (Glasgow: Brown, Son and Ferguson, 1977)

Dunlop, Bill, *Female Wits* (Belfast: Canto Press, 1990)

——, *Klytemnestra's Bairns* (Edinburgh: Diehard, 1993)

Evaristi, Marcella, *Mouthpieces* (St Andrews: Crawford Centre for the Arts, 1980)

——, *Commedia* (Edinburgh: Salamander Press, 1983)

Eveling, Stanley, *Come and be Killed* and *Dear Janet Rosenberg, Dear Mr Kooning* (London: Calder and Boyars, 1971)

——, *The Buglar Boy and his Swish Friend* (Edinburgh: Salamander Press, 1983)

——, 'Mister' in *A Decade's Drama: Six Scottish Plays* (Todmorden: Woodhouse Books, 1980)

Ferguson, Alistair, *Money a Slip: One Act Play* (Glasgow: Brown, Son and Ferguson, 1975)

Foggo, John, *Farewell Appearance: A Play* (Glasgow: Brown, Son and Ferguson, 1978)

Fraser, Jessica, *An Author in Search of Eight Characters: A Comedy in One Act* (Macclesfield: New Playwrights' Network, 1980)

Gallacher, Tom, *Mr Joyce is Leaving Paris* (London: Calder and Boyars, 1972)

——, *Revival!* and *Schellenbrack* (Glasgow: Molendinar Press, 1978)

——, *Jenny: A Play* (London: Samuel French, 1980)

——, *Our Kindness to 5 Persons: A Play in Two Acts* (London: Dr J. Van Loewen, 1981)

——, *The Only Street: A Play in Two Acts* (London: Dr J. Van Loewen, 1981)

——, *The Sea-Change: A Play in Two Acts* (London: Dr J. Van Loewen, 1981)

Glover, Sue, 'Bondagers' in *Made in Scotland: An Anthology of New Scottish Plays*, edited by Ian Brown and Mark Fisher (London: Methuen Drama, 1995)

Gunn, George, *Songs of the Grey Coast* and *The Gold of Kildonan* (Edinburgh: Chapman, 1992)

Hannan, Chris, *The Evil Doers* and *The Baby: Two Plays* (London: Nick Hern Books, 1991)

——, 'Elizabeth Gordon Quinn' in *Scot-Free: New Scottish Plays*, edited by Alasdair Cameron (London: Nick Hern Books, 1990)

Hardie, Amy, *Precarious Living* (Edinburgh: Polygon, 1985)

Hendry, Joy, *Gang Doun wi a Sang: A Play about William Soutar* (Edinburgh: Diehard, 1995)

High, Bernard G., *Ambush: A One-Act Play for Women* (Glasgow: Brown, Son and Ferguson, 1976)

Kelman, James, *Hardie and Baird and Other Plays* (London: Secker and Warburg, 1991)

Leonard, Tom, *If Only Bunty Was Here: A Drama Sequence of Totally Undramatic Non-Sequiturs* (Glasgow: Print Studio Press, 1979)

Lochhead, Liz, *Blood and Ice* (Edinburgh: Salamander Press, 1982)

——, *True Confessions and New Clichés* (Edinburgh: Polygon, 1985)

——, *Tartuffe: A Translation Into Scots from the Original by Molière* (Edinburgh: Polygon and Third Eye Centre, 1985)

——, *Mary Queen of Scots Got Her Head Chopped Off* and *Dracula* (Harmondsworth: Penguin, 1989)

McDonough, Joe, *Opening Night* (Glasgow: Brown, Son and Ferguson, 1982)

——, *Over the Rainbow* (Cumbernauld: Pedersen Press, 1992)

——, *No More Mondays* (Cumbernauld: Pedersen Press, 1993)

——, *Not Proven* (Cumbernauld: Pedersen Press, 1993)

Macdonald, Robert David, 'Chinchilla' in *A Decade's Drama; Six Scottish Plays* (Tormorden: Woodhouse Books, 1980)

Macdonald, Sharman, *When I Was a Girl I Used to Scream and Shout* with *When We Were Women* and *The Brave* (London: Faber and Faber, 1990)

——, *Shades* (London: Faber and Faber, 1992)

Macdonald, Stephen, *Not About Heroes: The Friendship of Siegfried Sassoon and Wilfred Owen* (London: Faber and Faber, 1983)

McGrath, John, *Random Happenings in the Hebrides or The Social Democrat and the Stormy Sea* (London: Davis-Poynter, 1972)

——, *Bakke's Night of Fame: A Play from the Novel 'Danish Gambit' by William Butler* (London: Davis-Poynter, 1973)

——, *The Cheviot, the Stag and the Black, Black Oil* (Kyleakin, Isle of Skye: West Highland Publishing, 1974)

——, *Little Red Hen* (London: Pluto Press, 1977)

——, *Fish in the Sea* (London: Pluto Press, 1977)

——, *Yobbo Nowt* (London: Pluto Press, 1978)

——, *Joe's Drum* (Aberdeen: Aberdeen People's Press and 7:84 Theatre Company, 1979)

——, *The Cheviot, The Stag, and The Black, Black Oil*, revised edition (London: Eyre Methuen, 1981)

——, *Two Plays for the Eighties: Blood Red Roses* and *Swings and Roundabouts* (Aberdeen: Aberdeen People's Press and 7:84 Theatre Company, 1981)

——, *Six-Pack: The Scottish Plays* (Edinburgh: Polygon: 1996)

McGrath, Tom, and Jimmy Boyle, *The Hard Man* (Edinburgh: Canongate, 1977)

McKay, John, 'Dead Dad Dog' in *Scot-Free: New Scottish Plays*, edited by Alasdair Cameron (London: Nick Hern Books, 1990)

McLean, Duncan, 'Julie Allardyce' in *Made in Scotland: An Anthology of New Scottish Plays*, edited by Ian Brown and Mark Fisher (London: Methuen Drama, 1995)

McLeish, Robert S., *'True Steel': A Covenanting Drama in One Act* (Glasgow: Brown, Son and Ferguson, 1979)

——, *Nothing Ever Happens: A Scots Comedy in One Act* (Glasgow: Brown, Son and Ferguson, 1980)

McLellan, Robert, *The Hypocrite* (London: Calder and Boyars, 1970)

——, *Jamie the Saxt: A Historical Comedy*, edited by Ian Campbell and Ronald D. S. Jack (London: Calder and Boyars, 1970)

——, *Collected Plays Volume 1* (London: Calder and Boyars, 1981)

MacMillan, Hector, *The Sash My Father Wore* (Glasgow: Molendinar Press, 1974)

——, 'The Rising' in *A Decade's Drama: Six Scottish Plays* (Todmorden: Woodhouse Books, 1980)

McMillan, Roddy, *The Bevellers: A Play* (Edinburgh: Southside Press, 1974)

——, *All in Good Faith* (Glasgow: Scottish Society of Playwrights, 1979)

Milligan, John, *A Place in Class* (Musselburgh: John Milligan, 1978)

——, *Up the Quango: A Fable of Revolution* (Musselburgh: John Milligan, 1979)

——, *Folk and the Land: A Play in Two Acts* (Musselburgh: John Milligan, 1980)

Munro, Rona, *Fugue* (Edinburgh: Salamander Press, 1983)
——, *Bold Girls: A Play* (London: Samuel French, 1991)
——, 'Saturday at the Commodore' in *Scot-Free; New Scottish Plays*, edited by Alasdair Cameron (London: Nick Hern Books, 1990)
Parker, Stewart, *Catchpenny Twist: A Charade in Two Acts* with music by Shaun Davey (New York: Samuel French, 1984)
Richardson, Alan, *Nicht O' the Blunt Claymore; A Jacobean Farce* (Glasgow: Brown, Son and Ferguson, 1975)
——, *Brodie the Broadsword: A Border Comedy* (Glasgow: Brown, Son and Ferguson, 1977)
——, *Farewell Ploy: A Border Comedy* (Glasgow: Brown, Son and Ferguson, 1977)
——, *The Black Ring: A Tale of Highway Robbery* (Glasgow: Brown, Son and Ferguson, 1978)
——, *The Auld Alliance: A Tale of the Napoleonic Times* (Glasgow: Brown, Son and Ferguson, 1979)
——, *A Tale o' Twa Undertakers: A Scots 'Black' Comedy* (Glasgow: Brown, Son and Ferguson, 1979)
——, *Liddesdale: An Episode from a Border Feud* (Glasgow: Brown, Son and Ferguson, 1980)
——, *A Fine Gentleman: A Scots Comedy Inspired by Molière's 'Le Sicilien'* (Glasgow: Brown, Son and Ferguson, 1980)
——, *Platform One: A One Act Comedy* (Glasgow: Brown, Son and Ferguson, 1984)
——, *The Comedy of the Marks: or a Funny Thing Happened on the Way to the Piazza* (Glasgow: Brown, Son and Ferguson, 1984)
——, 'A Pair of Feet' in *Triad 62* (Macclesfield: New Playwrights' Network, 1987)
——, *The Bailie's Stratagem: A One Act Scots Comedy* (Glasgow: Brown, Son and Ferguson, 1988)
——, *Perfect Partners: A Comedy* (London: Samuel French, 1992)
Roper, Tony, 'The Steamie' in *Scot-Free: New Scottish Plays*, edited by Alasdair Cameron (London: Nick Hern Books, 1990)
Rosie, George, *Carlucco and the Queen of Hearts* and *The Blasphemer* (Edinburgh: Chapman, 1992)
Scotland, James, *Union Riots: A Scottish Comedy in One Act* (Glasgow: Brown, Son and Ferguson, 1973)
——, *The Sorcerer's Tale: A Hallowe'en Bleeze* (Glasgow: Brown, Son and Ferguson, 1973)
——, *Baptie's Lass: A Caledonian Rant* (Glasgow: Brown, Son and Ferguson, 1973)
——, *Grand Finale: A Scots Comedy in One Act* (Glasgow: Brown, Son and Ferguson, 1974)
——, *The Daurk Assize: The Morality of Everyman Told in Scots* (Glasgow: Brown, Son and Ferguson, 1975)
——, *The Rape of the Mace: A Collegiate Comedy* (Glasgow: Brown, Son and Ferguson, 1975)
——, *Oh, Whistle and I'll Come To You My Lad: An Episode* (Glasgow: Brown,

Son and Ferguson, 1975)

——, *The Girl of the Golden City: A Play with Folk Music* (Glasgow: Brown, Son and Ferguson, 1975)

——, *Himself When Young: A Comedy* (Glasgow: Brown, Son and Ferguson, 1975)

——, *The Highlander: A Play in One Act* (Glasgow: Brown, Son and Ferguson, 1975)

——, *We'll Go No More A'Reivin: A Border Legend* (Glasgow: Brown, Son and Ferguson, 1975)

——, *The Burning Question: A Black-Edged Comedy* (Glasgow: Brown, Son and Ferguson, 1975)

——, *Hallowe'en: A Decameronian Adventure* (Glasgow: Brown, Son and Ferguson, ?1975)

——, *Fawcett: A Sabbatical Comedy* (Glasgow: Brown, Son and Ferguson, 1976)

——, *Day of Wrath: A Kind of Apocalypse* (Glasgow: Brown, Son and Ferguson, 1977)

——, *A Surgeon for Lucinda: A Glasgow Fairy Tale; Freely Adapted from Molière's Comedy 'L'Amour Medecin'* (Glasgow: Brown, Son and Ferguson, ?1977)

——, *The Friends of the People: A Comedy in Scots* (Glasgow: Brown, Son and Ferguson, ?1977)

——, *A Shilling for the Beadle: A Scots Comedy in One Act* (Glasgow: Brown, Son and Ferguson, ?1977)

——, *The Holy Terror: A Scots Comedy Freely Adapted from Molière's 'Tartuffe'* (Glasgow: Brown, Son and Ferguson, 1978)

——, *The Philosopher's Stone: The Third Sorcerer's Tale* (Glasgow: Brown, Son and Ferguson, 1979)

——, *Hogmanay: A Ne'erday Saturnalia* (Glasgow: Brown, Son and Ferguson, 1981)

——, *A Hundred Thousand Welcomes: A Comedy in Three Acts* (Glasgow: Brown, Son and Ferguson, 1982)

——, *The Merry Monks of Cambusdonald: The Fourth Sorcerer's Tale* (Glasgow: Brown, Son and Ferguson, 1984)

Schofield, Christine, *Red Wine in Crystal Glasses: A Comedy in One Act* (Glasgow: Brown, Son and Ferguson, 1976)

Smith, W. Gordon, *Jock: A Play* (Edinburgh: Cacciatore Fabbro, 1977)

——, *Mister Carnegie's Lantern Lecture: A Play* (Dunfermline: The Carnegie Dunfermline Trust, 1985)

Spence, Alan, *Sailmaker* (Edinburgh: Salamander Press, 1982)

——, *Space Invaders* (Edinburgh: Salamander Press, 1983)

Taylor, C. P., *Thank You Very Much: A Play in Two Acts* (London: Methuen Educational, 1970)

——, *Bandits!* (North Shields: Iron Press, 1977)

——, 'The Killingworth Play' in *3 North-East Plays* (North Shields: Iron Press, 1978)

——, *Live Theatre: Three Plays* (North Shields: Iron Press, 1981)

——, *Live Theatre: Four Plays for Young People* (London: Methuen in Association with Iron Press, 1983)

——, *Good* and *And A Nightingale Sang* . . . (London: Methuen Drama, 1990)
——, *The Plays of C.P. Taylor as Performed at the Edinburgh International Festival, 1992* (Edinburgh: Edinburgh Festival Society, 1992)
——, 'Walter' in *A Decade's Drama: Six Scottish Plays* (Todmorden: Woodhouse Books, 1980)
Ure, Joan, *Five Short Plays* (Glasgow: Scottish Society of Playwrights, 1979)
Waddell, George, *The Flesh and the Devil: A One Act Scots Play* (Glasgow: Brown, Son and Ferguson, 1971)
——, *The White Cockade: A One-Act Scots Play* (Glasgow: Brown, Son and Ferguson, 1971)
A list of recently-translated plays appears at the end of Bill Findlay's article, pp.196–7

II) CRITICAL TEXTS

Arnott, James, and Randall Stevenson, 'Drama' in *The New Companion to Scottish Culture*, ed. David Daiches (Edinburgh: Polygon, 1993).
Barnes, Philip, *A Companion to Post-War British Theatre* (London: Croom Helm, 1986)
Bennett, Susan, 'Debts and Directions: The Place of Robert McLellan's *The Changeling*', *Scottish Literary Journal* 19, no.1 (May, 1992), 28–34
Bold Alan, 'Part 3: Drama' in *Modern Scottish Literature* (London: Longman, 1983)
Boyd, Eddie, 'No Flowers, by Request', *Cencrastus*, 11 (New Year 1983)
Bryden, Bill, 'Bricks on our Shoulders', in *Theatre 74*, edited by Sheridan Morley (London, 1974)
Calder, R., 'Ideas in Scottish Theatre; A Compilation', *Chapman*, 3, no.1 (1974), 8–17
Calder, R., ed., 'Scottish Theatre 1 & 2', *Chapman*, 3, no.1 & 3 (1974)
Campbell, Donald, *A Brighter Sunshine: A Hundred Years of the Edinburgh Royal Lyceum* (Edinburgh: Polygon, 1983)
——, 'A Focus of Discontent: Scottish Literature and the Scottish Assembly', *New Edinburgh Review*, no.45 (Spring 1979), 3–5
Chambers, Colin and Mike Prior, *Playwright's Progress: Patterns of Postwar British Drama* (Oxford: Amber Lane Press, 1987)
Combres, C., 'Le Theatre de Stewart Conn, poète et dramaturge ecossais', *Caliban*, 17 (1981)
Conn, Stewart, 'Ways of Losing: The Radio Work of Iain Crichton Smith' in *Iain Crichton Smith: Critical Essays*, ed. Colin Nicholson (Edinburgh: Edinburgh University Press, 1992)
——, 'C. P. Taylor (1928–1981): Tempered by Tolerance', *Scottish Review*, no.25 (February 1982), 31–2
Coveney, Michael, *The Citzs: 21 years of The Glasgow Citizens Theatre* (London: Nick Hern Books, 1991)
Crawford, Robert, 'Drama' in *Literature in Twentieth-Century Scotland: A Select Bibliography* (London: The British Council, 1995)
Crawford, T, *Scottish Writing Today: Poetry, Fiction, Drama* (Aberdeen: Aberdeen Association for Scottish Literary Studies, 1972)

Edgar, David, *Contemporary British Dramatists* (London: British Council, 1992)

Edwards, Owen Dudley, *City of a Thousand Worlds: Edinburgh in Festival* (Edinburgh: Mainstream, 1991)

Eveling, Stanley, *The Total Theatre* (Edinburgh: Heriot-Watt University, 1972)

Findlay, Bill, 'Translating into Dialect' in David Johnston, ed., *Stages in Translation* (Bath: Absolute Press, 1996)

——, ed., *A History of Scottish Theatre* (Edinburgh: Polygon, 1996)

Friesner, Susan, 'The Plays of C. P. Taylor', *Contemporary Review*, 255, no.1487 (Dec. 1989), 309–11

Gallacher, Tom, *The Way to Write for the Stage* (London: Elm Tree Books, 1987)

Giesekam, Greg, 'Connections with the Audience; Writing for a Scottish Theatre' (Interview with Peter Arnott), *New Theatre Quarterly*, 6, no.24 (Nov. 1990), 318–34

Haase, L., 'New Battles at the Abbey; A Scottish Playwrights' Conference', *Theatre Quarterly*, 8, no.33 (Winter 1979), 67–73

Hayman, Ronald, *British Theatre Since 1955* (Oxford: Oxford University Press, 1979)

Hendry, Joy, ed., *Chapman*, Scottish Theatre Number, Vol viii, no.6 and Vol ix, no.1 (Spring 1986)

Hutchison, David, *The Modern Scottish Theatre* (Glasgow: Molendinar Press, 1977)

——, 'Roddy McMillan and the Scottish Theatre', *Cencrastus*, 2 (Spring 1980), 5–8

Itzin, Catherine, 'John McGrath and 7:84 Theatre Company' in *Stages in the Revolution: Political Theatre in Britain Since 1968* (London: Eyre Methuen, 1980)

Jager, Andreas, *John McGrath und die 7:84 Theatre Company Scotland: Politik und Regionalismus im Theater der siebziger Jahre in Schottland* (Amsterdam: Verlag B. R. Grun, 1986)

Koren-Deutsch, Ilona S., 'Feminist Nationalism in Scotland: *Mary Queen of Scots Got Her Head Chopped Off*', *Modern Drama*, 35, no.3 (Sept. 1992), 424–32

Lofton, R., 'The Idea of Scottish Drama' *Chapman*, 3, no.3 (1975), 18–24

McBain, Hugh, 'Bards of the Board Unite!' *Cencrastus*, 4 (Winter 1980–81), 23–4

McDonald, Jan, and Jenifer Harvie, 'Putting New Twists to Old Stories: Feminism and Lochhead's Drama', in *Liz Lochhead's Voices*, edited by Robert Crawford and Anne Varty (Edinburgh: Edinburgh University Press, 1993), 124–47

McGrath, John, *A Good Night Out: Popular Theatre: Audience, Class and Form* (London: Eyre Methuen, 1981)

——, *The Bone Won't Break: On Theatre and Hope in Hard Times* (London: Methuen Drama, 1990)

——, 'Better a Bad Night in Bootle . . .' *Theatre Quarterly*, 5, no.19 (Sept.–Nov. 1975), 39–54

——, 'The Theory and Practice of Political Theatre', *Theatre Quarterly*, 9, no.35 (Autumn 1979), 43–54

Mackenney, Linda, *The Directory of the Scottish Theatre Archive Collection* (Glasgow: Scottish Theatre Archive, 1982)

——, 'Scotland' in *The Cambridge Guide to World Theatre*, edited by Martin Banham (Cambridge: Cambridge University Press, 1988)

Mackenzie, D., 'The Dramatist in Scotland', *Akros*, 14, no.41 (August 1979), 28–32

MacLennan, Elizabeth, *The Moon Belongs to Everyone: Making Popular Theatre with 7:84* (London: Methuen, 1981)

McMillan, Joyce, *The Traverse Theatre Story* (London: Methuen, 1988)

Moffat, Alasdair, *The Edinburgh Fringe* (London: Johnston and Bacon, 1978)

Mikhail, E.H., *Contemporary British Drama, 1950–1976: An Annotated Critical Bibliography* (London: Macmillan, 1976)

Milligan, John, *Birth and Death of the Glossy Fringe Brochure in the Seventies* (Edinburgh: John Milligan, 1992)

Oliver, Cordelia, *Glasgow Citizens' Theatre, Robert David MacDonald and German Drama* (Glasgow: Third Eye Centre, 1984)

Ross, Raymond, 'The View from Eddie Boyd', *Cencrastus*, 27 (Autumn 1987), 4–13

Roy, Kenneth, *Scottish Theatre Directory* (Maybole: Kenneth Roy Publishers, 1979)

Scene: Magazine of the Scottish Community Drama Association and the Amateur Theatre in Scotland, 1967–

Scottish Drama (Edinburgh: Moray House), 1994–

Scottish Society of Playwrights: A Scottish National Theatre or Not; Report for the Conference in September 1977 (Glasgow: 1978)

Scottish Theatre Archive Newsletter (Glasgow: 1982–)

Scottish Theatre News (Glasgow: Scottish Society of Playwrights, 1981–7)

Scottish Theatre (Inverkeithing: 1969–1973)

Selerie, Gavin, ed, *The Riverside Interviews 6: Tom McGrath* (London: 1983)

Smith, Donald, ed., *The Scottish Stage: A National Theatre Company for Scotland* (Edinburgh: Candlemaker Press, 1994)

Stevenson, Randall, 'Scottish Theatre Company: First Days, First Nights', *Cencrastus*, 7 (Winter, 1981–2), 10–13

——, 'Scottish Theatre, 1950–1980' in *The History of Scottish Literature, vol 4, Twentieth Century*, edited by Cairns Craig (Aberdeen: Aberdeen University Press, 1987), 349–67

——, 'Looking for a Theatre, Looking for a Nation', *Graph: Irish Literary Journal* (Winter 1988)

——, 'Recent Scottish Theatre: Dramatic Developments?' in *Scotland: Literature, Culture, Politics*, edited by Peter Zenzinger (Heidelberg: Carl Winter/Universitätsverlag, 1989)

——, 'Re-enter Houghmagandie: Language as Peformance in Liz Lochhead's *Tartuffe*', in *Liz Lochhead's Voices*, edited by Robert Crawford and Anne Varty (Edinburgh: Edinburgh University Press, 1993), 109–23

Taylor, C. P., *Making A Television Play; A Complete Guide from Conception to BBC Production* (Newcastle-upon-Tyne: Oriel Press Limited 1970)

Theatre Research International Scottish Issue, 17, no.2 (Summer 1992)

Theatre Scotland (Edinburgh: 1992–)

Unwin, Stephen, Jenny Killick & A. Pollock, eds, *The Traverse Theatre 1963–1988* (Edinburgh: Traverse Theatre, 1988)

Varty, Anne, 'Scripts and Performances', in *Liz Lochhead's Voices*, edited by Robert Crawford and Anne Varty (Edinburgh: Edinburgh University Press, 1993), 148–69

Wandor, Micheline, *Drama Today: A Critical Guide to British Drama, 1970–1990* (London: Longman/British Council, 1993)

Wells, Patricia, *Scottish Drama Comes of Age* (Ann Arbor: Michigan University Microfilms International, 1987)

About the Contributors

Audrey Bain is currently researching a thesis on the mother in Scottish drama. After gaining her degree in Scottish Ethnology and English Literature at the University of Edinburgh in 1990, she worked as an oral historian for Dalmellington and District Conservation Trust, gathering material for an archive housed in Dunaskin Industrial Heritage Centre. Her interests span folklore, drama and women's studies. Recent projects include compiling a history of the Scottish Society of Playwrights and transcribing and collating material from Dr Emily Lyle's collection on Galoshins, the Scottish folk play.

Ian Brown comes from Alloa and studied at Edinburgh University, where his research degree concerned Shaw, dramaturgy and history. He subsequently taught drama degree programmes in Edinburgh and Cheshire and is currently Professor of Drama at Queen Margaret College, Edinburgh. A playwright as well as a teacher, he has chaired the Scottish Society of Playwrights both from 1973 to 1975, as founding Chairman, and again from 1984 to 1987. From 1986 until 1994 he was Drama Director for the Arts Council of Great Britain, and he has been an advisory board member for both arts and academic matters.

Ian Brown was director of The Cockpit in London, where he commissioned many new writers, then Associate Director of the Theatre Royal, Stratford East, before joining the TAG (Theatre About Glasgow) company as its Artistic Director in 1984. He has been Artistic Director of the Traverse since 1988, overseeing its move into its new theatre in Cambridge Street in 1992. His many productions for the Traverse – several of which have later transferred to other theatres – include *Moscow Stations, Unidentified Human Remains, Poor Super Man, The Bench, Hardie and Baird, Tally's Blood, Bondagers, Light in the Village* and *Loose Ends*.

Owen Dudley Edwards was born in Dublin and studied at Belvedere College, University College Dublin and the Johns Hopkins University. He has taught at the Universities of Oregon, California (at San Francisco), Aberdeen and – since 1968 – Edinburgh, where he is Reader in History. He is married to Bonnie Lee, whose family was immersed in theatre, and has been her fellow critic of the Edinburgh Festival – for *Festival Times*, *The Scotsman*, the BBC and the *Irish Times* – for over twenty years, with incursions on stage and in the press from their children Leila, Sara and Michael. His many books include *City of a Thousand Worlds: Edinburgh in Festival* (1991) and (with Robbie Jack) *The Edinburgh Festival* (1995).

Bill Findlay has translated with a Montrealer, Martin Bowman, five plays by Quebec dramatist Michel Tremblay: *The Guid Sisters*, *The Real Wurld?*, *Hosanna* and *Forever Yours, Marie-Lou* (all at the Tron Theatre): and *The House Among the Stars* (Traverse and Perth Theatre). Bowman and Findlay have also translated work by Quebec playwrights Michel Marc Bouchard and Dominic Champagne, and Bill Findlay has translated Gerhart Hauptmann's *The Weavers* for Dundee Rep.

Mark Fisher is the chief theatre critic for the *Glasgow Herald*, and a founder and managing editor of *Theatre Scotland* magazine. He was theatre editor on *The List* from 1989 to 1995 and co-edited (with Ian Brown of the Traverse) an anthology of plays for Methuen, *Made in Scotland* (1995). He has been published in the *Guardian*, the *Observer*, the *Scotsman* and the *Daily Telegraph*.

Femi Folorunso studied drama and literature at the University of Ife (now Obafemi Awolowo University), Ile-Ife, Nigeria, and taught dramatic and African literature there until awarded a Commonwealth Scholarship in 1994. He is currently researching contemporary Scottish drama at the University of Edinburgh.

David Hutchison is Senior Lecturer in Communication Studies at Glasgow Caledonian University. His published work has been concerned principally with media policy and Scottish theatre, and includes *The Modern Scottish Theatre* (1977). He was a governor of the Scottish Film Council 1990–95, and has been a member of the BBC's General Advisory Council since 1988. He has a particular interest in cultural and media comparisons between Scotland and Canada.

Alison Lumsden is British Academy research fellow for the Edinburgh Edition of the Waverley Novels. Her publications include articles on Alasdair Gray and Robert Louis Stevenson. She is currently editing Walter Scott's *The Heart of Midlothian* for the Edinburgh Edition.

John McGrath has been working in theatre, film and television since 1959, mainly as a writer, but also as a director of theatre and television.

He has written more than 45 plays for the theatre, directing many himself; founded the 7:84 Theatre Companies, England and Scotland, of which he was director until 1988; and in the 1990s has been making epic theatre on the one hand, and on the other writing one-woman shows for his partner, Elizabeth MacLennan. He has written many plays for television; directed many plays and films for TV; was founding director of the long-running *Z-Cars* series; and now runs his own production company, Freeway Films, based in Edinburgh. He has scripted around twenty screenplays, and received the BAFTA Writers Award. He recently produced the film *Carrington*, and the television version of the Scott enquiry, *Half the Picture*, which he also co-wrote.

Linda Mackenney was educated at New Hall, Cambridge. During the 1980s she carried out the research for 7:84's 'Clydebuilt' season, before being appointed to set up the Scottish Theatre Archive in Special Collections, Glasgow University Library. She edited 7:84 Publications' Scottish Popular Plays series and was a member of the company's Board of Directors from 1983 to 1988. She is currently a teacher at George Watson's College in Edinburgh.

Lindsay Paterson is Professor of Educational Policy at Moray House Institute, Edinburgh. He has written on the culture, sociology and politics of Scotland and has reviewed theatre for several Scottish publications. He is particularly interested in questions of national identity – what it is, how it changes over time, and what bearing it has on politics. His publications on this and related themes include *The Autonomy of Modern Scotland* (1994), and (with Alice Brown and David McCrone) *Politics and Society in Scotland* (1996). He is editor of the quarterly journal *Scottish Affairs*.

Sarah C. Rutherford is an award-winning freelance writer and broadcaster specialising in the arts. She graduated with a first-class degree in English Language and Literature from Merton College, Oxford, where she was awarded the Vaughan Morgan Medal and a Fowler Prize for outstanding scholarship. Her radio work has included daily features on the Edinburgh Festival, while her writing has taken her all over Europe. She is currently completing a Ph.D. at the University of Edinburgh, with the working title 'Black Farce in Jacobean and Nineteen-Sixties Theatre'.

Roger Savage was born in Kent and taught at the Victoria University of Wellington and at the University of Edinburgh, where he is currently Head of the Department of English Literature. He has published (*inter alia*) several essays on seventeenth- and eighteenth-century opera and music-theatre; written and presented a dozen features on BBC Radio 3; sat on several Edinburgh theatre boards; and directed quite a few shows (for the Scottish Early Music Consort, the Purcell Simfony and the Edinburgh University Opera Club).

Randall Stevenson covered Scottish Drama for *The Independent* in the early 1990s, and has reviewed for BBC Radio Scotland, and for the *Times Literary Supplement* since 1983. He has been a member of the Traverse Script Panel, and of the Board of Directors and Artistic Policy Committee of the Royal Lyceum Theatre. His publications include *Modernist Fiction* (1992), *A Reader's Guide to the Twentieth-Century Novel in Britain* (1993), and the chapter on 'Scottish Drama 1950–1980' in *The History of Scottish Literature*. He has lectured on literature and drama in many European countries, and in Nigeria, Korea, Egypt and Israel. He is currently Senior Lecturer in English Literature in the University of Edinburgh, and Associate Dean of the Scottish Universities' International Summer School.

Olga Taxidou is a lecturer in the Department of English Literature in the University of Edinburgh, where she teaches mainly drama courses. She has also taught in the Drama Department at the University of Exeter. Her main research interest is in performance and cultural theory and she has published on classical Greek drama, modernist performance, and contemporary epic and political theatres. Her study of the dramatic theories of Edward Gordon Craig is forthcoming with Harwood Academic Publishers. She has co-edited the journal *Studies in Theatre Production* and is also co-editing *Modernism: An Anthology of Documents and Sources* for Prentice Hall. She is a member of the executive committee of the International Federation of Theatre Research and has worked on several translations and adaptations – mainly from classical and modern Greek – for various theatre productions.

Gavin Wallace is a Course Tutor in Literature with the Open University in Scotland, and co-editor of the journal *Edinburgh Review*. His wide-ranging work as a teacher, lecturer and critic includes frequent book reviews for *The Scotsman*, and research and reviewing for BBC Radio Scotland. His many publications on Scottish literature and cultural affairs include contributions to *The History of Scottish Literature* (1987), and *The Scottish Novel since the Seventies* (1993), the latter co-edited with Randall Stevenson.

Peter Zenzinger teaches English Literature at the Technische Universität Berlin, where he also directs an English Language drama group. He wrote his thesis on Allan Ramsay (1977) and has published articles on medieval Scottish poetry, Carlyle, Stevenson, contemporary Scottish and English fiction and drama, and Scottish literary criticism. He is the editor of *Scotland: Literature, Culture, Politics* (1989) and co-editor (with Armin Geraths) of *Text und Kontext in der modernen englischsprachigen Literatur* (1991).

Index

Adaptations and translations are listed under the name of their original author.